Coriolanus
in Context

Coriolanus
in Context

Clifford Chalmers Huffman

LEWISBURG
Bucknell University Press

Associated University Presses, Inc.
Cranbury, New Jersey 08512

ISBN: 0-8387-1011-5
Printed in the United States of America

Dedication

TO CLARA

WITHOUT WHOM, NOT

Contents

Preface

Coriolanus opens with one famous formulation of the ancient body-state analogy. The first term, Coriolanus's private self or "character," has been the subject of frequent moral-philosophical investigation; but the other term, the state of Rome, has not fared so well, despite the fact that according to classical political thought, the public analogue of the study of man, politics is a large field in which to observe the practice of human nature. Critics have been remiss here, perhaps due to misconceptions about the wide range of attitudes toward government really available to members of a Jacobean theater audience. If past studies can be shown, first, to be inadequate to the demonstrated complexity of work by Shakespeare and others set in Rome and intended for professional dramatic presentation, and, second, to conflict with the sources from which the historical information of the plays is derived—and this is the burden of the second chapter—then a new study of *Coriolanus* is warranted. The critic must concern himself with Shakespeare's treatment of the continuous tradition of "mixed" government, one example of which is the government of Rome established in the popular insurrection of the play's first scene.

The approach must necessarily be contextual, and this book studies material from medieval, sixteenth-century, and immediately Jacobean England, from ancient Greece and Rome, and from Renaissance Italy. It is hoped that this will interest students of cultural history as well as literary scholars. Because much of the historical material is no longer current, I have adopted a full form for presenting the evidence and citing the sources. In doing so, incidentally, I have expanded contractions and regularized some eccentricities of older spelling, particularly with regard to *i, j, u, v* and *w*. References to Shakespeare's work other than *Coriolanus* are to the Kittredge edition (Boston: Ginn, 1936); the revision, edited by Irving Ribner, appeared too late for use here. The exception is *Coriolanus* itself. For the focal play I have used John Dover Wilson's "New Cambridge" edition (Cambridge, England: Cambridge University Press, 1960).

The many and varying debts to earlier studies are registered in the book's documentation. I should like to single out my own personal debt to S. F. Johnson, whose suggestions have always been valuable, and whose example has itself been a constant incentive to improve, to attempt to approach his ideal of scholarship. Here I should also like to record other debts: to John Unterecker, *radix bonorum;* to Wylie Sypher, for motiveless beneficence; to G. Robert Stange, Victor Harris, and Robert O. Preyer, for sympathetic interest; and to Irving Ribner, for patience, humor, and a sense of perspective. Last, for active encouragement, understanding, and innumerable kindnesses, I should like to thank John Hazel Smith.

Coriolanus
in Context

Epigraph

He who might lay claim to the title of steadfastness and constancy in his views would merit instead a reputation for imprudent resoluteness and thoughtless stubbornness since it is rather easily recognized by everyone, even those with superficial knowledge of things of state, that civil affairs are changeable, and subject to the impact and diversity of events just like the sea to the diversity of winds. Thus a man should moderate his opinions, just as a ship on a voyage sets its course according to the nature of the winds; nor must he always have the same opinion, but rather the same goal, the good and safety of the state.
Doge Leonardo Donà, 1606/7

1
Introduction

There is general critical agreement that English Renaissance history plays, of which Shakespeare's are the best-known, usually reflect the orthodox Tudor view of history, a reductive modification of medieval attitudes. The latter, anti-nationalistic, providential, apocalyptic, and periodized,[1] saw in history a rational pattern associated with God's will: a "cosmic background"[2] the God-ordained principles of which were felt to be necessary for the very existence of the universe. These principles, which can be summarized by the terms "Order" and "Degree," were seen in every stratum of life according to a series of correspondences;[3] in the world of men they would be insured by monarchy.

Irving Ribner has suggested that Renaissance Englishmen valued history for at least seven different functions

---

1. R. G. Collingwood, *The Idea of History* (Oxford: at the Clarendon Press, 1946), pp. 49–50; Tom F. Driver, *The Sense of History in Greek and Shakespearean Drama* (New York: Columbia University Press, 1960), chapter 1, analyzes Collingwood's ideas and relates them to drama.

2. E. M. W. Tillyard, *Shakespeare's History Plays* (London: Chatto and Windus, 1944), chapter 1.

3. See, *e.g.*, Hardin Craig, *The Enchanted Glass* (New York: Oxford University Press, 1936), pp. 2–3.

it could serve.[4] It instills patriotism, is concerned with current events in England and Europe, uses the past as a guide to present action or to document a secular political theory, and presents past political disasters as an aid to stoical fortitude in the present; in explicitly Christian terms, it illustrates God's providence in human affairs and demonstrates His rational plan. Nationalism, absolute obedience to the reigning monarch, order, and unity are paramount;[5] all were endorsed by the Tudors, who saw in threats of rebellion the imminent destruction of all order and therefore of all life. Plays tending to reflect any of the seven functions may be called history plays; and where English history is dramatized, the secular political theory supports strong monarchy. No other form of government is suggested as desirable to combat the chaos of democracy or tyranny.

History that is expected to furnish immediate and unequivocal political meaning amounts to propaganda. The stage was regarded as an important means of inculcating the civic virtues, and plays dramatizing English history regularly present "the unifying of the nation and the binding of the audience into the myth as the inheritors of that unity, set over against the disasters of civil war and weak leadership."[6] E. M. W. Tillyard concluded that "the orthodox doctrines of rebellion and of the monarchy were shared by every section of the community,"[7] and termed the specifically terrestrial application of the past that informs Shakespeare's history plays "the Elizabethan World Picture."[8]

4. *The English History Play in the Age of Shakespeare,* rev. ed. (London: Methuen, 1965), p. 24.

5. S. C. Sen Gupta, *Shakespeare's Historical Plays* (Oxford: Oxford University Press, 1964), p. 18.

6. Northrop Frye, *Anatomy of Criticism* (Princeton: Princeton University Press, 1957), pp. 283–84.

7. Tillyard, p. 64.

8. E. M. W. Tillyard's book of this title came out "of an attempt to write a larger one on Shakespeare's Histories." See *The Elizabethan World Picture* (New York: Modern Library, n.d.), p. vii.

R. W. Chambers's influential contribution to *Shakespeare's Hand in the Play of Sir Thomas More* reasonably sought to coordinate Elizabethan dramatic practice with political orthodoxy, and thereby to establish Shakespeare's authorship of an anonymous English historical play, *The Book of Sir Thomas More* (1593-1601).[9] Chambers based his argument on the similarity of the views in *More,* expressed particularly by the thoughtful manuscript lines (II.iii.1-172) perhaps in Shakespeare's handwriting, to political moments in several of Shakespeare's plays. He found consistently a humane treatment of the common people, concern for order, and fear of insurrection. Chambers saw similar, particularly clear positive expression of political tenets in the formulations of Ulysses's speech on Degree (*Tro.* I.iii.75-137) and in Menenius's fable of the Belly and the Members (*Cor.* I.i.95-153). The precepts and standards of behavior expressed by Ulysses and Menenius are, according to Chambers, strikingly like that of such a sixteenth-century Tudor propaganda piece as Sir John Cheke's *The Hurt of Sedition* (1549). This was written a generation earlier than Shakespeare's plays; and much later twentieth-century Shakespeare criticism has tended similarly to ignore the possibility of changes and divergences in sixteenth-century opinions.

In 1934 Alfred Hart proved that the *Homilies* were a source for political attitudes in Shakespeare's English history plays.[10] His study's real contribution, however, was the clear perception that traditional English government did not at all support the absolutist pretensions of the Tudors. The attitudes toward monarchy expressed

9. R. W. Chambers, "The Expression of Ideas—particularly political Ideas—in the three pages and in Shakespeare" in *Shakespeare's Hand in the Play of Sir Thomas More,* ed. A. W. Pollard et al. Shakespeare Problems, Series 2. (Cambridge, England: Cambridge University Press, 1923), pp. 142–88.

10. *Shakespeare and the Homilies* (Melbourne: Melbourne University Press, 1934).

in Shakespeare's plays set in the time of the War of the Roses are anachronistic: standards of the late sixteenth century are imposed on characters of the preceding century. These works, like Cheke's pamphlet, represent a constriction of views.

The Hurt of Sedition, an answer to the rebels of the 1549 Northern Rebellion, strongly supports the government's argument for civil order. However, this argument was part of a new note of harshness, marking a reversal of the liberal policies of Somerset;[11] Cheke deliberately narrowed his broad experience of humanist education to write a defense of royal supremacy, setting it within traditional political thought for a discontented population made up of nobility and gentry as well as of common people. It should be clear, therefore, that documents such as *The Hurt of Sedition,* responding to immediate situations of crisis, cannot be adduced for purposes of literary analysis before their place in the social writing of their historical period and their immediate propagandistic intentions are determined.

The speeches that Shakespeare wrote for Ulysses and Menenius, with their Christianized concerns for order and degree, are uttered in legendary Greek and Roman history. Again, it has become too common a critical practice to gloss over possibly radical distinctions, this time between plays set in classical antiquity and in England, and to see Shakespeare's plays set in pagan Rome to be Christian English Histories simply in changed dress. Despite Hart's citation of influential English writers whose endorsements of order were hardly endorsements of absolute monarchy,[12] J. E. Phillips, Jr., saw in Shakespeare's Greek and Roman plays only unaltered Tudor

11. Arthur B. Ferguson, *The Articulate Citizen and the English Renaissance* (Durham: Duke University Press, 1965), p. 268; W. G. Zeeveld, *Foundations of Tudor Policy* (Cambridge, Mass.: Harvard University Press, 1948), pp. 221–25.
12. Hart, p. 71.

doctrine: after all, the "raw materials of his expressions, however refined the latter, were those of his own time and place."[13] Since, according to Tudor orthodoxy, monarchy was divinely ordained, Shakespeare must have preferred it to aristocracy, the rule of the few, or democracy, the rule of the many, both of which violate order.[14] Phillips's discussion limits itself to Aristotle's discussions of these states; there is no other possibility, he implies in a footnote, for "I fail to find in Renaissance political literature the word 'polity' employed in its Aristotelian sense of rule by the many for the common welfare of all."[15]

Indeed such a narrow view has contemporary precedent, for the practicing playwright Thomas Heywood wrote:

> Playes are writ with this ayme, and carryed with this methode, to teach the subjects obedience to their King, to shew the people the untimely ends of such as have moved tumults, commotions, and insurrections, to present them with the flourishing estate of such as live in obedience, exhorting them to allegeance, dehorting them from all trayterous and fellonious strategems. . . . If wee present a forreigne History, the subject is so intended, that in the lives of *Romans, Grecians,* or others, either the vertues of our Country-men are extolled, or their vices reproved.[16]

This statement of 1608 (printed 1612) accords with Heywood's own peculiarly conservative dramatic prac-

---

13. *The State in Shakespeare's Greek and Roman Plays* (New York: Columbia University Press, 1940), p. 17.

14. *Ibid.,* pp. 104–11. A corrective appeared incidentally in R. Mohl's *Studies in Spenser, Milton, and the Theory of Monarchy,* (New York: King's Crown Press, 1949), p. 31, but even she looked at republican alternatives as outside political tradition.

15. Phillips, p. 106, n. 45; but cf. Sir Thomas Smith, *De Republica Anglorum* (1583) (Cambridge, England: Cambridge University Press, 1906), pp. 20–22.

16. Thomas Heywood, *An Apology for Actors* (written 1608, printed 1612), ed. R. H. Perkinson (New York: Scholar's Facsimiles and Reprints, 1941), sig. F3ᵛ.

tice, but is hardly binding on other playwrights. That he glosses over a clear and available distinction between England and Rome can be seen by looking at an early Shakespearean use of Rome, embedded in *2 Henry VI* (ca. 1591).

In IV. i, the Duke of Suffolk is about to be led off to execution. His captor, a Lieutenant, says:

> By devilish policy art thou grown great,
> And, like ambitious Sylla, overgorg'd
> With gobbets of thy mother's bleeding heart.
> (ll. 83–85)

Some lines later, Suffolk exits uttering these comparisons:

> A Roman sworder and banditto slave
> Murder'd sweet Tully; Brutus' bastard hand
> Stabb'd Julius Caesar; savage islanders
> Pompey the Great; and Suffolk dies by pirates.
> (ll. 135–38)

These quotations, which may reflect the reading of Plutarch,[17] use historical references dramatically, as historical parallels. The Lieutenant's citation of Sulla is not made from the commonplace monarchist point of view, which regarded his advent as providing a temporary solution to Rome's civil turmoil, a more permanent solution to which was provided by Augustus's accession later. Instead of praising Sulla, the Lieutenant places his emphasis on the commonwealth at large, which suffered from Sulla's ambition: by means of "devilish policy,"

---

17. The revised Arden edition of *2 Henry VI* cites Plutarch's *Cicero* as a source for the reference to sworder and slave ("Herennius a centurion, and Popilius Laena, tribune of the soldiers"), and *Brutus* for the suggestion of bastardy and the confusion over Pompey's murderers. See *2 Henry VI*, ed. A. S. Cairncross. Arden Shakespeare (London: Methuen, 1957), pp. 107–8. The reference to "Bargulus" (*2 Henry VI* IV. i. 108), which may come from Plutarch's *Pyrrhus*, would be another indication of Shakespeare's early knowledge of Plutarch's *Lives;* however Cairncross notes that "Bargulus" was available in Cicero, *de Officiis* ii. 11.

Sulla devoured his own country. The Lieutenant's view, established by means of a Roman reference, brings the actions of great heroes into question: it insists on judging them by their effects on the state.

His remark differs as greatly as possible from Suffolk's; the latter also refers to Roman history to find an analogy to the present situation, and fastens on the deaths of three Roman notables, two of whom opposed usurping Caesar and favored the traditional Republic; these men, Cicero and Pompey, are united by the irony of their fates, great men killed by base ones. But the remark is more fundamentally ironic than this, for the Lieutenant has just accused Suffolk of being the man who arranged Henry's marriage to the wrong woman, and caused him to break faith in the matter of his previous arrangement with Armagnac. Consequently, Henry lost Maine and Anjou and the loyalty of Picardy and Normandy. Further, Suffolk has been Margaret's lover, and the two are associated with a non-English tendency toward strong, unrestrained monarchy. All of these associations are borne out by Suffolk's actions onstage; but despite this evidence, he sees an injustice in that his death is at the hands of pirates! Shakespeare certainly does not present Suffolk's attitude for unqualified audience approval; although he may express a "popular medieval and Renaissance attitude," according to which Caesar's assassination, for instance, is clearly not the liberating republican act of overthrowing a tyrant,[18] the placement of the statement in Suffolk's mouth merely demonstrates his superciliousness. He is, the audience knows, radically different from a hero, and his views allow for derisive laughter from members of the audience whose sympathies are allied with the common good of the state.

"Rome" arrests the audience's attention for a mo-

---

18. Schanzer, *The Problem Plays of Shakespeare* (London: Routledge 1963), p. 23.

ment, but does not divert it from the English situation; the Roman reference does not complicate this play's action and values. The dramatic context of the quotations from *2 Henry VI* just sketched, however, indicates a tendency toward complication, rather than simplification, of political (and therefore of moral) attitudes. In plays dramatizing Roman situations, the suggestions of complexity are even stronger: England remains present by implication, and the relevance of the action to the audience is enforced by parallelism, a central concern with deep intention.

The passage cited from Heywood implies that historical plays are no more truly philosophical than Tudor propaganda, for both use history merely to illustrate a foregone conclusion; and criticism of the English history plays has contented itself in the main with enforcing the immediate relevance of the action to the precepts of orthodoxy. Only recently has there been a major movement against this approach: Sen Gupta is representative in judging that "Tudor political philosophy was indecisive, ambiguous, and confused,"[19] and that the narrow historical approach not only alters the full meaning of the plays but specifically does not allow the possibility of a skeptical or satirical presentation of an orthodox position. More theoretically, Dean argued against the view of plays as static *exempla:* when "reality is conceived as a process rather than as static perfection, then esthetic value becomes the harmony of tradition and change."[20] E. W. Talbert carried out such a "process" study of *Richard II* (ca. 1595), and found, in the period of the end of Elizabeth's reign, not total agreement with the official views of submission and monarchy, but a considerable and vital divergence of opinion.[21]

19. Sen Gupta, p. 17.
20. L. F. Dean, "Shakespeare's Treatment of Conventional Ideas," *SR* 52 (1944): 415.
21. *The Problem of Order* (Chapel Hill: University of North Carolina Press, 1962), *passim.*

When it has been recognized that the plays set in Rome differ from those set in England and require separate study with regard to both dramatic conventions and underlying philosophical and political ideas, interest in politics as a means of approach has not been great; and when the interest has at least been present, it has not been fruitful. J. C. Maxwell provides a useful summary of criticism of the Roman plays in the first half of the twentieth century, and finds a tendency among "recent" writers to stress "Shakespeare's 'political wisdom.' "[22] The phrase is L. C. Knights's, who introduces it only to disregard politics promptly and to probe the moral depths of the right relations between men. He finds a "mutuality" of relationship existing prior to the institution of political structures,[23] and derives from his reading of Aristotle's *Politics* the view that the city is of ultimate importance morally rather than politically. Within the city is the only possibility for a natural, human, and truly civilized life; without is nothing but monstrousness and meaninglessness, an absence of civilization and language.[24] But classical political philosophy defined man as primarily a social, and therefore a political, animal; for Aristotle as for Plato, politics is a large field in which to observe the practice of human nature. If the central issue of Shakespeare's *Coriolanus* is indeed "the disruption of the natural bonds and of the naturally inherent order of human existence,"[25] that disruption is presented in specifically political terms a critic cannot afford to avoid.

With Maxwell's survey appeared T. J. B. Spencer's

22. "Shakespeare's Roman Plays: 1900–1956," *SS* 10 (1957):1.
23. See L. C. Knights, *Shakespeare's Politics: with some Reflections on the Nature of Tradition.* British Academy Lecture (London: Oxford University Press, 1957).
24. Aristotle, *Politics* i. 2, 1252b–53a; also see D. J. Gordon, "Name and Fame: Shakespeare's *Coriolanus.*" *Papers Mainly Shakespearean,* ed. G. I. Duthie (Edinburgh: Oliver and Boyd, 1964), pp. 53–54.
25. H. Heuer, "From Plutarch to Shakespeare: A Study of *Coriolanus,*" *SS* 10 (1957):52.

discussion of Shakespeare's Roman plays in the light of
contemporary attitudes toward Rome and Roman politics.[26] Spencer's study is limited by his exclusive acceptance of the historical readings of such a pro-monarchist
as William Fulbecke (1560-1603?), who associates pre-
Imperial Rome with factions and dissension, the
"wounds of civil war." Other studies dealing with the
Roman background of the play have also tended to be
limited, like the English-history approaches,[27] by a passion for immediate relevance: the studies by Barroll and
Zeeveld share the approach and the limitation, although
the latter, studying *Coriolanus* against the background
of the new reign of King James I, presents material important for chapter 5.[28]

It seems safe to admit, at the beginning of this study
of *Coriolanus* and its contexts, that Shakespeare aimed,
with this play, at the same kind of immediacy that scholarship has recently been discerning in his other early-
Jacobean plays.[29] That "England" is present to some
extent when "Rome" is dramatized is a supposition warranted by historical enquiry:

26. "Shakespeare and the Elizabethan Romans," *SS* 10 (1957):27-38.
See also R. L. Anderson, "Kingship in Renaissance Drama," *SP* 41
(1944): 136-55.

27. B. Stirling, *The Populace in Shakespeare* (New York: Columbia
University Press, 1949), attempts to relate Shakespeare's plays to concerns of ca. 1590-1610, but agrees with his predecessors, herein outlined,
that the official view prevailed in Shakespeare's audience.

28. J. Leeds Barroll, "Shakespeare and Roman History," *MLR* 53
(1958): 327-43; W. G. Zeeveld, *"Coriolanus"* and Jacobean Politics,"
MLR 57 (1962):321-34.

29. See, *e. g.,* Josephine W. Bennett, *"Measure for Measure"* as *Royal
Entertainment* (New York: Columbia University Press, 1966); D. L.
Stevenson, *The Achievement of Shakespeare's "Measure for Measure"*
(Ithaca: Cornell University Press, 1966), pp. 142-44; Manfred Gross,
Shakespeares "Measure for Measure" und die Politik Jakobs I (Neu-
munster: Wachholtz Verlag, 1965); W. R. Elton, *King Lear and the
Gods* (San Marino, California: The Huntington Library, 1966); H. N.
Paul, *The Royal Play of Macbeth* (New York: Macmillan, 1950).

When his company became the King's men, his plays were, in effect, addressed *ad clerum* to practitioners in political affairs: this would at once encourage the use of political themes, and require that they be handled in a fashion both tactful and convincing.[30]

It is also warranted by the conventional substitution of a Roman name for an English one—"Tiber" for "Thames," and "Rome" for "England."[31] But there is a danger in being too specific: pointing a fancied correspondence between contemporary people and events and classical ones (a habit pervasive in such varied areas as parliamentary speeches, law cases, casual letters and historiography) does not mean that individual characters need necessarily represent living men. To see, for instance, in Coriolanus a topical reference to the Earl of Essex may be more distorting to Shakespeare's play than it is revealing, despite the fact that the analogy was pressed in one notable contemporary instance. In 1601 Bishop William Barlow, preaching a pro-government sermon from St. Paul's Cross, referred to Coriolanus as "a gallant young, but a discontented Romane, who might make a fit paralell for the late Earle, if you read his life."[32]

Such emphasis on a single character would seem to be appropriate in discussion of a tragedy; but critics who attempt to see the play in this light have had chronic difficulties with the character of Coriolanus, which Shakespeare has very deliberately placed within a tightly woven political fabric. When these critics attempt, as

30. John W. Draper, "Political Themes in Shakespeare's Later Plays," *JEGP* 35 (1936):70–71.

31. Ancient "Rome" was frequently used to mean "London" by contemporary writers. B. N. DeLuna, *Jonson's Romish Plot* (Oxford: at the Clarendon Press, 1967), p. 94, shows that the Roman Senate was used by Heywood (in the translation of Sallust, ca. 1608) to mean Parliament.

32. *A Sermon preached at Paules Crosse. With a short discourse of the late Earle of Essex* (1601), sig. C3ᵛ (STC 1454).

they must, to take politics and history into account, they fall back on the inheritance of the historical scholarship outlined above. Reuben Brower, O. J. Campbell, and H. J. Oliver have done so,[33] and in his discussion of the play's imagery, even Maurice Charney, who sees "the essence of the tragedy . . . in the grinding and pull of public and private motives, choices, and abilities,"[34] leaves the nature of these concerns unexamined, adding only that there is "some common ground between Shakespeare's English and Roman history plays, for both offer a sort of case book of illustrations for *Elizabethan* political theory."[35]

The fancied correspondence to which I have referred is not necessarily so specific as a topical reference. Bevington's observation, made in a different context, may apply a corrective: "Politics is germane to a remarkable percentage of Tudor plays, but in terms of ideas and platforms rather than personalities."[36] The more general correspondence is the parallelism seen between English government and others that resemble it from one or more points of view; the parallelism would of course be made in accordance with the author's particular intentions.

The adequacy of Heywood's statement, or the undifferentiating approach to "Shakespeare's English and

---

33. Reuben Brower, ed., *Coriolanus* ("Signet Classic Shakespeare": New York: New American Library, 1966), p. xlvii; O. J. Campbell, *Shakespeare's Satire* (London: Oxford University Press, 1943), p. 210; H. Oliver, "Coriolanus as Tragic Hero," *SQ* 10 (1959): 53–60. On discussions of Coriolanus's personal qualities, see chapter 6 below.

34. *Shakespeare's Roman Plays* (Cambridge, Mass: Harvard University Press, 1961), p. 217. Cf. M. Proser, *The Heroic Image in Five Shakespearean Tragedies* (Princeton: Princeton University Press, 1965), pp. 139–44; W. Rosen, *Shakespeare and the Craft of Tragedy* (Cambridge, Mass.: Harvard University Press, 1960), pp. 187, 206; and N. Rabkin, *Shakespeare and the Common Understanding* (New York: Free Press, 1967), p. 12.

35. Charney, p. 217; italics mine.

36. D. M. Bevington, *Tudor Drama and Politics* (Cambridge, Mass.: Harvard University Press, 1968), p. 25.

Roman history-plays,"[37] should be provable by consulting the Roman play *Coriolanus*. According to such a reading, actually proposed and relentlessly demonstrated by Phillips,[38] the common people, anywhere and anytime, by seeking a role in government (as they so clearly are doing in *Coriolanus* I. i), are guilty of trying to violate natural, universal, hierarchical order. The results of such a transgression follow swiftly: Coriolanus leaves Rome and then marches on it. This action, partly punishment and partly itself a resultant and further "departure from the pattern of society prescribed by natural law,"[39] is to be unequivocally condemned. This interpretation of the play would be inevitable only if the Tudor view had been accepted by all of Shakespeare's responsible contemporaries, as Tillyard suggests was the case.

Orthodox Tudor interests, Spencer rightly observed,[40] would admit relevance only in treating monarchs or monarch-analogues; however, William Fulbecke himself, in these words first written in 1584, praised, like many Englishmen of his time, the traditional government of the Roman Republic:

> The common-weale was brought to this good and temperate constitution, many profitable lawes were established, many victories followed, many monarchies sued for their favour, manie tyrants feared their puissance, and manie contreys dreaded their invasion. Then there flourished in Rome most admirable examples of abstinencie, modestie, justice, fortitude, and which was the seale of their securitie, an universall unitie and agreement.[41]

37. J. Dover Wilson, ed., *Coriolanus* by William Shakespeare. New Shakespeare (Cambridge, England: Cambridge University Press, 1960), p. xvii.

38. Phillips, pp. 153–71.

39. *Ibid.,* p. 169.

40. Spencer, p. 30.

41. *A Historicall Collection of the Factions, Tumults, and Massacres* (London, 1601), sigs. B2ᵛ-3ʳ (STC 11412).

This passage, taken in conjunction with the suggestion that the presence of "Rome" implies an expansion in the spectrum of political possibilities, indicates the need for a reassessing study of *Coriolanus*. The indication would be confirmed if most of the popular Roman plays up to the time of *Coriolanus* concern themselves significantly with the Roman Republic rather than with the Empire, and indeed if they support the concept of that republican, or, as it is more frequently termed, of that *mixed* government.

2
Dramatic Contexts

The corpus of other specifically Roman plays written by Shakespeare and the generally contemporary corpus of Roman plays written for the English popular stage are the immediate dramatic contexts of *Coriolanus*. The terminal date of each category is approximately 1611, the latest reasonable date for the focal play. Harbage and Schoenbaum's *Annals of English Drama, 975-1700* indicates that in addition to *Coriolanus*, the plays fitting the limitations imposed are as follows, arranged for the moment by date of dramatic setting:[1] Thomas Heywood's *Rape of Lucrece* (534-510 B.C.), Thomas Lodge's *Marius and Sylla: or, the Wounds of Civil War* (88-78 B.C.), Ben Jonson's *Catiline his Conspiracy* (63 B.C.), George Chapman's *Caesar and Pompey* (48 B.C.),

---

1. I have excluded the drama represented by the Countess of Pembroke's translations of Garnier (*Antony*, 1590), Thomas Kyd (*Pompey the Great, or Cornelia*, 1594), Samuel Daniel (*Cleopatra*, 1593, revised 1607), Samuel Brandon (*Virtuous Octavia*, 1598) and Fulke Greville (*Antony & Cleopatra*, destroyed); for this body of work see M. W. MacCallum, *Shakespeare's Roman Plays and their Background* (London: Macmillan, 1910), pp. 19-61. I have also excluded the body of academic drama deriving from the above, *e. g.*: William Alexander's *Julius Caesar* (1607), the anonymous *Tragedy of Tiberius* (printed 1607, written earlier), *Caesar's Revenge* (printed 1606, written probably 1592-96) and Matthew Gwinn's *Nero* (1603).

Shakespeare's *Julius Caesar* (44 B.C.) and *Antony and Cleopatra* (40-30 B.C.), Ben Jonson's *Sejanus* (A.D. 23-31) and Shakespeare's *Titus Andronicus* (perhaps A.D. fifth century). Within the Shakespearean canon, the dramatic date of the narrative poem *Lucrece* (510 B.C.) is closest to that of *Coriolanus* (494 B.C.), but their attitudes toward politics are most distinct. Of the non-Shakespearean plays cited, Ben Jonson's *Catiline* is closest to *Coriolanus* in date of composition; the radical difference between these virtually contemporaneous plays I reserve for discussion in the Epilogue.

Arranged in this manner, the plays show a recurring conceptual pattern. The civil wars between Marius and Sulla and their continuation, and the problems involved in imperial pleas for absolute power, present the threatening of freedom by tyranny; the former is identified with Republican Rome and associated with the welfare of the nation, while the latter is identified with potential or actual emperors and associated with their self-seeking interests. Only rarely is the pattern reversed: in Shakespeare's treatment of the revolt of the hero Junius Brutus, tyranny is clearly overthrown by liberty.

The works to be surveyed thus treat the government of Republican Rome as a moral-political positive. It would be well to look at this form of government briefly. The treatment is an inheritance from classical Greek political thought, in which the earliest reference to this form of government (although without name, and not Roman) is by Thucydides (ca. 460-ca. 400 B.C.). For him it is "the best which the Athenians ever enjoyed within my memory," a state in which "Oligarchy and Democracy were duly attempered."[2] Both Plato and Aristotle discuss governments which "attempered,"by balance or mixture, the elements present by nature in all states—

---

2. Thucydides, *The Peloponnesian War* viii. 97, in *The Greek Historians*, ed. F. R. B. Godolphin (New York: Random House, 1942), 1:996.

the monarch, the aristocracy, and the people. Although he too has some difficulty finding a name for this kind of government, Aristotle agrees with the historian both in praising the government and in locating its defining characteristic as a combination of oligarchy and democracy.[3] He offers this *locus classicus* on its structure:

> Some, indeed, say that the best constitution is a combination of all existing forms, and they praise the Lacedaemonian because it is made up of oligarchy, monarchy, democracy, the king forming the monarchy, and the council of elders the oligarchy, while the democratic element is represented by the Ephors; for the Ephors are selected from the people.
>
> (*Politics* ii. 69. 1265b)

The terms of Aristotle's analysis are specifically Spartan; since, however, all states were understood by classical political thought to be made up of three elements, the monarchic one might variously be termed the monarch, king, prince, duke, doge, emperor, or the consuls; the aristocratic might be termed the lords or nobles, the elders, patricians, or senators; the democratic might be termed generally the people or the commons, but was usually represented by parliamentary officers, such as Members of the House of Commons in England, or, elsewhere, by ephors, tribunes, even *avvocatori*. The degrees of power represented by these three ubiquitous divisions of society varied from state to state, from time to time, and from observer to observer. The varieties of mixture are thus enormous.

Although such influential historians as Dionysius of Halicarnassus, Livy, and Plutarch discuss mixed governments, for Antiquity as for the Renaissance the recognized authority on the theory and structure of its Roman form was Polybius (ca. 203-ca. 130 B.C.); his views and attitudes pervade the later work of his many later

---

3. *Politics* iv. 8–9, v. 7, 1293b–94b, 1306b–8a.

readers.[4] According to his analysis, in fully Republican Rome each of the ubiquitous three elements, through self-interest, sought to dominate the others, but was only powerful enough to check the attempts of each of the other two to take control. The mixture was a series of balances between one element and the other two: two would join together to protect themselves against the ambition of one.[5] The first element, the monarchic, was represented by the two consuls. For this position to work well, it needed to respond to "commonweale" pressures: it depended on the support of the Senate and of the people. The Senate was in charge of renewing the appointment of the consul at the expiration of his term of office; this was normally automatic, since the consul was usually a member of the aristocratic class. The people had to be consulted before peace could be ratified, and the consul had to give them an account of his actions before laying down his office.

The people exercised power through their elected representatives, the tribunes. As a practical matter, the people were under pressure to agree with the Senate for fear of reprisals, but generally the people and the Senate were closer, although hardly cordial, than the people and the consuls; the consuls tended to be in absolute control in military matters (vi. 17, pp. 307-9), an area which tends to augment differences rather than similarities. In the very structure of the state, then, "mixture" takes the form of a balance: the balancing of the consuls

4. A partial English translation by C. W[atson]., of Book One of the *Histories* appeared in 1568 (STC 20097). Watson annexed "an abstract of the worthy acts perpetrate by King Henry the fift," presenting material dramatized by Shakespeare in *Henry V* (cf. *Histories,* sigs. 05ᵛ–06ʳ with *Henry V* I. i. 1–19). The analogy Watson enforces is between the wisdom of England's attacking Scotland rather than France, and Rome's wisdom in attacking nearby Sicily rather than far-off Gaul (sigs. P7ᵛ–8ʳ).

5. Polybius, *Histories,* vi. 10, trans. W. R. Paton. Loeb Classical Library (Cambridge, Mass.: Harvard University Press, 1954), 3: 289-93. References will be to this edition.

and aristocracy on the one hand, and the people on the other, or, perhaps, of the extremes of consul and people by the mean, the aristocratic Senate. Only in later Italian formulations, such as Giannotti's, does the Greek concept of "balance" give way to that of a more complex "mixture."

The Roman tribunes, often viewed as parallel or analogous to the Spartan ephorate, were a "piece of institutionalized revolution,"[6] a countermagistracy with power to annoy and prod the rest of government. The tribunate had been instituted not only to redress specific grievances, but for general safety, as a measure of protection for private citizens against the arbitrary and oppressive actions of the patrician aristocracy and its servants. The institution of the tribunate was an expression of the plebeian view that government is alien and dangerous by its very nature. Accordingly, the tribunes, by protecting the people from tyranny, guarded the real interests of the state; however, from the aristocratic point of view, the tribunes were seditious by their very existence, the welfare of the state being identified with the aristocracy.[7]

Mixed government, unlike the three traditional simple states and their perverse counterparts inherited from Greek political theory, was considered stable in its very essence; it was invented in Sparta by Lycurgus, who saw its possibilities for both stability and longevity.[8] After his death, popularly elected ephors were added, in order to control the aristocracy. According to Polybius, the mixture in question was really a sort of balanced coexistence:

---

6. K. Von Fritz, *The Theory of the Mixed Constitution in Antiquity* (New York: Columbia University Press, 1954), pp. 103-4, 201.

7. See F. W. Walbank, *A Historical Commentary on Polybius* (Oxford: at the Clarendon Press, 1957), 1: 674.

8. Polybius, vi. 10, 48, 50, pp. 289-93, 377-81, 383. Praise of the mixed state had been commonplace since Plato, who also attributed its invention to Lycurgus of Sparta.

The three kinds of government that I spoke of above all shared in the control of the Roman state. And such fairness and propriety in all respects was shown in the use of these three elements for drawing up the constitution and in its subsequent administration that it was impossible even for a native to pronounce with certainty whether the whole system was aristocratic, democratic, or monarchical. This was indeed only natural. For if one fixed one's eyes on the power of the consuls, the constitution seemed completely monarchical and royal; if on that of the senate it seemed again to be aristocratic; and when one looked at the power of the masses, it seemed clearly to be a democracy.[9]

Polybius thought Sparta the only fit parallel for Rome, matching her in political structure and success (vi. 48-50, pp. 377-83). It is to this structure that his book attributes Rome's remarkable success in the years 220-168 B.C., when, after a long period of adjustment, the "constitution of Rome reached its point of perfection."[10] Shakespeare's Horatio calls this period of the late Republic "the most high and palmy state of Rome,/A little ere the mightiest Julius fell" (*Hamlet* I. i. 113-14); and it is this structure that the works now to be surveyed use for a moral-political positive.

Shakespearean Contexts

The 1590s saw two treatments of the Lucrece story that place it in a political context. Shakespeare's early effort was apparently composed in the plague-years 1592-

---

9. Polybius vi. 11, in 3: 295-97; Paul Pédech, *La Méthode historique de Polybe* (Paris: Société d'Edition "les belles lettres," 1964), p. 319, understands this passage to be an early attempt to formulate the existing peculiar government of Rome in terms of the theory of simple states since there was no adequate vocabulary: Plato, *e.g.*, varies the interpretation and shows the difficulty involved, for he did not know what to call government which was tyrannical by the Ephors, aristocratic by the royalty, and in other ways democratic (*Laws* iv. 712 c-d).
10. Pédech, p. 431; see also Polybius vi. 11, pp. 293-97.

93, during much of which the theaters were closed; the printed text is thought to have been carefully checked by the author, for whom nondramatic writing was a new venture. *Lucrece,* printed by Richard Field, Shakespeare's townsfellow, in 1594, and reprinted in 1598, twice in 1600, 1607, 1616, 1624, and yet twice more before the Restoration, was enormously successful. Although this learned poem was intended as a serious literary work, possibly to establish Shakespeare as a nondramatic poet, and was aimed at an educated and sophisticated class of readers, critics have generally had a more difficult time accounting for its popularity than is the case with its companion, *Venus and Adonis* (1593).

The poem's sources are Ovid and Livy, but the story of Lucrece was available elsewhere as well;[11] the description of Troy, which has seemed unnecessary to some critics,[12] comes from the *Aeneid:* "the 'pictura inanis' from the first book, the fall of Troy from the second."[13] Gabriel Harvey draws attention to the direction taken by Shakespeare's treatment by writing, "the younger sort takes much delight in Shakespeare's Venus, and Adonis; but his Lucrece, and his tragedie of Hamlet, Prince of Denmark, have it in them, to please the wiser sort."[14] Taken in conjunction with a Roman-Trojan setting ha-

---

11. The usual list of sources includes Ovid, Livy, Dionysius of Halicarnassus, Gower, and Chaucer. Chaucer combines Ovid and Livy, and Renaissance editions of Ovid commonly had *variorum* notes. Thus T. W. Baldwin, in *On The Literary Genetics of Shakespeare's Poems and Sonnets* (Urbana: University of Illinois Press, 1950), pp. 100, 107, 153 and 382–83, suggests that Shakespeare used the Marsus *variorum* edition of Ovid (Basle, 1550) which incorporated material from Dionysius of Halicarnassus and Livy.

12. See *e.g.,* Louis R. Zocca, *Elizabethan Narrative Poetry* (New Brunswick: Rutgers University Press, 1950), p. 49.

13. D. C. Allen, "Some Observations on the *Rape of Lucrece," SS* 15 (1962): 94–95.

14. *Gabriel Harvey's Marginalia,* ed. G. C. Moore Smith (Stratford: Shakespeare Head Press, 1913), p. 232.

bitually interpreted allegorically during the Renaissance,[15] this remark suggests that the political stratum running through the poem was potent to the poem's educated readers. The nature of that stratum also suggests why the poem was reprinted less frequently in the later Jacobean years.[16]

The "argument" cites events preceding the opening lines of the poem: Lucius Tarquinius Superbus, "contrary to the Roman laws and customs, not requiring or staying for the people's suffrages, had possessed himself of the kingdom."[17] Tarquin is identified as a usurper who imposed his will on Rome and was overthrown: in presenting this action, Shakespeare committed himself to a point in history at which that nation threw off her tyrannic kings and became free, with a mixed state.

The political setting is continued into the poem. Lucrece is described heraldically (l. 64), a manner pointing outward from the personal catastrophe of rape, a direction also indicated by the long, formal complaints to Night, Opportunity, and Time (ll. 764-1036). The rape itself, the ultimate tyrannic act, is referred to as the sack of the house of Lucrece's soul (ll. 1170-76), and Tarquin identified with Sinon (ll. 1541-47). The "skil-

---

15. D. C. Allen, pp. 95–96.

16. E. P. Kuhl, "Shakespeare's *Rape of Lucrece,*" *Renaissance Studies in Honor of Hardin Craig* (Stanford: Stanford University Press, [1941]), pp. 160–68, argues convincingly that *Lucrece*'s political theme was recognized and appreciated by contemporaries. He points out that Lydgate's *Serpent of Division,* reprinted with *Gorboduc* in 1590, begins with the banishment of the Tarquins, and he draws attention also to the extracts from *Lucrece* that appear in a political context in the widely-read *England's Parnassus* (1600). *Lucrece* was understood to be a political poem at least until after its appearance in a supplementary fourth volume of *Poems on Affairs of State* (London, 1707).

17. Cf. Plutarch, "king Tarquine surnamed the prowde, being come to the crowne by no good lawfull meane, but contrarylie by indirect and wicked wayes . . . ," *Publicola* 1, *Plutarch's Lives of the Noble Grecians and Romans Englished by Sir Thomas North* (1579). The Tudor Translations (London: Nutt, 1895), 1: 249. References will be to traditional chapter divisions, herewith supplied, followed by volume and page numbers in this edition.

ful painting" Lucrece looks at is the siege or rape of Troy, caused by "sly" Ulysses (ll. 1394-1400), Paris's "lust" (l. 1473) and Sinon's "false creeping craft and perjury" (l. 1517). Like Hamlet, who also at a moment of personal crisis turns to something external, past, and Trojan, in the Player's recitation of Aeneas's tale to Dido of the death of Priam and sorrow of Hecuba (*Hamlet* II. ii), so here Lucrece finds an external parallel to her private condition. Troy, caught treacherously by the treacherous Greeks, is sacked, as Lucrece, caught by the treacherous Sextus, is sacked metaphorically. The parallelism transcends the realistic distinction between city and woman by means of the allegorical *psychomachia:* the woman, already clearly emblematic, with propriety stands for Troy. The military action, a parallel to Lucrece's situation, causes her to ask:

> Why should the private pleasure of some one
> Become the public plague of many moe?
> Let sin, alone committed, light alone
> Upon his head that hath transgressed so;
> Let guiltless souls be freed from guilty woe.
> > For one's offence why should so many fall,
> > To plague a private sin in general?
> > > (ll. 1478–84)

Lucrece lists some of the significant casualties, direct and indirect, of the war, and implicitly answers her own question: for individuals of this stature, the private and public worlds are indissolubly linked. For the same reason, her own private situation has public consequences, presenting the fundamental nature of, and objection to, tyranny; under tyranny there is neither the possibility of impartial justice nor that of freedom.

Faced with having to offer a political solution to this situation, a writer might have proposed actions ranging from stoic fortitude to violent revolution. In the popular theater, the conventional solution was to advocate passive obedience; but this poem, addressed to a more literate audience, approves the violent overthrow of the rulers and the attempt to establish a just state.[18] This is the extremist course selected by Lucrece's family and their friends; after her husband Collatinus and her father Lucretius come in answer to her message, accompanied by Junius Brutus and Publius Valerius (Publicola),[19] Brutus informs the Roman people of the rape, and incites them against the king:

> They did conclude to bear dead Lucrece thence,
> To show her bleeding body thorough Rome,
> And so to publish Tarquin's foul offence;
> Which being done with speedy diligence,
>   The Romans plausibly did give consent
>   To Tarquin's everlasting banishment.
>   (ll. 1850–55)

As a result, the "argument" reads, "the people were so moved, that with one consent and a general acclamation the Tarquins were all exiled, and the state government changed from kings to consuls." At the end of the action, Brutus is still alive, supported not only by the Roman aristocracy but also by the people. Although the government is not as yet technically fully mixed, for it has no tribunes, nevertheless the stress on popular support makes it in effect mixed.

 Shakespeare's poem shares both title and initial popularity with Thomas Heywood's play *The Rape of Lucrece*, which went through three printings in 1608-9. The play may therefore be considered here. Alan Hola-

---

18. For the difficulties involved in Lucrece's parallel violent overthrow, her suicide, see D. C. Allen, pp. 90–91, 97.

19. Renaissance readers would have known from Livy or Plutarch that the Roman people chose Collatinus and Junius Brutus to be consuls and, when Collatinus proved unsatisfactory (he was related to the Tarquins), chose Publicola to replace him. In *Coriolanus,* Shakespeare chooses the name Valeria, that of Publicola's daughter, for Virgilia's friend. See Plutarch, *Publicola* 19, in 1: 270.

day has termed it loosely connected and a series of scenes[20] (despite a revision in 1607). First written in about 1594, it is a popular[21] counterstatement to Shakespeare's learned poem of that year, and adheres closely to orthodox Tudor doctrine. This adherence is indicated circumstantially by Heywood's own references immediately following the passage quoted above and by his largely unsophisticated audience at the popular theaters; internally it is indicated by the important and clear thread of politics running through this action, as it does through Livy's source-account. Despite similarities to Shakespeare's poem, and indeed to a number of Shakespearean plays,[22] Heywood's greater emphasis on the political background highlights remarkable differences.

The beginning of the play makes abundantly clear that Tarquin's assumption of power is a usurpation. His subsequent tyranny will have evil results at large, morally as well as politically: it will "beget a weak impotence" in the state that will

> so becalme us that wee have not aire
> Able to raise our plumes, to taste the pleasures
> of our own Elements.
>
> (ll. 479–80)

The moral degeneration is immediately to be seen in Tullia's desecration of her father's body, and, in the world at large, in the progressive degeneration of the manhood of the Roman heroes, which creates a world in which the rape of Lucrece is the inevitable result, and in fact the emblem. The revolution is inspired by this act of personal tyranny.

---

20. Thomas Heywood, *The Rape of Lucrece,* ed. Alan Holaday ("University of Illinois Studies in Language and Literature, vol. 34, no. 3"; Urbana: University of Illinois Press, 1950), p. 37.
    21. *Ibid.,* pp. 27–29.
    22. Irving Ribner, *Jacobean Tragedy* (London: Methuen, 1962), pp. 59–71.

The beginning of the return of order to the chaotic land is signaled by the oracle at Delphi, who says,

> Then *Rome* her ancient honours wins,
> When she is purg'd from *Tullia's* sins.
> (ll. 711–12)

Speaking as it were for divine providence, the oracle sanctions revolutionary action that will purge evil and end the play by reestablishing natural relations. Collatine, Lucrece's husband, steadfastly utters the orthodox "Leave all to Heaven" (l. 1221), thus exhibiting an approved passive obedience which Heywood incorporates in several of his English History plays.[23] However, this view is no longer sufficient. Early in the action, Brutus questioned the gods' intentions (ll. 378-80); in disguise as the humorous Brutus, he waits for the right moment, the occasion signaled by the oracle's obscure disclosure, "He that first shall kisse his mother/ Shall be powerfull, and no other" (ll. 743-44). When Brutus kisses the earth, he and his followers at last have warrant for direct action. In opposition, Sextus invokes the Tudor commonplace threatening the revolutionaries with the gods' punishment (ll. 2557-60). He is answered by the anointed agent of providence, Brutus, whose "vertues did thy sinne exceed" (l. 2587), and who proclaims himself consul, since henceforth the name of king is "odious/ Unto this nation" (ll. 2581-82). The usurper Tarquin's rightful punishment is to be crushed; an immediate result is that the degenerate M. Scevola (ll. 1003-5) is regenerated and performs acts of incredible bravery in defense of Rome (ll. 2620-22).

In this process, Brutus's death at the hands of Sextus, whom he in turn kills, is dramatically necessary.[24] Brutus

---

23. Irving Ribner, *The English History Play in the Age of Shakespeare*, rev. ed. (London: Methuen, 1965), pp. 221, 273-77.

24. Ribner, *Jacobean Tragedy*, p. 70, calls this "extraneous"; however, it follows Plutarch's account, according to which Brutus's antagonist is Tarquin's son Aruns.

has put off his antic disposition to engage in action; like Hamlet, he is the revenger acting in accordance with the wishes of providence to purge a rotten state, and like Hamlet too, he dies in personal combat. He achieves no philosophical transcendence of such opposing claims as those of appearance and reality, or passion and reason, a transcendence which frequently implies death in tragedy;[25] Brutus dies simply for upsetting the state. In Heywood's orthodox view there can be no moral justification for rebellion, regardless of the motivation; however, once dead, Brutus is a hero. The state he leaves behind is ruled by Collatine, who in Plutarch is judged to be inadequate. In Heywood's treatment, and in a state as yet without tribunes, he is an approved monarch-analogue: the final emphasis is on the resurgence of heroism and order, not of freedom.

Titus Andronicus was printed by John Danter in 1594, the same year as Shakespeare's *Lucrece*. The dramatic time is not indicated with precision, but the simultaneous presence of Bassianus (possibly the Emperor Caracalla, d. A.D. 217) and Gothic invasions (actually culminating in the sack of Rome, A.D. 410) sufficiently indicates that the play's action takes place in late-Imperial Rome. The eighteenth-century prose tale, thought by some to be a late version of a source for the play,[26] locates the action in the time of the Eastern Emperor Theodosius (A.D. 378-95). Although the play's sources (Ovid's *Metamorphoses* and Seneca's *Thyestes*) are otherwise considered to be nonhistorical and nonpolitical, the appearance of suggestive Roman names indicates that Shakespeare also used Plutarchan material, gathered principally from *Scipio Africanus* and *Coriolanus,* and the *Comparison*

25. S. F. Johnson, "The Regeneration of Hamlet," *SQ* 3 (1952): 207.
26. R. Sargent, "The Source of *Titus Andronicus,*" *SP* 46 (1949), 167–83, and Geoffrey Bullough, *Narrative and Dramatic Sources of Shakespeare* 6 (London: Routledge, 1966): 7; the text is on pp. 34–44.

between Scipio and Hannibal,[27] in an attempt to make
Titus "a Roman play with political implications."[28]
Such an intention is revealed by references and parallels
to *Lucrece*[29] and by certain patterns of action occurring
also in both Plutarch and in Shakespeare's later play
Coriolanus.

As in the case of *Lucrece,* politics forms an element
running through the play. Act One opens with the problem of power disputed by two claimants. Saturninus, the
older son of the deceased Emperor, seeks support from
the Senators and the people for his "successive title"
(I.i.4.). Bassianus, the younger son, requests rather
that the imperial seat be filled by one elected by free
Romans, arguing that such choice will exclude dishonor
(thus suggestively associated with primogeniture and
Saturninus) from approaching a throne dedicated to
"virtue. . . ./ To justice, continence, and nobility" (I.i.
14-15).[30]

The rivalry is interrupted by the tribune Marcus Andronicus, the people's "trust" (l. 181), who holds up
the crown and announces that the people of Rome have
resolved the difficulty posed by the aristocratic striving
by factions:

> Know that the people of Rome, for whom we stand
> A special party, have by common voice
> In election for the Roman empery
> Chosen Andronicus.
>
>   (I.i.20–23)

---

27. *Scipio* and *Hannibal* are really post-Plutarchan, but appeared in
the 1579 edition of the *Lives.* See the articles by R. A. Law, "The Text
of Shakespeare's Plutarch," *HLQ* 6 (1943): 197–203; "The Roman
Background of *Titus Andronicus*" *SP* 40 (1943): 145–53.

28. Bullough, 6: 7.

29. References and parallel passages are given in *The Poems,* ed.
F. T. Prince. Arden Shakespeare (Cambridge, Mass.: Harvard University Press, 1960), p. xxxvii, n.

30. See A. Sommers, "'*Wilderness of Tigers*': Structure and Symbolism in *Titus Andronicus,*" *EIC* 10 (1960): 278–79.

Titus's past heroism is recounted conventionally, but he is not attracted to power; an equally conventional Roman view of the vanity of glory causes him to ask,

> What should I don this robe, and trouble you?
> Be chosen with proclamations to-day,
> To-morrow yield up rule, resign my life?
>
> (I.i.189–91)

He asks the people for "a staff of honour for mine age,/ But not a sceptre to control the world" (ll. 198-99).

In order to ensure his own installation on the throne, Saturninus begins to incite a disturbance which is quieted when the tribune says that the people will accept whomever Titus selects to rule. The tribune, nominally representing the people, is quite clearly intended to have a strong voice in the political affairs of Rome; and even though Bassianus has lost the imperial throne, he praises the tribune's "uprightness and integrity" (l. 48). This view of the virtuous tribunate is questioned only by Saturninus, who calls Marcus "proud and ambitious Tribune" (l. 202). The charge is understandable in the situation, for Saturninus wants the empery and the tribune seems to him to be forcing it on an unwilling Titus; but dislike of the tribunate is a characteristic of those who embrace tyrannic rule. In this first scene, Shakespeare deliberately shows the tribune fulfilling well his function, and not misleading the people, but rather safeguarding their interests by pressing their choice of ruler.

Titus declines power for himself and chooses the emperor's elder son Saturninus. Although initially Shakespeare's Elizabethan audience would have approved this choice, the new ruler soon begins to show tyrannic qualities of fickleness and willfulness, which are encouraged by Tamora, formerly the Gothic queen, now "incorporate in Rome" (I.i.462). Under this government, the political climate of Rome changes: the tribunes become

of less use than stones (III.i.33-47). Now a "wilderness
of tigers" (III.i.54), the city unjustly preys on the An-
dronici.

Tyrannic Rome becomes "ingrateful" (V.i.12) and
disregards Titus's past service;[31] but the military hero
Titus nevertheless remains loyal to the commonwealth.
He exemplifies other early-Roman virtues as well: he is
stern, unmoved by appeals to pity, and, motivated by a
"cruel, irreligious piety" (I.i.130), kills his son Mutius
for opposing his will. The combination of this national
loyalty, willingness to kill his son, and his later feigned
madness are reminiscent of the great republican Lucius
Junius Brutus, who feigned madness in order to fool
Tarquin,[32] who preserved justice by overthrowing tyranny, and who is reported to have executed his sons for
plotting to restore it. The state of tyranny is represented
in a manner parallel with that in *Lucrece*. Lavinia, whose
very name is symbolic (it is the name of Aeneas's second
wife, after whom he named Lavinium), is raped and
mutilated by forces associated with Saturnine's tyrannic
and oppressive government. Brought before her father
Titus and uncle Marcus, she stands, in III.i, an emblem
for raped and dismembered Rome; young Lucius then
exits with the intention of requiting her wrongs (l. 297).
His actions are thereafter parallel to a recognizable
Plutarchan pattern; they are also parallel to the actions
of Shakespeare's Coriolanus, with the exception that

---

31. Heywood's mention of the pattern indicates that Roman "ingratitude" was a commonplace view: "Hast thou of thy Country well
deserved? and art thou of thy labour evill requited? to associate thee
thou mayest see the valiant *Roman Marcellus* pursue *Hannibal* . . .
and presently (for his reward) banisht his Country into Greece. There
thou mayest see *Scipio Affricanus,* now triumphing for the conquest of
all Affrica, and immediatly exil'd the confines of *Romania." An Apologie
for Actors* (1612), ed. R. H. Perkinson (New York: Scholar's Facsimiles
and Reprints, 1941), sig. G1r. On Roman ingratitude, see chapter 6
below and, on James I's reference to Scipio Africanus, chapter 5.
32. Plutarch, *Publicola* 3–7, in 1:252–57; cf. *Lucrece,* ll. 1807–20 and
Henry V II.iv.37.

Lucius's are unequivocally approved. He returns leading Gothic troops, and "threats in course of his revenge to do/ As much as ever Coriolanus did" (IV.iv.67-68). Tamora, like the women in *Coriolanus* V.iii, plans to "pluck proud Lucius from the warlike Goths" (IV.iv. 110), but fails. Lucius's description of his own situation with relation to Rome offers a counterpart to Coriolanus's (cf. *Cor.* IV.v.71-95):

> myself unkindly banished,
> The gates shut on me, and turn'd weeping out
> To beg relief among Rome's enemies;
> Who drown'd their enmity in my true tears
> And op'd their arms to embrace me as a friend.
> I am the turned forth, be it known to you,
> That have preserv'd her welfare in my blood
> And from her bosom took the enemy's point,
> Sheathing the steel in my advent'rous body.
> (V.iii.104–12)

Lucius's march, seeking to save Rome from tyranny, is victorious; audience approval of this is assured when his Gothic troops, after all enemies of Rome, virtually disappear in accordance with the last lines quoted. Lucius's direct revolutionary action heals Rome; the public resolution of Act V, which involves Rome's renewal, is presented as a fitting ending for the play.[33] This account of it illustrates the tribune Marcus's lesson, which shows the Romans

> how to knit again
> This scattered corn into one mutual sheaf,
> These broken limbs again into one body.
> (V.iii.70–72)

By omitting the consequences of an invasion of foreign troops, the Coriolanus-pattern is anticipated without tragic results.

---

33. See my essay *"Titus Andronicus:* Metamorphosis and Renewal."

That a loyal tribune should express concern for Rome's health is characteristic of Shakespeare's early dramatic use of the tribunate. *Titus Andronicus* has presented republican vestiges in late-Imperial Rome in approving terms consistent with *Lucrece*. Shakespeare's *Lucrece* and *Titus Andronicus* share an overt anti-tyrannic bias; but the knowledge of history demanded of the intended educated reader of the first, and the emphasis on Rome's regeneration in the second, indicates that neither of these works rests finally on "revenge." Rather, revenge is in both cases subsumed by the political temperance implied by mixed government.

Shakespeare's next treatment of Rome was more severely political. *Julius Caesar* was first printed in the 1623 Folio; it uses factual material from Plutarch's *Caesar, Brutus, Antony,* and *Cicero*[34] in dramatizing the assassination of Caesar (44 B.C.) and the final moments of the Republic. Contemporary Renaissance attitudes toward this period ranged from condemning, pro-Empire views to extreme, pro-Brutus republicanism;[35] the playwright thus had considerable latitude in deciding the kind of political treatment appropriate for his play.[36] At the beginning of Act One Caesar's triumph is celebrated by the people of Rome. That triumph, however, is undercut

34. See T. S. Dorsch, *Julius Caesar* Arden Shakespeare (Cambridge, Mass.: Harvard University Press, 1955), pp. vii–xix; and Bullough 5 (London: Routledge, 1964) :36.

35. T. J. B. Spencer, "Shakespeare and the Elizabethan Romans," *SS* 10 (1957) :34, refers to the full biographies of Caesar by Hubert Goltz (1563) and Stephano Schiappalaria (1578). For a recent summary on the range of attitudes Shakespeare could appeal to, and some twentieth-century scholarship on the subject, see David Bevington, *Tudor Drama and Politics* (Cambridge, Mass.: Harvard University Press, 1968), p. 248 and notes.

36. For a brief survey of contemporary pro-republican literary attitudes, see S. F. Johnson, review of Dorsch, in *SQ* 8 (1957) :393–94. Brutus, whose strong statement (II.i.10–34) was suggested by Plutarch's *Comparison* of Brutus and Dion (see E. A. J. Honigmann, "Shakespeare's Plutarch," *SQ* 10 (1959) :25–33) was much given to reading and annotating Polybius (Plutarch, *Brutus* 4, in 6:185; cf. Shakespeare, *Julius Caesar* IV.iii.252–74.

by the tribunes of the people, Flavius and Marullus, who chide the celebrants for praising one who brings only Roman captives, countrymen defeated in civil war. The validity of the people's joy is undercut by the revelation that only recently they had celebrated the victories of Caesar's adversary, Pompey (I.i.55-56). After dispersing the people, the tribunes make plans to go through Rome to "disrobe the images" that are "dek't with ceremonies" in Caesar's honor (ll. 69-70). The next the audience hears of the tribunes, "for pulling scarfs off Caesar's images, [they] are put to silence" (I.ii.288-89).

Between these two events, Caesar appears and then leaves the stage; during the following moments, Cassius and Brutus speak onstage, interrupted by offstage shouts marking moments at which the people approve Caesar's rejection of kingship. This sequence of action establishes simultaneous presentation of Rome the republic, providing freedom and belittling Caesar, and Rome the imminent Empire, rewarding ambition by approving Caesar.[37] The people shout and clap as he refuses the crown three times—yet, ominously, he refuses it "every time gentler than other" (I.ii.229). This offstage action is of course reported, and hence filtered through a character's unsympathetic perception of it. The effect is to stress the more immediate action, the conversation between Brutus and Cassius, which concentrates on belittling the Caesar whom the audience has so briefly and so magnificently seen. As a result, to that appearance adhere a number of reductive associations: sterility (I.ii.8-9), weakness in swimming (ll. 100-15), fever (ll. 119-27), partial deafness (l. 213), and epilepsy (ll. 249-57).

Such is the man, Cassius's equal in birth, who seeks to become king. This action, undoubtedly ambitious (for

---

37. In *Coriolanus*, the Senate-dominated state is presented simultaneously with the new fully mixed state. See below, chapter 6.

he threatens to destroy the balance of the republic), is the cause of his death.[38] Thereafter the role of the ineffectual tribunes is assumed by the Roman praetor, Marcus Brutus. Brutus, the descendant of Lucius Junius Brutus, who overthrew the Tarquins (I.ii.159-61; II.i. 53-54), and son of the Junius Brutus dramatized by Lodge, is ideologically and congenitally republican. Further, he is married to Portia, daughter of Cato Utican, and thus associated with a family of idealized republican examples of virtue. For these reasons he can say:

> Set honour in one eye and death i' th' other,
> And I will look on both indifferently;
> For let the gods so speed me as I love
> The name of honour more than I fear death.
>
> (I.ii.86–89)

It is precisely the "honour" of the conspirators that is effectively discredited by Antony in the Forum scene. The forces that replace Caesar to defeat Brutus and Cassius are more politically able than they; it is Rome's tragedy that these forces are also unscrupulous and base, robbing the people of their rightful "legacies" bequeathed them by Julius Caesar (IV.i.8-9). The end of the play acknowledges the fact of Octavius's historical victory, but does not rejoice at it. Antony praises Brutus:

> This was the noblest Roman of them all.
> All the conspirators save only he
> Did that they did in envy of great Caesar;
> He, only in a general honest thought
> And common good to all, made one of them.
> His life was gentle, and the elements
> So mix'd in him, that Nature might stand up
> And say to all the world, "this was a man!"
>
> (V.v.68–75)

---

38. A. Venezky, *Pageantry on the Shakespearian Stage* (New York: Twayne, 1951), pp. 133–34, draws attention to the fact that Caesar's death is like the downfall of a proud and unjust king; see also Plutarch's *Caesar* 57, 60, in 5:57, 60–61.

His words are not challenged by Octavius; but at the end, the qualities inherent in "honest thought," "gentle" life, and interest in "common good" are, like Brutus, dead.

In *Julius Caesar* and *Titus Andronicus,* as in *Coriolanus,* initial triumph leads only to final funeral; in the two later plays, which stress the political dimension of these deaths, the presentations of both deaths and the future of Rome are tinged with irony.

Between *Julius Caesar* and *Coriolanus,* Shakespeare's only Roman Plutarchan play is *Antony and Cleopatra* (1607-8), in which politics has generally been regarded as incidental. P. L. Rose has recently discerned a political dimension: "the political attitudes of Antony, of Caesar, and of Cleopatra are all basically archetypal of conflicting sixteenth-century views on kingship."[39] Each character can be distinguished by his attitude toward power: for Caesar, it is an instrument for peaceful social order; for Antony, a means for attaining, and maintaining, valor. Cleopatra's power, by contrast, is "naked, hereditary, and despotic" (p. 382).

The politics of Empire allow no justification for rebellion: but it is in the minor themes of civil war and foreign invasion that traditional republican politics figures. Sextus Pompey's rebellion and its attendant sympathetic civil unrest in Rome are mentioned (I.iii.45-54, II.i.3-11) and arguments for it presented (II.vi.10-23). Sextus Pompey identifies his cause with that of his father and his friends:

>   what
> Made the all-honour'd honest Roman, Brutus,
> With the arm'd rest, courtiers of beauteous freedom,
> To drench the Capitol, but that they would
> Have one man but a man?
>   (II.vi.15–19)

---

39. P. L. Rose, "The Politics of *Antony and Cleopatra,*" *SQ* 20 (1969):381.

Civil insurrection against Octavius Caesar is associated
with Antony by the mention of the activities of his wife
Fulvia and his brother Lucius (II.i.38-42, II.ii.42-47).
Antony's creation of independent kingships within the
Empire is one of Octavius's charges against him (III.vi.
1-19). Last, Antony uses foreign troops to combat
Rome. Understated though it is, the political dimension
is an important contributing element in this great tragedy.

Non-Shakespearean Contexts

The Wounds of Civil War was, like Shakespeare's
Titus Andronicus, printed by John Danter in 1594, but
according to the title page Thomas Lodge's play had
already been acted by the Lord Admiral's Men, presumably in the period 1585-91.[40] The play deals with
the period of rivalry between Marius and Sulla in the
years 88-78 B.C. Lodge subordinates politics to an interest in demonstrating the role of Fortune in human
life; the conquests and defeats of the heroic Marius and
Sulla alternate as their fortunes rise and fall. Both characters seek private remedies for the goddess's fickle
behavior, yet their public actions involve them both in
the politics of divided Rome. Although it is a background
interest, the subject is handled consistently.

As in *Titus Andronicus,* Rome at the outset is split
into two factions which support Marius or Sulla for
designation as general to lead Roman troops against
King Mithridates. Marius's faction includes Cinna, Lepidus (father of Lepidus the triumvir), Lucius Scipio, and
Junius Brutus, "a magistrate" (historically the father of

---

40. Joseph W. Houppert, ed., *The Wounds of Civil War,* by Thomas
Lodge. Regents Renaissance Drama (Lincoln: University of Nebraska
Press, 1969), p. xii.

Caesar's assassin); on the other hand, Sulla is joined by Quintus Pompey, Mark Antony the orator, and Gnaeus Octavius. The tribune Sulpitius nominates Marius, and is opposed by Pompey, who points out that Sulla has already been made general "by lot and by election" (I.i. 52). According to Pompey, an unnecessary new election would be the result of Rome's "unstable government" and would deprive Sulla unjustly of his rightful post; this he calls "injury" and "disgrace" (ll. 55, 57). Junius Brutus appeals to the great public power of the Senate to "appoint, dispose, and change" (l. 59) its individual generals; he then refers to Sulla, whose "haughty pride and swelling thoughts puff'd up/ Foreshows the reaching to proud Tarquin's state" (ll. 61-62). Sulla is thus associated with the kind of self-regarding behavior banished in Roman politics with the overthrow of Tarquin's tyranny by Brutus's ancestor Junius Brutus; the latter's descendant and namesake appeals to the traditional center of power, the Senate, the "pillars" of the state, in contrast to Sulla's derogatory address to "trustless Senators and ingrateful Romans" (l. 160).

Brutus suggests a compromise whereby Sulla would rule in Rome and Marius would be general; but this reasonable solution is no sooner held out than it is dismissed by one of Sulla's uncompromising followers, who predicts that Sulla's party "first will make the towers of Rome to shake/ And force the stately Capitol to dance/ Ere any rob him of his just renown" (ll. 89-91). For Sulla, personal reputation is more important than Rome; but the Senate resists intimidation. Consul, Senate, and tribune join to confirm Marius's appointment.

The sides are clearly defined: on the one hand is Marius, the older Roman hero designated by the patrician government of Rome to lead the army, and on the other hand Sulla, the younger, more rash hero who threatens

Rome with slaughter and destruction before he will yield up his titles. Marius, identified with the interests of the commonwealth, brands his rival a "traitor" and calls all those who love "the Senate and Marius" to oppose Sulla. Mark Antony notes commonplace dangers of division, and, joined by Merula and Granius, laments that Fortune has raised Rome only to make her fall through "civil discords and domestic broils" (l. 302) resulting from "foul ambitious thoughts" (l. 307) that do not care about the good of Rome. Both Marius and Sulla are the offspring of Rome, although neither fully represents it; Rome remains the prize, and only government that has the approval of a virtuous Senate can be approved by the play's audience.

Immediately following Marius's seeming victory, Sulla enters "triumphant" (II.i.S D); Granius, distinguishing between "ambitious pride and princely zeal" (l. 82), appropriately associates Sulla with "a fortunate, but froward, governance" (l. 87). Sulla is designated general, and his first action is to demand that the Senate "take away the scandal of this state,/ Banish the name of tribune" (ll. 193-94). After the Senate agrees, Marius is declared a traitor and his party outlawed. From this point on, the consuls and Senate become partisan, and "commonweale" values are subordinated to rival claims of power.

As Marius's fortunes continue to decline, he relies on internal "magnanimity . . . and fortitude" (II.ii.27-28) to counter Fortune's adversity, escapes assassination, and travels to the Numidian mountains, where he lives at the lowest point on the Goddess's wheel, feeding on roots, until he meets his son and they prepare to return to Sulla's Rome, intending to upset that government. Sulla, still fortunate, appears in III.iii parading in triumph in a golden throne drawn by Moors, and threatening Rome with destruction for harboring plots against him. He asserts that he "never feared fate" (l. 65) and whimsically orders the death of his captives, challenging them, "When we meet in hell,/ Then tell me, princes, if I did not well" (ll. 103-4). The contrast between Marius's orthodox and approved fortitude in the face of adversity and Sulla's excessive and irresponsible bravado is clear.[41]

Next it is Marius's turn to triumph: when he enters a Rome which now supports him, he reestablishes not a normal Senatorial government, but rather himself orders the death of his enemies, justifying his actions by referring to a natural "just revenge" (IV.i.62). The consul Octavius prays for Sulla's arrival, and, mirroring Granius, defies the new conqueror as a tyrant (l. 141). Marius, who is installed in the consul's chair when Octavius is killed, wants Sulla proclaimed traitor as he himself had been. Despite this precise and deliberate parallelism of action, however, Marius emerges as less disapproved than Sulla; the disapproval attendant upon the killing of the consul is qualified by Marius's kind treatment of Sulla's wife and daughter (IV.i.242ff). It remains true, nevertheless, that the interests of the commonwealth are served by neither man. The remainder of the play is not political: Marius's miraculous death is reported, and shortly thereafter Sulla, newly in power, is caused by "a sudden thought" (V.v.80) to retire to the country where he dies. Both men have been heroes, and after their deaths Rome returns to normality under the combined government of Pompey, the consul Flaccus, and the Senate.

Although the spectacle of the rise and fall of the two heroes is the play's primary concern, the rivalry between them has clear political implications. Marius, identified with the interests of the commonwealth, is the approved

41. Bevington reverses the role of Sulla by seeing him as the approved leader in Rome and Marius as only the fomenter of a "counter-rebellion." See *Tudor Drama,* p. 235.

hero; Sulla is ambitious, a threat to the health and unity of the state. Since Sulla's real threat to the republic, arranging to have himself made perpetual dictator, is not presented in detail, the play fails to go beyond generalities which are really Tudor commonplaces on the evil effects of a divided state. Rome is subject to Fortune rather than to human action; at the end of the play the city rises again to prosperity and is placed in the hands of her rightful rulers.

A greater freedom from orthodox views characterizes Ben Jonson's *Sejanus,* printed for Thomas Thorp in 1605, but composed in 1603; it was acted by the newly formed King's Men, with Shakespeare in the cast. The quarto contains commendatory verses by Jonson's friends and fellow dramatists, including George Chapman, who may be the "second pen" referred to in the "address to the reader."[42] The play covers the years A.D. 23-31, making its dramatic time the latest of the non-Shakespearian Roman plays examined in this chapter, and the farthest removed from the Roman Republic. Since Tiberius was Emperor in A.D. 14-37, the action covers only part of his reign; the events leading to the downfall of Sejanus are but one series within the general movement away from the Republic and toward the expanding Empire.

Sejanus opens with Silius and Sabinus declaring that they, "no good inginers" (I.4), should not be in court, and they point to two "clients" (presumably Romans not unusually evil[43]) of the "great Sejanus" who have em-

---

42. Jonson indicates that the quarto text "is not the same with that which was acted on the publike Stage," *Ben Jonson* 4, ed. C. H. Herford and P. Simpson (Oxford: at the Clarendon Press, 1932) :351. References to the text of Jonson plays will be to this edition. *Sejanus* III.302-10 is an anti-tyrannic note that may have escaped excision until the 1616 folio; see *ibid.,* 2 (1925) :4-5.

43. Honig, "Sejanus and Coriolanus," *MLQ* 12 (1951) :416, cites Satrius and Natta as "Sejanuses in miniature," two of "scores of lesser men" like them.

braced duplicity (ll. 23-41). Sabinus remarks that senators, consuls, and praetors have all so degenerated that Emperor Tiberius himself, "who least the publique liberty could like,/ As loathly brook'd their flat servilitie" (ll. 54-55) and had even cried publicly "ô race of men,/ Prepar'd for servitude" (ll. 52-53). Jonson adds to this comment, in passages not derived from his main source, Tacitus's *Annals,* the causes for the growth of tyranny and its results:

> We, that (within these fourescore yeeres) were borne
> Free, equall lords of the triumphed world,
> And knew no masters, but affections,
> To which betraying first our liberties,
> We since became the slaves to one mans lusts;
> And now to many: every ministring spie
> That will accuse, and sweare, is lord of you,
> Of me, of all, our fortunes, and our lives.
>
> (I.59–66)

The political difficulties are the results of an internal degeneration. Arruntius, the most outspoken critic in the play, blamed men rather than the times:

> Where is now the soule
> Of godlike CATO? he, that durst be good,
> When CAESAR durst be evill; and had power,
> As not to live his slave, to dye his master,
> Or where the constant BRUTUS, that (being proof
> Against all charme of benefits) did strike
> So brave a blow into the monsters heart
> That sought unkindly to captive his countrie?
> O, they are fled the light.
>
> (I.89–97)

This view of Rome's decline is established as choric by an appeal to Cordus, whose work of Roman history from the time of Pompey and Gaius Caesar to "the present state"—a subject "somewhat queasie to be toucht" (ll. 79, 82), and in fact the "fourescore yeeres" just mentioned—is published between the events of Acts One and Three. Cordus's enemies define the political possibilities in Rome: "Is he or *Drusian?* or *Germanican?*/ Or ours, or neutrall?" (ll. 80-81). Arruntius quotes Cordus's phrase, which will be used against him at his trial (III.392): *"Brave* CASSIUS *was the last of all that race"* (I.104). The republican heroes are dead, and the last hope of freedom resides in the "sons" of Germanicus. He, grandson of Augustus's wife Livia and among the most cultured and approved patrician Romans, is made the embodiment of virtue and the ideal:[44] "If there were seedes of the old vertue left,/ They liv'd in him" (ll. 119-20). He surpassed Alexander the Great and resembled the great, stern Romans of the past, for he had "POMPEI's dignitie,/ The innocence of CATO, CAESAR'S spirit,/ Wise BRUTUS temperance" (I. 150-52). But the world of Tiberius is a Rome that has expanded by foreign conquests that have yielded only luxury and selfishness; the most obvious result is the unregulated ambition of Sejanus. The only hope for the state is that "the name TIBERIUS/ . . . will keepe; how ere he hath fore-gone/ The dignitie, and power" (ll. 244-46).

Tiberius is to be measured against the old republican virtue, with its political concomitant in the freedom produced by the republic. When he appears on stage for the first time, he styles himself "the servant of the *Senate*"; but, lest the audience be deceived, Cordus immediately adds, in an aside, "rarely dissembled" (ll. 393, 395). Silius, who accepts the fact of the new Rome, makes it

---

44. See Jonas A. Barish, ed., *Sejanus* by Ben Jonson ("Yale Ben Jonson": New Haven: Yale University Press, 1965), p. 11. Honig, p. 413, refers to the republican standards as "traditions of an earlier golden age" which are "a glass in which contemporary deformities must be seen." The word "contemporary" must refer both to Tiberian Rome and Jacobean England.

clear that under certain conditions an empire could be politically virtuous; but this would require a different, virtuous emperor, one who had a "mind allied unto his words" (l. 401). If such were the case,

> We could not thinke that state, for which to change,
> Although the ayme were our old liberty:
> The ghosts of those that fell for that, would grieve
> Their bodies liv'd not, now, againe to serve.
> "Men are deceiv'd, who thinke there can be thrall
> "Beneath a vertuous prince. Wish'd liberty
> "Ne're lovelier lookes, then under such a crowne.
>
> (ll. 403–9)

Tiberius, thus, lacks virtue and dissembles; he publicly repeats that he is the "creature" of the Senate, and holds power only by its election (ll. 439-43). Only in a rare moment of honesty does he exclaim to Sejanus:

> As if there were that *chaos* bred in things,
> That lawes, and libertie would not rather choose
> To be quite broken, and tane hence by us,
> Then have the staine to be preserv'd by such.
>
> (II.313–16)

In answer to later dissembling, in which Tiberius ironically wishes for anonymity, Sejanus yet more ironically (for the audience) couches his objection in terms analogous to orthodox Tudor ideas on sovereignty:

> But *Rome,* whose bloud,
> Whose nerves, whose life, whose very frame relyes
> On CAESAR's strength, no lesse then heav'n on ATLAS,
> Cannot admit it but with generall ruine.
>
> (III.128–31)

These early scenes establish the political and moral limits of the play. Under the circumstances, virtue is represented by the discontented nobility allied to the house of Germanicus's widow Agrippina. Silius, Sabinus, Arruntius, Gallus, Furnius, Regulus, and others gather, and must be destroyed if Tiberius and his line are to be firmly established—and if Sejanus, who recognizes the opposition (II.191-94), is to be successful in his own bid for imperial power.

In Act Three Silius is accused; when it becomes apparent that he will be condemned (l. 297), he in turn accuses the ineffective Senate, the "hands of fortune" (l. 324), and, opposing the power of Tiberius, commits a noble suicide (ll. 337-39) reminiscent of Cato's before Caesar's victory. The next to be accused is Cordus, who "paralels/ The times, the governments, a profest champion,/ For the old libertie" (II.310-12). Cordus defends himself against the true charge that he praised Brutus and Cassius by citing the freedom that the "deified JULIUS, and no less AUGUSTUS" (III.436) allowed to Livy and other historians who openly praised the republican heroes Pompey, Brutus, and Cassius. Cordus argues that he has given no cause to "incense the people in the civil cause,/ With dangerous speeches" (ll. 451-52); the argument is cogent and forces the accusers, who represent an evil far more base than any ascribed to Julius Caesar, to delay his fate to a later time; but Cordus too is "fore-doomed."

The persecuted circle around Agrippina hopes "that bright flame/ Of libertie might be reviv'd againe" (IV. 143-44), but is unable to take action. Here Jonson seems to reach a limitation of permissible stage action: Latiaris's suggestion of taking the active role,

> if men would change
> The weari'd arme, and for the waightie shield
> So long sustain'd, employ the ready sword,
> (ll. 152–54)

is a threat of rebellion quickly overborne by the orthodox

Sabinus, who remarks, "No ill should force the subject undertake/ Against the soveraigne" (ll. 163-64). He goes on to espouse a stoical acceptance of adversity: "A good man should, and must/ Sit rather downe with losse, then rise unjust" (ll. 165-66). To this acceptance, however, he adds a qualification:

> Though, when the *Romanes* first did yeeld themselves
> To one mans power, they did not meane their lives,
> Their fortunes, and their liberties, should be
> His absolute spoile, as purchas'd by the sword.
>
> (ll. 167–70)

In this world, the virtuous nobles can look forward only to extermination. Arruntius, for instance, finds it difficult to believe that he remains alive (IV.274-76), and also embraces "plaine, and passive fortitude,/ To suffer, and be silent" (ll. 294-95).[45] Thus the group of approved malcontents making up the Germanican party can neither preserve the traditional values of Rome nor overthrow their antagonist, the "new man" Sejanus.

Sejanus would dethrone other traditions too: the orthodox gods of Rome, and with them fear and all scruples. He worships Fortune, keeping in his house an image of her that belonged to the Roman king Servius Tullius (V.84-87). Sejanus's attempt to use "policy" to secure power for himself fails, ironically: for he is destroyed by the still more ruthless "policy" of Tiberius and his servant Macro. The latter, more effective than Sejanus, is to be "a greater prodigie in *Rome,* then he/ That now is falne" (V.752-53). The crowd wreaks vengeance on

---

45. J. I. De Villiers finds the suggestion of rebellion and its prompt dismissal to be a failure on Jonson's part: see "Ben Jonson's Tragedies," *ES* 45 (1964):433-42. If the *Sejanus* of 1603 explored the possibility of rebellion further than Latiaris's remarks, that fact would adequately account for Jonson's citation before the Privy Council on a charge of treason; see Barish, pp. 15-19. The burden of the passage just quoted should be contrasted to the views of James I, who is quoted below in chapter 5.

Sejanus and his family as if they embodied the evil of Rome; but because he was only a representation of that evil, Rome remains at the end of the play still in the hands of evil. The play thus clearly dramatizes the decline of civic freedom. The individual characters are creatures spawned by Rome, and could have been bred at any time; but the play really concentrates on the social order as a whole.[46] Jonson establishes with great clarity the play's republican political and moral values, and the relations of his characters to them. The values and the technique show that Jonson and Chapman agreed on fundamental issues.

George Chapman's single Roman tragedy, *Caesar and Pompey*, was first printed in 1631, but, although written "long since," it "never touched . . . at the stage."[47] Scholars have assigned dates for its composition that range between 1603 to 1605 on the one hand,[48] and 1612-13 on the other.[49] Appraisals of its success vary also, recent opinions ranging from relative praise, calling attention to it as "an introspective play with integrity and clarity of meaning"[50] to disparaging it as "dull," full of noise, and finally a "muddle."[51]

The play, which relies on Plutarch,[52] deals with the outbreak of the civil war between Julius Caesar and Pompey, culminating in the battle of Pharsalia (48 B.C.) and the consequent deaths of Pompey and Cato. Immediately in the background of the action is the world of

---

46. K. M. Burton, "The Political Tragedies of Chapman and Ben Jonson," *EIC* 2 (1952) :397.

47. Dedication to the Earl of Middlesex, in *The Plays and Poems of George Chapman: The Tragedies,* ed. T. M. Parrott (London: Routledge, 1910), p. 341.

48. Ennis Rees, *The Tragedies of George Chapman* (Cambridge, Mass.: Harvard University Press, 1954), p. 130; Charlotte Spivack, *George Chapman* (New York: Twayne, 1967), pp. 144–45, 150.

49. Millar MacLure, *George Chapman: a Critical Study* (Toronto: University of Toronto Press, 1966), p. 151 and notes.

50. Spivack, p. 150.

51. MacLure, pp. 151–52.

52. Rees, p. 126.

the Catilinian conspiracy Jonson dramatized; Caesar and Cato reappear and some of the conspirators are still alive and imprisoned. Deciding their fate provides grounds for initial disagreement between Cato, who calls for the death penalty, and Caesar, who argues against it (I.ii.40-130); as in *Titus* and *Wounds,* the play begins with a radically divided Rome. The tribune Metellus calls for the admission of Pompey's army into Italy so that

> his forces here
> As well as he, great Rome may rest secure
> From danger of the yet still smoking fire
> Of Catiline's abhorr'd conspiracy:
> Of which the very chief are left alive,
> Only chastis'd but with a gentle prison.
> (I.ii.34–39)

As in *Wounds,* neither of two heroes is entirely approved: Catiline seeks "to make/ One tyrant over all the state of Rome," and Pompey wants the same thing (ll. 45-48). Together they "beat one sole path and threat one danger" (l. 72). Cato remains opposed to Pompey's entry, although he feels that Pompey does not seek power for himself (l. 134). It is the impartial Cato who argues against tribunal advice, and his initial distrust is never refuted; it marks a crucial reservation. In the face of Caesar, Pompey may become the military force fighting for the republic, in whom "the hopes of all good republicans, of whom Cato is one, center";[53] yet he is favored only as the lesser of two evils facing the state.

Caesar defends the prisoners and stresses his loyalty to the state by referring to his past deeds; he protests that he seeks Rome's good. During the remainder of the scene the question of admitting the two armies comes to a head: Caesar attempts to have Cato arrested, and Pompey supports Cato, who retires into the background.

---

53. *Ibid.,* p. 136.

The sides are clear by the end of the scene, for the first consul's authoritative word brands Caesar a "thief to Rome" and commands him to disband his army or be an acknowledged "open foe" (ll. 297-98). This initial scene parallels the opening of *Wounds;* but Chapman does not subordinate the action to Fortune.

A brief summary of the action will demonstrate that Cato is the moral and political spokesman in the play. At first Pompey is victorious, and Cato advises him to spare lives and to cause as little damage to the commonwealth as possible, for in a civil war "their loss is yours" (II.iv.6). Forced by his allies to turn down Caesar's offer of peace, Pompey disregards Cato's advice, attacks his adversary, and loses Pharsalia. Pompey's outward defeat causes him to turn inward, to Cato's traditional philosophical position on the vanity of glory. He decides to search out Cato at Utica, and on the road attains the stoic position (IV.iii.71-75). Caesar too suffers, seeing destruction all around, and decides to find Cato. The play ends paradoxically at Utica: Cato, personally and politically defeated, is victor, whereas Caesar, seemingly the conqueror, has been conquered:

> Caesar now is conquer'd in his conquest,
> In the ambition he till now denied,
> Taking upon him to give life, when death
> Is tenfold due to his most tyrannous self;
> No right, no power given him to raise an army
> Which in despite of Rome he leads about,
> Slaughtering her loyal subjects like an outlaw;
> Nor is he better.
>
> (IV.v.32–39)

Dramatic attention is focused at last on Cato's home and his suicide. As Chapman promises, the play presents "such a tragedy/ As all the princes of the earth may come/ To take their patterns by the spirits of Rome" (II.ii.41-43).

Cato, the major figure, is at one extreme of the play's polarity: he is approved, a "senecal saint" who is committed to the commonwealth. Although he is not given an active role, and is offstage for three acts, his presence, like that of Rome, is felt throughout; he represents the republic which dies, as he does, at the end of the play. In this way Chapman's ethical drama, which has a public manifestation in the stage's political and military events, endorses the proposition of the play's "Argument" that "only a just man is a free man." Cato stands for public justice based on an internal law of traditional Christian-stoical faith; the difficulty of living out this moral positive is shown by Pompey. Since he is inadequate, Cato's spiritual triumph must occur in the face of the fall of the republic.

Cato's opponent is Caesar, who is also both a character and a moral-political pole standing for tyranny and subjection. Caesar disclaims any intention of seeking to become tyrant (III.ii.111-38) although he has just been called "imperial Caesar" (III.ii.3); he then reiterates his identification of Rome's good and glory with his own (ll. 123-38). Pompey, who himself disclaims reliance on Fortune (I.ii.178), associates Caesar with that goddess (I.ii.167-77); this statement, despite Caesar's denial (II.iii.10), is enough to place him among Chapman's "proud, self-seeking individuals who, instead of humbly submitting to religious and civil law, are only too willing to go irrationally beyond their human limitations."[54] Pompey is supported on the field by the two Roman consuls, Brutus, and five kings; with such allies, Pompey might well hope to make Fortune steady, but because he, like Rome itself, swerves from Cato's teaching, the cause of the republic is defeated.

The end of the play, presenting the end of the Republic, also presents a world in which it is no longer

---

54. *Ibid.,* p. 135.

possible to be just. The virtuous man commits suicide, advising his son against engaging in the politics of Empire, since for Chapman virtue there is not possible and may be corrupted. This view is as pessimistic as that of Jonson. Although Jacquot is right in saying that Elizabethans would approve an ending which suggests a new unity in Rome,[55] they could not have approved very warmly a unity that dramatists explicitly labeled tyranny. Caesar, the least scrupulous of Chapman's three main characters, brings with him an injustice that robs men of freedom, the result of justice and the condition of virtue. The nature of Caesar's victory is made ambiguous (as it is in Shakespeare's *Julius Caesar*), for the embodiments of Rome, Cato and the two consuls, as well as her military guardian Pompey, are all dead; Caesar is effectively a tyrant. Only Brutus joins Caesar, and Cato, before dying, remarks that his daughter Portia, Brutus's wife, would not have done so (V.ii.105-6). Chapman uses politics for their ethical worth and leaves untouched the politics of the mixed state; republican Rome exists only as a past, idealized polity, supported by the dead Cato, whom Chapman idealizes, following Plutarch, like the latter's other earnest student, the young Montaigne.[56]

The non-Shakespearean plays endorse values that promote the interests of the Roman state as a whole, and condemn partisan activity that would result in the sub-

---

55. Jean Jacquot, *George Chapman* (Paris: Société d'Editions "les belles lettres," 1951), p. 185.

56. See *Essays* I.37, "Of Cato the Younger." P. Villey, ed., *Essais* 1 (Paris, 1930) :440, summarizes: the "admiration se voit encore dans les essais I.xliv, II.iii et II.xiii notamment. Mais, assez vite, semble-t-il, d'autres modèles ont remplacé Caton d'Utique: il y a déjà quelques réserves dans le chapitre II.xi; et dans le chapitre II.xxxvi Caton n'est pas au nombre des 'trois plus excellents hommes'; après 1580, il n'est plus nommé que rarement, et quelquefois il est critiqué; et tandis qu'avant 1580 huit emprunts étaient faits à la *Vie de Caton* par Plutarque, on n'en relève qu'un après cette date."

jection of the free people to the power of a single man. In political terms, the plays clearly endorse mixed-state government, a form that ensures freedom by allowing every element some power in deciding issues that affect the whole state. It would, however, be incorrect to say that these dramatists presented the mixed state as a working ideal. Everywhere republican Rome is failing or has failed, despite the presence of men who exemplify the personal virtues associated with republicanism. Shakespeare's Roman work of the 1590s shares these values. The latest of the plays, *Julius Caesar,* is deliberately complex and avoids an unambiguous preference with regard to the vexed question of approval of the assassination of Caesar; but after that moment, those forces representing "Caesarism" are presented as thieves. The later *Coriolanus* (ca. 1608-11) marks a reversion to the directness of treatment in the earlier work; this very different play will be treated at length in the final chapter.

The plays studied confirm the "liberalization," the widening of spectrum of the political possibilities suggested by the introductory chapter above. They have in common an endorsement of an anti-tyrannic attitude, which takes a variety of specific forms ranging from a direct expression of Tudor orthodoxy, the need for just, strong rule (Heywood and Lodge), to a specifically pro-republican position (Shakespeare, Chapman, and Jonson). But even in the former instances, the central power must be supported by the community at large: the ultimate reference is the "commonweale."

The English plays found in the narrations of classical historians a source not only for facts but also for attitudes toward them. It remains to show how thoroughly these attitudes permeated Elizabethan understanding of the Greek and Roman past. Among the accounts of Tacitus, Livy, Lucan, and Plutarch, the last, combining moral

philosophy with exciting stories, particularly appealed
for dramatization, and was also, we know, enormously
popular among Elizabethan readers. He himself refers
to other historical writers, including Dionysius of Halicarnassus, Livy, and Polybius;[57] he took over (and modified slightly) Polybius's unqualified admiration of the
mixed state and his view of historical parallels, grounded
on similarity in structure of the state, geography, events
in men's lives, and even organization of the army.[58] For
the English readers of the sixteenth and seventeenth
centuries, whether professional dramatists or simply, to
use A. B. Ferguson's happy phrase, "articulate citizens,"[59] the classical historians, and preeminently Plutarch, represented variations of a single major attitude
that endorsed republican states and stressed contemporary relevance by insisting on parallels.

Renaissance readers of Plutarch found in the *Parallel
Lives* more than the twenty-three pairs that scholarship
has subsequently assigned to the Greek writer. The post-
Plutarchan additions, consisting of biographies of such
men as Hannibal, Scipio Africanus, Epaminondas, Plato,

---

57. Dionysius was a widely-used model for rhetorical exercise in the
curriculum of English Renaissance schools: see T. W. Baldwin, *William
Shakspere's Small Latine and Lesse Greeke* (Urbana: University of Illi-
nois Press, 1944), 1:310, 312–13. Dionysius's account is the basis of
Plutarch's *Camillus* and *Coriolanus:* cf. Dionysius of Halicarnassus,
Roman Antiquities vi.93 ("Loeb Classical Library": Cambridge, Mass.:
Harvard University Press, 1943), in 4:131–35, with *Coriolanus* 9, in
2:151–52. Plutarch mentions Dionysius elsewhere, *e.g.: Romulus* 16,
in 1:90; *Comparison* of Alcibiades and Coriolanus 2, in 2:191;
Pyrrhus 16 and 21, in 3:134 and 141. Bullough 5:463, suggests that
Dionysius was more important for Plutarch than Livy was. Plutarch
refers to Livy a number of times: *Camillus* 6, in 1:327; *Marcellus* 12,
24, 30, in 2:346, 364, 373, and *Comparison* 1, in 2:375; *Flaminius* 18, 20,
in 3:101, 104; *Sulla* 6, in 3:274; *Lucullus* 28, 31, in 3:403, 408; and
Caesar 47, 63, in 4:49, 65. Last, Plutarch relies on Polybius, and refers
to him directly in *Aemilius* 15, 16, 18, in 2:212, 214, 218 (passages which
follow the *Coriolanus*); *Cato the Elder* 9–10, in 3:13, 15. There are
other references as well: *Aratus* 38, in 6:277; *Cleomenes* 25, 27, in
5:221, 224; *Pelopidas* 17, in 2:307, and *Comparison* 1, in 2:375; *Philo-
poemon* 16, 21, in 3:68, 76, and *Brutus* 4, in 6:185.
58. Pédech, chapter 9.
59. See above, chapter 1, n. 11.

Augustus, and even Plutarch himself, testify to the vogue of paired biographies and to the ease with which new lives might be included in a moralized pattern of parallels. Plutarch placed less overt emphasis on Rome's political structure than Polybius did, but made it clear that, in the lives of men who played important roles in their times, statecraft plays a large part. Since the states presented are often other than monarchic, Plutarch's book is in effect something of an encyclopedia of practical political experience. The variety of experience is not held tightly in a consistent political attitude; Plutarch accepts the structure of a state as he finds it in his sources, without expressing preconceived judgments.

The first *Life* that Plutarch wrote is now lost, but in a sense remains the culmination of the collection; it is the biography of Augustus, under whom the Roman world was unified after the long civil wars. In the composition of the other Roman *Lives,* Plutarch filled out a sequence of political concern that moves forward in time. The earliest lives deal with the legendary Roman kings, Romulus and Numa Pompilius, who are paired with two equally legendary Greeks, the semi-divine Theseus and Lycurgus. Following this basis for the establishment of government come the still-legendary lives of Publius Valerius Publicola, Camillus, and Coriolanus, covering the early days of the republic and broadly paralleling Lycurgus' difficulties in reforming Sparta. Thirteen Roman *Lives* fall in the later period, 133-30 B.C., the civil war years which culminated in the unification of the known world by Roman conquest.

These years are known to have been of great interest to the Elizabethans because the historical movement so closely paralleled the history of their own country: civil dissension calmed and unified by the accession of Henry VII. The sympathy Elizabethans must have felt with this reading is indicated by "W. B." 's Preface to the

1578 English translation of Appian's *Civil Wars*, which describes the political chaos in Rome during the wars between Marius and Sulla:

> Some there were, in power like princes, and as Monarkes, made leaders of seditious armies; some would not leave the army that was delivered them of the people: some without authoritie, would levie straunge souldiers against their enimies, striving whether of them should first get the Citie, in word against the contrary faction, but in deede against the countrey: for they invaded it, as an enemy. Cruell murders were used in some, in others proscriptions to deathe, banishments, confiscations, and torments intollerable, so as no kinde of crueltie was left undone.[60]

English readers found, however, that Plutarch did not wholly endorse monarchy as the preferred, stable alternative to this confusion. Toward the crucial assassination of Caesar, for instance, his attitude is not simple. He disapproves of Caesar's ambition, although he seems to have felt that he was not a tyrant: Caesar was a "Man of Destiny" whose role in attempting to unify and heal Rome was the work of a superhuman force which destroyed the assassins.[61] Shakespeare deliberately developed this ambivalence to write a "problem play."[62] Part

---

60. *Shakespeare's Appian,* ed. Ernest Schanzer ("English Reprints Series No. 13": Liverpool: Liverpool University Press, 1956), pp. 6–7.

61. Ernest Schanzer, *The Problem Plays of Shakespeare* (London: Routledge, 1963), pp. 12–13.

62. The question of Shakespeare's use of Plutarch is complicated. In addition to the suggestions mentioned above (chapter 1, n. 17; chapter 2, n. 17), Shakespeare's long and wide acquaintance with the Greek writer is apparent from the character of Theseus and the names of Demetrius and Lysander in *A Midsummer's Night Dream* (1595), which derive from Plutarch's *Theseus* and *Romulus* (see Bullough 1 (London: Routledge, 1957):368–69). The later plays *Julius Caesar* and *Antony and Cleopatra* use Plutarch's *Caesar, Brutus, Mark Antony, Cicero, Alcibiades* and the post-Plutarchan *Augustus,* actually by Simon Goulart (1543–1628), appearing in the 1603 edition of Plutarch. F. Chappell has shown that Shakespeare was acquainted with the biography of Cato the Elder: "Shakespeare's *Coriolanus* and Plutarch's Life of Cato," *Renaissance Papers 1962* ("Southeastern Renaissance Conference," 1963), 9–16. Shakespeare also used the *Comparisons:* E. A. J. Honigmann,

of the root of the "problem" is the complexity of Shakespeare's allowance of the validity of the appeal to the good of Rome, the "commonwealth" view espoused by Brutus. Such a claim to validity would have been handled gently in a play about kingship: *Richard II,* for instance, is known to have been considered incendiary, and Bullough feels that the events surrounding the Essex uprising caused the hiatus in Shakespeare's political exploration between the composition of *Julius Caesar* and *Coriolanus.*[63] By contrast, the variety in Roman history afforded the playwright a wider and safer area to work in.

Of Shakespeare's three Plutarchan plays, *Julius Caesar, Antony and Cleopatra* and *Coriolanus,* two are set within a few years of Caesar's assassination. His only other classical settings in plays of these years are *Timon* and *Troilus,* only the former of which is Plutarchan, being partially based on the Lives of *Antony* and *Alcibiades.* However, neither of these works has the organizing political structure of the earlier, or later, Plutarchan play. Thus *Coriolanus* marks a return to an overtly political concern after approximately ten years; in returning, Shakespeare also went back to an earlier period in Roman history, and relied more heavily than ever on Plutarch's account. The early, legendary *Lives* are among the more political, dealing with the establishment of a variety of forms of government and with successive changes in them. Plutarch's *Coriolanus* appears in this context.

Among the legendary men who founded or reformed states, Solon, Romulus, Lycurgus, and Publicola contrib-

---

"Shakespeare's Plutarch," *SQ* 10 (1959):25–33, "Timon of Athens," *SQ* 12 (1961):1–20; and, in addition, C. M. Eccles draws attention to his use of Jacques Amyot's "Address to the Reader," in "Shakespeare and Jacques Amyot: Sonnet 55 and *Coriolanus,*" *N & Q,* NS 12 (1965): 100–102. See also below, chapter 6.

63. Bullough 5:217–18.

uted to the final elaboration of the mixed state; the biographies of these men make up a self-contained political history within the *Lives*. The standard according to which judgment is passed on political action within the state is the "commonweale" standard. Plutarch's ideal ruler is the Spartan Lycurgus, who was born to rule but (unlike Julius Caesar) did so solely in the interests of the commonwealth. Lycurgus had a "natural grace and power to draw men willingly to obey him,"[64] and was so good that he voluntarily stepped down from power and left the country for the continued good of the state. Finally, to insure an unchanged continuation to his mixed state, Lycurgus killed himself.

Plutarch's *Lycurgus,* the subject of which is mentioned in *Coriolanus* II.i.54 in a confrontation between a patrician and the tribunes, presents the change of a state "as one should geve some easie medicine, to purge an overthrowen bodye with all humours and disseases."[65] The new state he formed was commonly understood to promote stability and personal virtue, a virtue most effectively present in the nobility, for Sparta, like Solon's Athens, permitted the people to debate only matters propounded to it. Plutarch's conception of the nature of the state's mixture understood the balance to exist, not, as in Polybius, between equally powerful elements, but rather with one of them supreme: the Senate was "(as Plato sayeth) to be the healthfull counterpease of the whole bodye of the Common weale," or a "stronge beame, that helde both these extreames in an even ballance."[66]

Because political stability and civic virtue were concomitant with, or resulted from, the mixed state, Plutarch and later writers favored "constitutional republics

64. Quoted in *Plutarch,* 1:xxvi.
65. *Lycurgus* 5, in 1:124.
66. *Ibid.,* p. 125. The marginal note refers to Plato, "De Leg 3."

and opposed . . . hereditary monarchies."[67] Only a
superhuman destiny, such as Caesar's, could make them
accept Empire. However, although this was Plutarch's
inclination, he could not entirely approve the key element of the mixed state, the tribunate, which in Roman
history as again later in the sixteenth and seventeenth
centuries raised questions of great importance on obedience to legally constituted authority. In the widely-
read *Moralia,* Plutarch presents a statement about the
questionable political and moral role of the office:

> Like as some oratours and lawiers doe hold, that exception in
> law is no action, considering it doth cleane contrary to action;
> for that action intendeth, commendeth, and beginneth a pro-
> cesse or sute; but exception or inhibition, dissolveth, undoeth,
> and abolisheth the same: semblably, they thinke also, that the
> Tribunate was an impeachment, inhibition, and restraint of a
> magistracie, rather than a magistracie itselfe: for all the au-
> thority and power of the Tribune, lay in opposing himselfe,
> and crossing the jurisdiction of other magistrates, and in di-
> minishing or repressing their excessive licentious power.[68]

Of the tribune himself, Plutarch then remarks "the more
submisse he is in outward appeerance, the more groweth
hee and encreaseth in puissance," indicating the combination of subservience and ambition latent in the office
for the unscrupulous to command.

Like Plutarch, later English and European thought
understood that as a practical matter one element of the
mixed state ought to be stronger than the others; depending on the particular instance, the government might be
said to incline toward monarchy, aristocracy, or democracy. The mixed state could, and did, take a variety of
specific forms, as we shall see. In all cases, however,

---

67. Wyndham, in *Plutarch,* 1:xxvii.
68. "Roman Questions," No. 81, *The Philosophie, commonlie called,
The Morals,* trans. Philemon Holland (London: Hatfield, 1603), sig.
Eeee[r] (p. 877). (STC 20063.)

overly strong assertions by either monarchic or popular power would threaten chaos and in sixteenth- and seventeenth-century England moderate men stressed the need for limitations on both elements.

Even a cursory reading of Shakespeare's *Coriolanus* demonstrates that the play is distinct from most of those looked at in this chapter and from the spirit of Polybius and Plutarch. Although it shares with all the plays other than Heywood's a tendency to irony, its moral-political positives are less fully elaborated and less fully present. Apparently neither Coriolanus's plea for power nor the opposition of the tribunes, representing the people, is approved—and withholding approval from the tribunate while at the same time granting that, to some extent at least, authority stems from the people, marks a major departure from both the other Roman plays and from Plutarch's biography. *Coriolanus* thus reverses both a dramatic trend and the leaning of its source. The nature of the specific changes imposed and the reasons for making them need to be accounted for. This is possible, for they lie in the substratum of any work of dramatic literature: this is the range of contemporary attitudes—in this case on the subject of mixed governments—that would determine the ways in which a professional author, truly responsive to his audience, treats material they have inherited in common. To this subject we now turn.

3
English Sources

The Jacobean age inherited an active body of native English political and legal thinking from frequent sixteenth-century discussions of the nature of English government. When under James I it became necessary for law cases to attempt definitions of the rights of king and of individuals, they did so by referring to precedent, to decisions of the past which were kept thereby in currency and incorporated into textbooks and dictionaries. One such dictionary is Cowell's *Interpreter* (1607), which was the subject of a parliamentary investigation in 1610: a conference was appointed by the House of Commons to examine "dangerous matter against the authority of the Parliament" contained in the pro-monarchist definitions of the terms "subsidy," "king," "Parliament," and "prerogative," all terms that will concern us.[1]

Between 1608 and 1611, when Shakespeare, the major playwright of the King's Men, came to compose a play

---

1. See the entries in *Parliamentary Debates in 1610,* ed. S. R. Gardiner (Westminster: Camden Society, 1862), p. 19. The definitions in Cowell's book were used as a matter of course by Francis Bacon and Edward Coke: see E. H. Kantorowicz, *The King's Two Bodies* (Princeton: Princeton University Press, 1957), p. 405; and C. H. McIlwain, *The Political Works of James I* (Cambridge, Mass.: Harvard University Press, 1918), pp. lxxxvii–lxxxix.

in which politics was to be essential, he wrote for an
audience many members of which had experience in both
theoretical and practical aspects of the subject; and he
had to take into consideration also that King James
himself had certain quite set ideas about the free play
of monarchic rule and the proper limitations on would-
be counsellors that had, if anything, hardened during
the first four years of the reign. The historical setting
of *Coriolanus*—early Rome shortly after the expulsion
of the kings (II.ii.85-99)—would elicit from the
audience not one, but a variety of attitudes formed toward a nexus of analogous English political concerns.
Certainly an audience that accepted Tudor propaganda
without question would react with horror to civil disorder, the establishment of popular tribunes, the exile
of the consul-elect, and his return leading an enemy army.
But acceptance was not total.

In an appendix to his book on English history plays,
Irving Ribner separates two strands of political opinion
about England current in Shakespeare's time: first, an
orthodox government view discussed by the historical
criticism of Shakespeare surveyed above, and second, an
opposing, radically anti-absolutist view, presumably illegal and subversive, embodied by rebels such as John
Knox, John Ponet, Jean Hotman, and the anonymous,
notorious tract *Vindiciae contra Tyrannos* (1579) that
appeared under the pseudonym of "Junius Brutus."[2] It
is indeed true that during the reigns of the Tudors, that
is, during the stresses of the English Reformation, of
the Marian period of renewed Catholicism, and of the
subsequent period which feared the threat of a Continental Catholic invasion, these two opposing views held the
center of the stage. But it will be the purpose of this

2. I. Ribner, *The English History Play in the Age of Shakespeare,*
rev. ed. (London: Methuen, 1965), pp. 305–12.

chapter to establish the existence, and identify the nature, of a mean, in effect an equally traditional but minority view held by educated men; because of the unfamiliarity of much of this material, I will try to incorporate descriptions of the evidence and include in the notes full citations of sources. During the period in question, this view was effectively eclipsed, but it was not destroyed. It merely retreated from the field of practical government to the study. Although the view was flexible and permitted a variety of individual stresses, and might approach either of the other two dominant views, this one remained independent, and understood English government to be a mixed state, analogous to contemporary Venice and to classical, pre-Imperial Rome.

In seeking native legal precedents, Jacobean lawyers searched out the medieval roots of English Common Law. According to these constitutional formulations, laws could be made only with the consent of the entire community, which therefore had to be present at the law-making assembly. This was held to be the case in the invocation of the Crown, which embodied "all sovereign rights . . . of the whole body politic."[3] The Crown was, then, abstract, in that it was passive, mystical, and corporational. It had to be cared for, as a perpetual legal minor, and its guardians were the king along with the composite body of king and magnates, all working together to represent it.[4]

The medieval formulations might be based on classical as well as biblical studies, applied to contemporary situations. In 1338 Walter Burley's *Commentary* on Aristotle's *Politics* showed that when the king, the powerful, and the wise are summoned together to parliament, they rule together with the king, "as it appears today

3. Kantorowicz, pp. 381–82.
4. *Ibid.*, pp. 363–64.

with regard to the king [Edward III] of the English."[5]
In 1401, the Speaker of the House of Commons, profit-
ing from the close connection between religion and government, compared the body politic, made up of King,
Lords spiritual and temporal, and Commons, to the
Holy Trinity: a "trinity in unity and unity in trinity"
(p. 227).[6] He further extended the parallel by compar-
ing the procedures of parliamentary behavior to the
Mass! His point was in fact well taken, of course, for
English government was believed to be a secularized
reflection of the composite yet unified nature of divine
authority, just as the world at large represented God's
order. According to Bishop Russell's formulation of
1483, "the body politic . . . of England was defined not
by the king or head alone, but the king together with
council and parliament."[7]

The composite and constitutional medieval theory of
government that permitted analogy to the Trinity is
distinct from divisive, absolutist views, also available in
England, that became most characteristic of Continental
formulations.[8] These insisted on the separation of the
king from the other elements in the state: and from
this separation developed the opposing views of ruler-
supremacy and people-supremacy characteristic of seventeenth-century European political developments. The in-

---

5. *Ibid.,* p. 226, quoting and translating Burley from S. Harrison
Thomson, "Walter Burley's Commentary on the *Politics* of Aristotle,"
Mélanges Auguste Pelzer (Louvain: Bibliothèque de l'Université, 1947),
p. 577. Burley's formulation already had precedent in the work of
Henry de Bracton (d. 1268).

6. Arthur Hall was therefore not innovating but significantly re-
formulating when "he said the Lower House was a new person in the
Trinity, and (because these words tended to the derogation of the state
of this house giving absolute power to the other) he was therefore
committed." This is referred to by Sir Francis Bacon in a speech of
1601: *The Works of Francis Bacon* 10, ed. J. Spedding, R. L. Ellis, and
D. D. Heath (London: Longman, 1869) :37.

7. Kantorowicz, p. 225.

8. Fortescue, *The Governance of England,* ed. Plummer (Oxford: at
the Clarendon Press, 1885), chapter 3.

clusive flexibility of the mixed state came to be caught
between these two opposing tendencies, and could be
approved of or disapproved of by men (Hotman, Al-
thusius) advocating people's sovereignty; and approved
of or disapproved of by men (Molina, Suarez, Bodin)
advocating ruler's sovereignty.[9] In practical terms, it
was the concrete fact of the meetings of parliament that
saved English composite sovereignty from assimilation
by one or the other of the Continental extremes.[10] The
parliamentary association of king, as head, and lords,
knights, and burgesses as members, illustrated the commonplace organic metaphor of the state and made visible
the *"corpus morale et politicum"* of the realm.[11]

Among the medieval writers who based their studies
at least in part on Aristotle, St. Thomas Aquinas, or
more precisely Ptolemy of Lucca, the continuator of the
unfinished *De Regimine Principum*,[12] discussed "imperial
domination," the government of Imperial Rome and of
Israel's Judges. Because the Roman Emperor was supreme lawgiver, and yet the succession was not ordered
by a hereditary rule (as Shakespeare correctly indicated
in *Titus*), the Imperial government held a mean between
"political" and "regal" forms of government. This view
was developed by Lord Chief Justice Sir John Fortescue
(d. ca. 1477), who remained influential enough in the
early seventeenth century for Sir Walter Ralegh to term
him "that noble Bulwarke of our lawes."[13] Fortescue,
historically the Lord Chief Justice in Shakespeare's *2*

---

9. Otto Gierke, *Natural Law and the Theory of Society: 1500–1800,*
trans. E. Barker (Cambridge, England: Cambridge University Press,
1950), pp. 236–37, n. 41.

10. B. Wilkinson, "The 'Political Revolution' of the 13th and 14th
Centuries in England," *Speculum* 24 (1949):504.

11. Kantorowicz, pp. 447, 382.

12. St. Thomas wrote only as far as II.4; the rest was the work of
Ptolemy of Lucca.

13. *History of the World* II.4.16, *The Works of Sir Walter Raleigh*
(Oxford: at the Clarendon Press, 1829), 3:147.

Henry VI, freed himself from the medieval Aristotelian tradition of the mirror of princes, always more or less irrelevant to specifically English concerns,[14] and saw a third example in England's government.[15]

St. Thomas had been intent on constructing a theoretical formulation which would secure a state against tyranny. In the influential *De laudibus legum Angliae* (probably composed in 1468-70), Fortescue in turn distinguished between *dominium regale,* or absolute kingship whereby the people give to the king their authority to make law—the king becoming in effect a tyrant—and *dominium politicum et regale,* a combination of "politique" and "regal" government whereby the people retain that authority which is only administered by a king.[16] Fortescue had first seen the possibility of three forms of government: *dominium* that was *politicum,* or *regale,* or *politicum et regale.* This idea, expressed in the early *De Natura legis naturae* I.16 (composed probably in 1461-64), indicates that the last, combined form he finally endorsed was indeed a well-balanced mixture of opposing alternatives.[17] It was also an accurate description of English practice.[18]

---

14. A. B. Ferguson, *The Articulate Citizen and the English Renaissance* (Durham: Duke University Press, 1965), pp. 24–25, 87.

15. The view of history as a succession of world empires was common in both the Middle Ages and the Renaissance; see E. R. Curtius, *European Literature in the Latin Middle Ages,* trans. W. Trask (New York: Pantheon, 1953), pp. 27–30. On the relevance of this to *Titus Andronicus,* see above, chapter 2, n. 33.

16. John Major was to emphasize the same view in *History of Greater Britain* (1521): "the king holds his right as king of a free people," and people may deprive him of this right; quoted in W. S. Hudson, *John Ponet* (Chicago: University of Chicago Press, 1942), pp. 171–72.

17. Felix Gilbert, "Sir John Fortescue's '*Dominium regale et politicum*'" *Mediaevalia et Humanistica* 2 (1943):94–95 and *Governance,* pp. 83–84.

18. It has been stressed that Fortescue did not advocate "republican" government principles: Felix Gilbert, *ibid.,* p. 95n, and C. H. McIlwain, *The Growth of Political Thought in the West* (New York: Macmillan, 1932), p. 359n. However Gierke, *The Political Theories of the Middle Age,* trans. F. W. Maitland (Cambridge, England: at the University

De Laudibus was extremely popular in England during Tudor and early Jacobean times: between 1537-46 it was printed in Latin by the Marian exile Edward White-church, then translated into English by Robert Mulcaster and printed by Tottel in 1567. This text was reprinted in 1573, 1575, and 1578, under the title *A learned Commendation of the Politique Lawes of England.* Three further editions appeared in Shakespeare's lifetime, in 1599, 1609, and 1616.

In this work Fortescue is quite clear where he thinks ultimate authority lies:

> Semblably in a body politik the intent of the people ys the first lively thing, having within it bloud, that is to say, politike provision for the utility and wealth of the same people, which it dealeth forth and imparteth aswell to the head as to the members of the same bodye whereby the body is nourished and mainteined.[19]

Good health in the body politic is assured by preventing the unrestrained exercise of the king's will; he cannot change the laws, which belong to the people in the same sense as private property does. Indeed the king cannot "withdraw from the same people their proper substance against their wills" (sig. $E1^r$). Subjection of all to good law is Fortescue's major theme, and with it the inalienability of people's rights (sig. $C1^r$); the king exists to defend the law, adherence to which is the greatest guarantee of personal felicity (sig. $B5^v$). The body of law, he says,

> under whiche a multitude of men is made a people, representeth the semblance of sinewes in the body natural, because like as

Press, 1927) pp. 30, 45, and 151–52, n. 165, cites relevant Italian republican views; "republican" or not, Fortescue was advocating a mixed state.

19. Sir John Fortescue, *A learned Commendation* . . . (London: Tottel, 1573), sigs. $D8^{r-v}$.

by the sinewes the joyninge of the bodye is knitt and preserved together.

(sigs. D8^{r-v})

The proper role for parliament was to provide counsel, in fact mostly information, to the king, a service more efficiently performed by, ideally, a permanently meeting council with representatives from all estates. Looking about for governments embodying these ideas, Fortescue cites Venice, traditionally identified with justice (sig. E8^r). Looking backward in time, in *The Governance of England* (composed 1471-75 and existing in ten manuscripts, but printed 1714), he found Rome and, second to it, the constitution established by the Lacedemonians.[20]

A Tudor writer whose views on England coincided with those of Fortescue was Christopher St. German (1460?-1540). St. German's dialogue, popularly entitled *The Doctor and Student,* was printed in Latin in 1523, and in English in numerous sixteenth-century editions after 1531.[21] The book, called by Baumer "the basic handbook for law students up to the time of Blackstone,"[22] was involved in justifying the Reformation of Henry VIII. In arguing the differences between Church and State,[23] St. German stressed the power of the secular government, which he understood to be wielded by Parliament:

There is no statute made in this realm but by the assent of the lords spiritual and temporal, and of all the commons, that is to say, by the knights of the shire, citizens and burgesses, that be chosen by assent of the commons, which in the parliament represent the estate of the whole commons.[24]

20. *Governance,* pp. 150, 87-94.
21. See STC nos. 21559-588, all but seven of which are sixteenth-century editions.
22. F. LeV. Baumer, "Christopher St. German," *AHR* 42 (1937):631.
23. See R. Pineas, *Thomas More and Tudor Polemics* (Bloomington: Indiana University Press, 1968), pp. 192-213.
24. *Doctor and Student,* p. 240, quoted in Baumer, p. 641.

St. German attacked the prerogative and privileges of the clergy much as later English Parliaments were to attack the privileges and prerogative of the King. The government of England is *"jus regale politicum,"* a clear repetition of Fortescue. Under the stresses of the Reformation, however, St. German formulated "an extension of the representative idea of which Fortescue had never dreamed" (p. 641), an argument that was easily turned into a doctrine of parliamentary sovereignty.

The native strand of political thought merged with an acquaintance of Italy and classical antiquity in the circle of humanists Cardinal Wolsey collected for Cardinal's College, Oxford. Among those involved in this project for the advancement of learning and the Papal cause as well as personal advancement in state affairs, were Reginald Pole, the cousin of Henry VIII, Thomas Starkey, and Thomas Lupset. After Wolsey's fall in 1529, continuity is provided by Pole, who will concern us at a later stage in this discussion; however, we may note here the bearing on England of two products of the Pole circle, books by Thomas Starkey and Pole himself.

Starkey, who had been in Padua with Pole and wrote that his reason for going abroad was to get a perspective on English laws and institutions,[25] returned to England to be chaplain to Pole's mother, Lady Salisbury. While there, he wrote *A Dialogue between Reginald Pole and Thomas Lupset* shortly after 1534 and before the great social changes inaugurated by the dissolution of the monasteries had made themselves felt in the realm. In the dialogue Pole and Lupset are made to discuss the gov-

25. Thomas Starkey, *England in the Reign of Henry VIII,* ed. J. M. Cowper (London: Early English Text Society, 1878) :x, lxxiv. This is the dialogue's first printing; that it was not printed in the sixteenth century has been taken to indicate that it represents attitudes current only in Starkey's enlightened circle, and that it follows its argument "beyond the limits acceptable in Henrician England" (Ferguson, p. 171). Indeed, Ferguson even suggests that Somerset may have been influenced by some of the dialogue's suggestions (p. 247).

ernment of England under Henry VIII with a view to practical reform.[26] Starkey, through Pole, pleads for recognition of England as a "mixed state,"[27] for which, he feels, ultimate authority exists in the people: they should elect, and, if necessary, depose, the ruler.[28] This reliance on the people is "one of the most distinctive contributions of Starkey's Pole to the discussion of the commonwealth of the time."[29] Like Fortescue, Starkey saw the chief danger to England to be the degeneration of despotism into tyranny; and "to avoid all tyranny . . . we must provide that by no prerogative he [the King] usurp upon the people any such authorized tyranny which the acts of parliaments in time past, under the pretence of princely majesty, hath granted thereto in our country." The responsibility of preventing tyranny lies with the people's representatives in parliament. Ideally, of course, the best safeguard would be an elective monarchy. But because Starkey also believes in national traditions and laws, he suggests that the latter must overcome the personal likes and dislikes of a strong ruler who is a potential tyrant ruling after "his own liberty and will" (pp. 164-65). In this way the entire commonwealth can enforce counsel.

In developing this line of thought, Starkey refers to English history and the office of the Constable of England, who could "singly counterpoise" the power of the prince much as one Roman consul could check the other in the Republic. The office of Constable had been

---

26. Starkey, *A Dialogue between Reginald Pole and Thomas Lupset,* ed. K. M. Burton (London: Chatto and Windus, 1948), p. 13.

27. OED's earliest entry for the phrase "mixed state" is from this treatise; see *ibid.,* p. 153.

28. Starkey is of course not referring to all the people: he rejects the inexperienced, unconsidered opinions of the multitudes, as do most sixteenth-century thinkers. See W. G. Zeeveld, *Foundations of Tudor Policy* (Cambridge, Mass.: Harvard University Press, 1948), pp. 90–91 for Starkey's expression of this idea in a short discourse preserved in the Public Record Office.

29. H. C. White, *Social Criticism in Popular Religious Literature of the Sixteenth Century* (New York: Macmillan, 1944), p. 66.

the cause of strife and faction in England because it was so powerful and potentially so dangerous. By the early sixteenth century, the office had fallen into disuse, but Starkey calls for its reestablishment in a new form. He proposes a group of fourteen men, to be made up "of the Constable as head, of the Lord Marshall, Steward and Chamberlain of England, with four of the chief judges, four citizens of London, and two bishops, London and Canterbury" (p. 166). This body would be in session when parliament was not, and would be a permanent safeguard of the realm against tyranny. This small group, actually an equivalent of Parliament, should in turn elect ten persons to be a council for the prince. The council is to be made up of two doctors of divinity, two of civil law, two of common law, and four members of the nobility. The King should be head when he chose to sit with it, and it would have power to make all appointments to bishoprics and great offices in the realm, thereby insuring to virtue its proper reward and securing peace: "for where virtue is not rewarded worthily, then it rebelleth sturdily; then riseth disdain and hate; then springeth envy and malice" (p. 166). The results of this rule would be immediate, as he proves by referring to Venice: "for as in Venice is no great ambitious desire to be there Duke, because he is restrained to good order and politic, so with us also should be our king, if his power were tempered after the manner before described" (p. 167). According to him, Venice is the precise analogy to English government.

Starkey, whose education at Padua and Venice was classical, knew the writings of Plato, Cicero, and Polybius; and the terms in which he saw English government are suggested by his advice that English intellectuals help to order society following "the example of Plato, Lycurgus . . . and of Solon."[30] If the *Dialogue*'s Pole relies on reason in his analysis, Lupset adds recognition

---

30. *Dialogue,* pp. 21–22.

84   *Coriolanus in Context*

of the practical demands of reality; altogether the work
shows the maturation of a century and a half of classical
scholarship[31] (especially Italian), and knowledge of contemporary republican Venice, which was sufficiently like
England to be cited as an analogy.

G. R. Elton has observed that in practical affairs a
doctrine "of an ultimate legislative supremacy vested in
King-in-Parliament . . . was half-grasped and wholly
practised after the constitutional revolution of the
1530's."[32] Holinshed gives an account of a striking case
of 1543, in the judgment of which Henry VIII concluded: "We be informed by our judges that we at no
time stand so highly in our estate royal as in the time of
Parliament, wherein we as head and you as members
are conjoined and knit together into one body politic"
(Elton, p. 270). The closeness of this to the mixed state
of the classical past and of contemporary Italy is implied
by the views recorded a few years later, under Edward
VI, by Petruccio Ubaldini, a Florentine *littérateur,* in
his manuscript *Relazione d'Inghilterra* (1552). The
essay, apparently written to acquaint a classically educated Italian with the English form of government, relates that when the health of the nation is in question,
the votes of nobles and the people are called for, so that
"la Republica Inglese [pare] essere ordinata, et com-
posta secondo l'openione di Platone; poichè in tal modo,
trè governi in un solo uniti, soprasedendo un giusto
Monarca, fanno una unione perfetta."[33]

31. Ferguson, pp. 375–76.
32. G. R. Elton, ed., *The Tudor Constitution* (Cambridge, England:
Cambridge University Press, 1960), p. 14.
33. The text is printed in G. Pellegrini, *Un fiorentino alla Corte
d'Inghilterra nel Cinquecento: Petruccio Ubaldini* ("Studi di Filologia
Moderna N.S. 7": Torino: Bottegha d'Erasmo, 1967); this passage
appears on p. 101. Ubaldini also recognizes the tendency of kings to
desire to rule unhindered: if kings "potesse con debito decoro, et utile
reggere senza il mezzo della Nobiltà, non è dubbio alcuno, che il Rè
anderebbe à poco spegnendola, come cominciò a fare Henrico Ottavo,"
(pp. 149–50). On Ubaldini and Machiavelli in England, see chapter 4.

Although in life Pole and Starkey remained on friendly terms, their disagreement on Henry's assumption of sovereignty in Church matters was profound. Pole chose, like More, to remain constant to the Roman Church, and his history thereafter is, except for the last few years of his life, in Italy. But in 1536 he wrote a thoroughly traditional treatise, the *Pro Ecclesiasticae Unitatis Defensione,* which is strikingly similar to the views of Starkey on some points. He argued that people appoint their kings and have the right to demand from them accounts of their administration; in calling on the Emperor Charles V to mobilize against Henry VIII, he promises that Englishmen who preserve the traditions whereby the people can remove a ruler who had violated the constitution of the realm or encroached upon the subjects' rights will come to his aid.[34] That Pole, who disagreed with Starkey's other views on the need for unity under the rule of Henry, could remain on friendly terms is characteristic of the earlier Tudor period. Later it was not so. The religiously committed Marian exiles emphasized, especially between 1553-56, that aspect of mixed state theory that concentrated on the limitation of monarchic power.[35] This concentration made Pole's work, otherwise a piece of orthodox Roman Catholic polemics, ironically apt for their purposes. The book was recirculated in 1555 as part of the exiles' pamphlet war aimed at Mary's (and Pole's) government, edited by Pierpaolo Vergerio and including other works by Martin Luther, Melanchthon, Bucer, and Calvin.[36]

Leaving England, the exiles went to Switzerland, the

---

34. (Rome, 1536), sigs, E1ᵛ, R5ᵛ.

35. The exodus was perhaps planned with the tacit approval of some in Mary's government: see C. H. Garrett, *The Marian Exiles* (Cambridge, England: at the University Press, 1938), pp. 2–15; Hudson, p. 67, n.21, outlines suggestive qualifications to this view.

36. J. G. Dwyer, ed., *Pole's Defense of the Unity of the Church* (Westminster, Md.: Newman Press, 1965), p. 342, gives further background of this, but does not draw these conclusions.

Low Countries, France, and Italy; the most significant number, some 361 men with their wives and children, went to Germany.[37] Once established there, these men intensified a political concern about monarchic rule which they treated not at all theoretically. For them, monarchic rule raised the most immediate, and therefore most extreme, of questions; their answers denied absolute power to the new Catholic Queen of England. The Marian Exile produced a variety of works on government that advocated the sharp limitation of monarchic power. But few went beyond advocating this, to achieve the moderate, balanced view that saw a proper place for subjects, nobility, and king within one government. Achieving this view is the distinction of the work of one of the most distinguished of the exiles, John Ponet (1516?-1556), Bishop of Winchester. Ponet wrote the *Short Treatise of Politike Power,* printed in 1556 *sine loco.*[38] The composition can be dated precisely by its reference to Cranmer's martyrdom (March 21, 1556), by its reference to the kidnapping of Sir John Cheke, news of which arrived in Strassburg on May 22, 1556,[39] and by Ponet's death in that city on August 2, 1556, perhaps of the plague then raging (sig. A1ᵛ).[40]

Ponet finds the origins of government in the imperfection of man; after the Flood, God found it necessary to enforce his commandments by establishing laws and magistrates to execute them. Various forms of government are possible and acceptable, depending on the people involved, so long as a given state adheres to the

---

37. Garrett, p. 39.

38. The book is thought to have been printed in Strassburg: see A. F. Johnson, "English Books Printed Abroad," *The Library,* 5th Series, 4 (1949–50) :275–76.

39. *A Short Treatise of Politique Power* (1556), sig. I6ᵛ. The date of the arrival of the news is noted by Peter Martyr Vermiglio in a letter to Bullinger; see Hudson, p. 85.

40. The printer expresses uncertainty whether the author is still alive or not. For the date of Ponet's death see Garrett, p. 258.

purpose of all states: to safeguard the welfare of those
for whom rulers have assumed responsibility (sigs.
A4^{r-v}). To the three traditional, simple states Ponet
adds one in which King, nobility, and commons ruled
together; this form of government "men by long continuance have judged to be the best sort of all. For wher
that mixte state was exercised, ther did the common
wealthe longest continue" (sig. A5^r).

He stresses the importance of counsellors, especially
those with sufficient experience to see the traps set for
the people by their potential enemy, the kings. Royal
counsellors must be wise and brave and must respond to
the pleas of the people; if they do not, the people are
justified in turning to their ministers and to such biblical
precedents as would encourage action. Members of Parliament are also counsellors, and those who always agree
with the monarch's wishes are dangerous to the commonwealth (sig. A3^v). Therefore if one is called to Parliament, one should serve fearlessly and with independence
(sig. A7^v). Ponet also cites a republican ideal, the Venetians, who are known for their honesty in running the
government (sig. K1^r).

Without "politike power and authoritie," civilized life
would become chaos; but the commonplace image of such
chaos as he invokes, "the great fish [eat] up the small"
(sig. A5^v), is not the prospect of the small fish rising
up against authority. Rather, danger lies in the unrestrained greed of kings like Tarquin (sig. A5^v), whose
instinct for oppression can be countered only by such
legitimate officers of the state as the Ephors of Sparta
or Tribunes of Rome, rightful representatives of the
common people:

> For as among the *Lacedemonians* certain men called *Ephori*
> were ordayned to see that the kinges should not oppresse the
> people, and among the Romaynes the *Tribunes* were ordayned
> to defende and mayntene the libertie of the people from the

pride and injurie of the nobles: so in all Christian realmes and dominiones God ordayned meanes, that the heads the princes, and governours should not oppresse the poor people after their lustes, and make their willes their lawes. As in Germanye betwene the emperour and the people, a Counsail or diet: in Fraunce and Englande, parliamentes, wherin ther mette and assembled of all sortes of people and nothing could be done without the knowlage and consent of all. . . .

(sigs. A6r–v)

This formulation indicates a close relationship between the exiled humanists and the Calvinists, for it reads like a paraphrase of the following well-known passage in Calvin's *Institution of the Christian Religion,* in Thomas Norton's 1562 translation:

I speake always of private men. For if there be at this time any Magistrates for the behalfe of the people (such as in old time were the Ephori, that wer set against the kinges of Lacedomonia or the Tribunes of the people against the Roman Consuls or the Demarchi, against the Senate of Athens: and the same power also which peradventure as thynges are now, the three estates have in every realme, when they holde theyr principle assemblies) I do so not forbidde them according to their office to withstande the outragyng lycentiousnesse of kynges, that I affirme that if they winke at kynges wilfully ragyng over and treadyng down the poore communaltie, their dissembling is not without wicked breache of faith, bicause they deceitfully betray the libertie of the people, whereof thei know themselves to be appointed protectors by ordinance of God.

(IV.20.31)

This passage bears the marginal note "Parliamentes," indicating Norton's understanding of its applicability to England. Calvin was delicate in his treatment of resistance to secular authority; but the matter was handled less delicately by the Marian exiles, much to Calvin's embarrassment upon occasion.[41]

41. The Puritans were associated with such views, although Calvin denied any knowledge of them; see his 1559 letter to Cecil: *Zurich Letters,* ed. H. Robinson (Cambridge, England: at the University Press, 1846), pp. 76–78.

For Ponet, rulers have quite definite limitations: "the ende of their authoritie is determined and certain to maintene justice, to defende the innocent, to punishe the evil" (sig. B3ʳ). They are subject to the laws of the realm (sig. C6ʳ⁻ᵛ). To illustrate his conception of the obedience rightfully due the ruler, Ponet, like Fortescue and Starkey before him, chooses a mean; he illustrates it by the analogy of the sinews of a man's body. If the sinews are strained, the man is in pain; if they are too loose, he cannot move. Both too much and too little obedience cause evil and disorder in the state. Those who show too much obedience are the English Papists; those who show too little obedience, the Anabaptists (sig. C8ʳ).[42] In order to secure the welfare of the people a mean between two extremes must be struck; it is necessary for the people to obey rulers only in decisions that conform to God's word (sig. D3ᵛ). In this plan, allegiance is due the commonwealth before any single element (sigs. D7ʳ⁻ᵛ), including the king. The people must judge in this matter; if they decide that the ruler is a tyrant, they are justified in taking action against him,[43] as had happened before in England, with Edward II and Richard II (sigs. G1ᵛ-G3ʳ). Thus Ponet's views are virtually those of Starkey; and like Starkey, Ponet proposes a safeguard against tyranny by referring to English precedent: he tells of the old office of High Constable, which was empowered to summon the king before Parliament, or even to commit him to ward (sig. G5ᵛ).[44] The treatise ends with a lengthy exhortation to the people—to Lords and Commons of England seen in the image of the exiles themselves, as a "politically

42. Despite the religious polemics, this discussion follows such traditional formulations as that of Fortescue very closely, particularly in the use of the analogy of obedience due the rightful ruler.

43. Garrett, p. 257, discusses the close relation between Ponet's views and those of Hotman, important in French political thought of the period. On the closeness of the views of Ponet and Starkey, see Zeeveld, pp. 247-49.

44. Cf. Starkey, *Dialogue,* p. 166.

responsible coalition of all classes,"[45] to unite to end the particularly English plague of civil strife (sig. L2^r). No element can prosper if the whole body of the state dies; better times will come, he promises, if the government of England overthrows the Roman Catholic government and returns to that of Edward's time (sig. L3^r).

As might be expected from a Cambridge-educated ecclesiastic, Ponet's mixture of classical and biblical references is applied to the contemporary English political situation. It strongly supports both limitation of monarchy and indicates the desirability of the mixed state.[46] Among the sources are the works of Fortescue, St. German, John Major, Sir Thomas Elyot, Erasmus, St. Thomas Aquinas, Duns Scotus, Plato, and in particular Aristotle's *Politics,* Cicero's *Oration in defense of Milo,* John of Salisbury's *Policraticus,* Marsiglio of Padua's *Defensor Pacis,* and Reginald Pole's *De Unione Ecclesiastica.*

When, after Queen Mary's death in 1558, the exiles returned, their attitude toward the Elizabethan government was an ambivalent mixture of gratitude for a non-Catholic monarch and distrust of any monarch. The attitude of the government of the country to which they returned, which solicited their support, was itself not unmixed with distrust. Garrett summarizes:

As a political faction, a group of disaffected country gentlemen, for the most part closely related, left England in 1554:

45. Zeeveld, p. 247.
46. Other exiles whose views clearly resembled Ponet's are John Aylmer, whose *Harborowe for Faithful and True Subjects* (1559) advocates an important role for Parliament in English government, especially to restrain the monarch; and Lawrence Humphrey, later the influential Calvinist president of Magdalen College, Oxford, whose *De Religionis Conservatione et Reformatione Vera* (1559) expressly limits the power of the monarch and accords revolutionary power to magistrates. Other sympathizers, such as Christopher Goodman (later chaplain to Sir Henry Sidney) and John Knox, agree with Ponet's constitutional views but concern themselves mostly with anti-tyrannic action. See Hudson, pp. 181–92, 219–20, and below, chapter 4.

as a political party they returned to it again in 1558, augmented in numbers; allied for party ends with a body of protestant ministers experienced in self-government untrammelled of bishops; trained in effective methods of propaganda; and actuated by a political philosophy that looked askance at the prerogative of kings.[47]

The extremist writers were not allowed to return to England; the more moderate, such as John Hales, were. The attitudes associated with the exiles were not acceptable to Elizabeth's government, and Ponet's book was not reprinted until the eve of the English Revolution, in 1639 and 1642.

Ponet's formulation of traditional views was determined by the stresses of the exile. A more moderate presentation was achieved by his tutor at Cambridge, Sir Thomas Smith (1512-77). Smith was a Fellow of Queen's College, which had been associated with Luther and Erasmus, and while there he had formed a circle of friends that included, after Ponet, Cheke, John Aylmer, Walter Haddon, Roger Ascham, William Cecil, and Edmund Grindal,[48] many of whom later fled to Strassburg. From 1539 to 1542 Smith traveled in France and Italy, earning the doctorate at the University of Padua and returning to be the first Regius Professor of Civil Law at Cambridge; there he promoted the new pronunciation of Greek advocated by Erasmus, and practised it, significantly, in his lectures on Aristotle's *Politics*.[49] Under Mary, Smith did not go into exile, but lived in retirement.

The extremism of the Marian exiles made them suspect to Elizabeth, for in asserting the people's rights

---

47. Garrett, p. 59.

48. John Strype, *Life of Sir Thomas Smith* (Oxford: at the Clarendon Press, 1820), pp. 13, 20.

49. Hudson, p. 8. Smith had Aristotle in mind in writing his work; see the letter of April, 1565, quoted in Sir Thomas Smith, *De Republica Anglorum*, ed. L. Alston (Cambridge, England: at the University Press, 1906), p. xiv.

they had raised the problem of obedience to legally constituted monarchs, and had decided against unthinking
submission. Although as a practical matter she favored
such submission, Elizabeth nevertheless sent Smith to
France in 1562 as the English ambassador. When he
returned in 1565, he had completed his book *De Republica Anglorum; the Maner of Government or Policie of
the realm of England,* which he wrote in both Latin[50]
and English. The work circulated in manuscript until it
was printed posthumously in London in 1583. It was
reprinted in 1584 and, a further attestation to its popularity, was enlarged and reprinted in 1589 under the
title *The Commonwealth of England.* This was reprinted
in 1594, 1601, 1609, 1612, and still four more times
before the Civil Wars opened.

Smith's book, like Ponet's, grew out of an academic
environment.[51] It was intended to be a guide for the
comparative study of government, both contemporary
and classical. He understood England's government to
exist between the opposite poles of mob rule, without
order or permanence, and, on the other hand, tyrannic
rule under which the people were slaves. To Smith,
England was "a society or common doing of a multitude
of free men collected together and united by common
accord and covenauntes among themselves for the con-
servation of themselves as well in peace as in warre"
(p. 20).

---

50. That Smith ever wrote a Latin version, which is the tradition
since Strype, has been questioned: see Smith, *ibid.,* p. 145. A study of
Smith, using newly discovered manuscript texts, is promised by Mary
Dewar, *Sir Thomas Smith* (London: Athlone Press, 1964), p. v.

51. E. W. Talbert, *The Problem of Order* (Chapel Hill: University
of North Carolina Press, 1962), p. 22; Hudson, pp. 4–8. Smith's knowledge is not surprising for a man whose library, the inventory of which
was taken on August 1, 1566, contained Livy, Greek and Latin editions of Plutarch's *Lives,* Dionysius of Halicarnassus, Bembo's *Historia
Veneta,* "Herodoto et il Principe di Machiavelli," the latter's *History of
Florence* and *Discourses,* and Aristotle's *Politics.* See Strype, appendix
6, pp. 275–78.

Technically Smith favors monarchic rule, although he is aware of many forms of government. His traditional English view represents the sovereignty as actually residing in "King-in-Parliament"; and his moderation causes him to recognize that the monarch in England is "farre more absolute than either the dukedome of Venice is, or the kingdome of the Lacedemonians was" (p. 59). His views on English government accord with the classic formulations of the great spokesman for Elizabethan government, Richard Hooker. For Hooker, Parliament

> is that whereupon the very essence of all government within the kingdom doth depend; it is even the body of the whole realm; it consisteth of the king, and of all that within the land are subject to him: for they are all there present, either in person or by such as they voluntary have derived their very personal right unto.
>
> (VIII.vi.11, not printed until 1648)

In according both king and subjects rights that must be maintained, Hooker demonstrates an attitude toward the essentially composite nature of English sovereignty that avoids the partisan biases of later Elizabethan times, and continues the tradition of the Middle Ages emphasizing unity. To understand Smith, or any of the authors studied in this chapter, to be insisting on the separability of sovereignty which would provoke competition between the opposing claims of King and Parliament, is to read sixteenth-century writing as partisan writers of the seventeenth century did, against the background of the developing conflict between extremists that resulted in the Civil War and of the political tracts of that later age.[52]

---

52. Such an error has historical precedent, for Smith's book had a second life as a work of political propaganda in the cause of the Puritan movement, which culminated in the establishment of the English republic in 1649: see Z. S. Fink, *The Classical Republicans* ("Northwestern University Studies in the Humanities No. 9": Evanston: North-

The popularity of Smith's work and of the line of thought traced in this chapter means that some members of Shakespeare's audience would have condemned such elements of *Coriolanus* as the civil strife and the establishment of tribunes only if these elements were, for some reason, presented as essentially dangerous to the welfare of the state. To present them in such a way in a Roman play would mean, we have seen, altering dramatic conventions and distorting historical interpretations received from classical sources; it would also mean countering the sympathetic attitude toward mixed government that this chapter has surveyed. Even should this prove to be the case, *Coriolanus* would no longer be explicable in the terms of J. E. Phillips, for example, who argues that the play's Rome is a monarchy in which the Senate and consuls rule together as one king,[53] and according to whom the people (whose plight he recognizes [p. 154]) are wrong to seek to redress their grievances by taking action, since the common person is treated only as he is "spurred by political ambitions, attempting to rise out of his degree" (p. 153).

Only in representations of *English* government on the public stage did Shakespeare consistently express Tudor orthodoxies, thereby avoiding problems that might have caused trouble to himself or the actors by prosecution of the authorities. In the *Histories* written before the turn of the century, he is careful to dramatize events in ways reconcilable with Tudor formulations. An attempt to dramatize the problems inherent in kingship in *Richard*

western University Press, 1945), p. 100n. The book began with a concern for Milton's political pamphlets. G. L. Mosse points out resultant errors in "The Influence of Jean Bodin's *République* on English Political Thought," *Mediaevalia et Humanistica* 5 (1948):74.

53. Phillips, p. 152. Cf. p. 108; the term "monarchy" was flexible in the sixteenth and early seventeenth centuries, and Phillips quotes Latimer, *Seven Sermons* (1549): "it maketh no matter by what name the ruler be named." In Shakespeare's *Coriolanus* there are not "consuls," as there were in historical Rome, but rather a single consul: see below, chapter 6.

II resulted in a play—suggestively a very popular one—that caused the acting company difficulty at the time of the Essex rebellion.

But even the English *Histories* allow the people a stronger role than Phillips suggests. Nowhere in these plays does Shakespeare show the government of England to be mixed, but he does accord to the common people some demonstration of their loyal counsel. In one such demonstration, they are at pains to deny any interpretation of insurrection, yet the implications of their proposed actions could be extreme. In *2 Henry VI,* following the murder of Humphrey of Gloucester, the people's requests are transmitted to Henry VI by the Earl of Salisbury: from "love and loyalty" and without intention "to contradict your liking," (III.ii.250, 251) they intend to protect the king, and despite any order to the contrary,

> Were there a serpent seen with forked tongue
> That slily glided towards your Majesty,
> It were but necessary you were wak'd,
> Lest, being suffer'd in that harmful slumber,
> The mortal worm might make the sleep eternal.
> And *therefore do they cry, though you forbid,*
> *That they will guard you, whe'r you will or no,*
> From such fell serpents as false Suffolk is.
>   (ll. 259–66; italics mine)

The matter, presented within the framework of a well-meaning commonalty, is expressed to William de la Pole, the Duke of Suffolk, at whose extremist attitudes we glanced in the first chapter. The reply of this direct ancestor of Reginald Pole calls the commons "rude unpolish'd hinds" and "a sort of tinkers" (ll. 271, 277); he is clearly disloyal and dangerous to the commonwealth.[54] The urgency of the people's repeated demands

---

54. The Pole family may have been associated with a kind of national and religious disloyalty, provoked probably by Reginald Pole's attempt, as Roman Catholic Archbishop of Canterbury under Queen Mary, to bring England back to the Church. It is ironic that Pole's

and Henry's acceptance of them in banishing Suffolk attests to their effectiveness; and slightly later, Richard takes the commonwealth into account in *Richard III,* III.vii, although he easily manipulates the Mayor and through him the common people at large. The English plays set in Rome present political situations of such a nature and of such complexity that they could not be dealt with fully by invoking the official governmental propaganda of the Tudors and Stuarts.

---

attack on tyranny in the *Pro Ecclesiasticae,* aimed at Henry VIII, should have been published separately in 1560 as *The Seditious and Blasphemous Oration of Cardinal Pole* (STC 20087).

4

Italian Sources and Analogues

According to Sir Philip Sidney (1554-86), the sweetness of Arcadia is largely due to the contentedness of the inhabitants of that primitive community:

> This countrie Arcadia among all the provinces of Greece, hath ever beene had in singular reputation: partly for the sweetnesse of the ayre, and other natural benefites, but principally for the well tempered minds of the people.[1]

This would seem to be nonpolitical, an impression that appears to be borne out when Sidney goes on, a few pages later, to point to a related quality of the people: "Ordinary it is among the meanest sorte, to make Songes and Dialogues in meeter, either love whetting their braine, or long peace having begun it, example and emulation amending it" (p. 28). This passage replaces the introduction to the First Eclogues of the 1580 text:

> The manner of the Arcadian shepherds was when they met,

<hr />

1. *The Countesse of Pembrokes Arcadia,* in *The Complete Works of Sir Philip Sidney,* ed. Albert Feuillerat. 4 vols. (Cambridge, England: at the University Press, 1912–26), 1:19; cf. 4:i.

together, to pass their time either in such music as their rural education would afford them, or in exercise of their body.

(IV.52; also see I.26)

The literary sources and traditions of similarly well-tempered, harmonious *Arcadia* have of course been extensively studied;[2] but, Elizabeth Dipple has recently shown, another dimension is provided by the existence among these sources of the Greek historian Polybius.[3] In the course of discussing the Roman occupation of Arcadia and neighboring Lacedemonia (Sparta), with the intention of bringing his reader up to date on history, he describes the country and its inhabitants in this way:

> The Arcadian nation on the whole has a very high reputation for virtue among the Greeks, due not only to their humane and hospitable character and usages, but especially to their piety to the gods. . . . For the practice of music, . . . it is hardly known except in Arcadia, . . . in the first place the boys from their earliest childhood are trained to sing in measure the hymns and paeans in which by traditional usage they celebrate the heroes and gods of each particular town.[4]

Rome's territorial conquest overwhelmed ancient Greece; in art as well as in life, harsh reality breaks in to complicate the arcadian ideal.[5]

Against the pastoral background, which exists as a contrasting setting in Sidney as in Polybius, the main plot of *Arcadia* presents the story of Basilius, who humanly and fallibly yields to vain curiosity by impiously seeking to learn the future from an oracle. The consequences are

2. These have been studied, with full references to earlier scholarship, by Walter R. Davis, "A Map of Arcadia: Sidney's Romance in its Tradition," *Sidney's Arcadia* by W. R. Davis and R. A. Lanham (New Haven: Yale University Press, 1965), pp. 1–179.

3. "Harmony and Pastoral in the *Old Arcadia*," *ELH* 35 (1968): 309–28.

4. Polybius, *Histories* iv.20, trans. W. R. Paton. Loeb Classical Library (Cambridge, Mass.: Harvard University Press, 1954), 2:349.

5. See E. Panofsky, "Et in Arcadia Ego," *Cassirer Festschrift* (Oxford: at the Clarendon Press, 1936), pp. 223–54.

that he passively retires, in his resultant fruitless uncertainty, thereby inviting confusion within himself, his family, and, most important for the present purpose, the state at large. Thus Sidney imports some of Polybius's specific interests, and firmly anchors the Arcadia in the early historian's concerns with affairs of state.

Amidst the complicated action, there are two striking moments of political turmoil. First, at the gathering of people when Basilius is presumed dead,

> some there . . . cried to have the state altred, and governed no more by a Prince; marry in the alteration, many would have the *Lacedemonian* government of fewe chosen Senatours; others the *Athenian,* where the peoples voyce helde the chiefe aucthoritye. But these were rather the discoursing sorte of men, then the active, being a matter more in imaginacion then practise.
>
> (II.131; cf. IV.300)

Here, at a moment of confusion when all things are potentially possible, Sidney surveys alternatives to monarchy. He is suggestive and accurate in his historical references.[6] Second, to the older text he added an enlargement of political concern in the more significant treatment of the rebellion of the Helots against their Lacedemonian overlords.

Although the presentation of this rebellion has been much debated by critics,[7] it seems clear that at least initially Sidney treats it as a thoroughly justified outbreak against usurpers; and he even gives the Helots one of the protagonists, Pyrochles, to fight for them. In any event, the peace, when it comes, establishes an approved new government which is to combine the two peoples, is to keep king and nobility, but is to allow the

6. Davis, pp. 153–55.
7. See the summary in the notes to E. W. Talbert's valuable *The Problem of Order* (Chapel Hill: University of North Carolina Press, 1962), pp. 89–117.

common people to elect magistrates (I.46-47). Irving
Ribner accurately terms this "a limited monarchy or
mixed state";[8] the terms are not, we have seen and shall
see again, mutually exclusive. The English Renaissance
saw—as Sidney himself did when on his Continental
voyages in 1572-75—a famous example of mixed government in Venice, and several studies of the structure
were available;[9] but these tended to be formulated in the
terms of the definitive theoretical one by Polybius, in
Book vi of his *Histories*.

Regardless of Sidney's attitude toward extreme situations of rebellion and civil disobedience, it seems clear
that Sidney's spectrum of political information, with
which he expected his readers to be familiar, is inclusive,
and that he felt that good government should reflect the
harmonious and "well-tempered minds of the people."
It would do so if it were itself "tempered"—and this
word, which, as we may recall, Herodotus had used,
implies several elements within the government, mixed
together and limiting each other's pleas for absolute
control. Even in the arrival of Euarchus, who is an
approved monarch, and in his strong monarchic rule,
there is a crucial reservation: Euarchus cannot enforce
arbitrary decisions. He is approved precisely because
he recognizes that as king he is bound to the laws of
nature; he is what Bodin termed the "royal monarch."[10]
Euarchus's arrival, then, is not Sidney's monarchist
"statement." Like Basilius's "resurrection" and the sub-

8. "Machiavelli and Sidney: The *Arcadia* of 1590," *SP* 47 (1950):
165. Talbert, p. 107, suggests that Sidney's refusal to use the term
"mixed state" reflects his reading of Jean Bodin, whose *Methodus*
(1566) he apparently recommended to his brother Robert (letter of
October 18, 1580).

9. See the discussion of Venice in Z. S. Fink, *The Classical Republicans*. Northwestern University Studies in the Humanities No. 9 (Evanston: Northwestern University Press, 1945), chapter 2.

10. Jean Bodin, *The Six Bookes of a Commonweale*, tr. Richard
Knolles (1606), ed. K. D. McRae (Cambridge, Mass.: Harvard University Press, 1962), p. 204.

sequent marriages, it is included in the complexity of the total work, and is literary rather than political: it is appropriate for the fifth act of a tragi-comedy.[11]

Sidney's familiar and inventive use of historico-political material is in part the result of being raised in an early-Elizabethan circle of relatives and family friends which approved of mixed government.[12] Members of this group include Hubert Languet, Sidney's father-in-law Sir Francis Walsingham, and his uncle Peter Wentworth, notorious, as we shall see, in the House of Commons. There was also Christopher Goodman, the Marian exile who settled in Strassburg with John Ponet and Piermartire Vermiglio. He was one of the translators of the Geneva Bible and author of *How Superior Powers ought to be Obeyed* (Geneva, 1558); he was allowed to return only to Scotland, as escort to John Knox's wife, in 1559, and to England, as chaplain to Sir Henry Sidney, in 1565. Another member, George Buchanan, wrote the anti-tyrannic *De Iure Regni apud Scotos* (composed ca. 1568, printed 1579), similar in tendency to Ponet's treatise. The Sidney circle liked the book for what J. E. Phillips terms its "doctrines of limited monarchy, popular sovereignty, and the right of tyrannicide."[13] At the same time that it appeared, the Sidneys were opposing Elizabeth's possible marriage to the Duc d'Alençon, on the grounds that England's "moderate form of Monarchie"—its mixed form of government—might thereby be changed to a "precipitate absoluteness."[14]

---

11. William A. Ringler, Jr., ed., *The Poems of Sir Philip Sidney* (Oxford: at the Clarendon Press, 1962), pp. xxxvii–xxxviii.

12. J. E. Phillips, "George Buchanan and the Sidney Circle," *HLQ* 12 (1948): 23–55; see also R. Howell, *Sir Philip Sidney* (Boston: Little, Brown, 1968), pp. 153–63.

13. Phillips, p. 37.

14. The words are Fulke Greville's, in the *Life of Sir Philip Sidney,* ed. N. Smith (Oxford: at the Clarendon Press, 1907), p. 54. On Greville see below.

In addition to such family acquaintances, Sidney had access to a wide variety of books in several languages. On 19 December 1573, during his travels on the Continent, he wrote Languet, asking whether the latter had received a shipment of books that included "il stato di Vinegia scritto da Contareni, et da Donato Giannotti."[15] The book referred to is a volume apparently binding together Gasparo Cardinal Contarini's *De Magistratibus et Republica Venetorum* (first printed 1543) with Giannotti's *Libro de la Repubblica de' Viniziani* (first printed 1540). These books, informed by classical political attitudes already surveyed, are products of Continental pre-Counter-Reformation Catholic thought; as such, they present ideals which could be shared by Englishmen who maintained, like Sir Thomas Smith, a moderate path in religion and politics. In themselves and in their representative nature, these works are important for an appreciation of English awareness of Italy during the sixteenth century, and, more specifically, for an illustration of an actual avenue by which political alternatives to Tudor despotism were made available to Englishmen. Interest in contemporary Italy and classical Rome was a response to pressing problems that confronted both Europe and England in the sixteenth century—and, we shall see, in the early seventeenth.

Since the thirteenth century, Englishmen considering themselves students had taken up contemporary residence in Italy, but in the mid-fifteenth century the movement became virtually a small migration,[16] which was continued, after 1487, by Thomas Linacre and those who gathered around him at Padua in the Veneto, at

---

15. *Works,* 3:81.
16. George B. Parks, *The English Traveller to Italy* (Stanford: Stanford University Press, 1954), 1:429–35.

Rome, and at Florence. With Linacre in Italy were William Lily (later the first headmaster of St. Paul's school, father of George, Reginald Pole's Chaplain, and grandfather of John, the dramatist), William Grocyn, John Colet, and William Latimer. In Italy Linacre studied with Leonico Tomeo, and this contact "made Padua the focal point for a whole generation of English humanists."[17] Like Leonico, Linacre is said to have been a tutor of Pole, a cousin of Henry VIII of England and later the last Roman Catholic archbishop of Canterbury under Queen Mary. Pole's Italian visits will concern us shortly. But whether the story is true or not,[18] the Anglo-Italian relation still exists, for Latimer was Pole's tutor at Oxford in about 1513. The Englishmen in Italy during these years—and there was continuity from the end of the fifteenth century through the first thirty years of the sixteenth century and beyond, in Florence, Rome, Venice, Padua, Urbino,[19] and other places—were in the presence of a body of Italian historical, moral, and political philosophy which they could hardly ignore, and which was, to boot, highly developed.

The earliest written history of Florence, for instance, the anonymous *Chronica de Originis Civitatis* (thirteenth century), traced the founding of the city to Roman colonization under Julius Caesar. Building on legends, history derived from ancient writers, and popular beliefs,

17. *Ibid.,* p. 461.
18. *Ibid.,* pp. 460–61.
19. C. H. Clough, "The Relations between the English and Urbino Courts, 1474–1508," *Studies in the Renaissance* 14 (1967): 202–18, discusses this rather neglected subject. The connections between England and Urbino in 1474–75 and 1504–08 partly account for the space devoted to that city in William Thomas's *History of Italy* (1549) and for the apparent popularity of Sir Thomas Hoby's 1561 English translation of Baldassare Castiglione's *Il Cortegiano* (1528). In Book IV, Pietro Bembo, who otherwise speaks little on that day, argues that "Commune weales well in order" keep liberty better than monarchy, and, like Machiavelli, argues that the people are less likely to be corrupted than a single Prince. See *The Book of the Courtier,* trans. Sir Thomas Hoby. The Tudor Translations (London: Nutt, 1900), pp. 311–12.

Florentines,[20] like Tudor Englishmen,[21] formulated their own providential view of history: the Florentine traditions, dating back to Rome but now decaying, would be renewed under God. Such renewal implied private and public moral virtue, which, from the earlier fifteenth century onward, writers identified with Florence's native republicanism, civic loyalty, and solidarity with the Church, rather than with territorial expansion of the state on the model of Imperial Rome. Giovanni Villani's *Cronica* (ca. 1300), reprinted in Venice in 1537,[22] is characteristic of his time in attributing Florence's greatness to its republicanism and the private virtue of its citizens.[23] In the early years of the fifteenth century, in the confrontation of Republican Florence with the imperial claims of Giangalleazzo Visconti (d. 1402), Florence's tradition of republican government was crystallized anew; Florence emerged from this controversy with a strengthened sense of the central importance of civic liberty.[24]

Florence's republican government ended in 1434, when the Medici took control of the state. They ruled for fifty years, when, after their overthrow, a *Parlamento*

---

20. Donald Weinstein, "The Myth of Florence," *Florentine Studies: Politics and Society in Renaissance Florence,* ed. Nicolai Rubinstein (London: Faber and Faber, 1968), p. 21.

21. E. M. W. Tillyard, *Shakespeare's History Plays* (London: Chatto and Windus, 1944), pp. 40–54.

22. A copy of this edition is No. 1141 in the Lumley Library; on this collection, see below.

23. Weinstein, p. 24.

24. Hans Baron, *The Crisis of the Early Italian Renaissance* (Princeton: Princeton University Press, 1955), 1:2–37, 67–68. Republicanism in "the Quattrocento was to become characteristic of Florentine historiography," Baron observes in *Humanistic and Political Literature in Florence and Venice* (Cambridge, Mass.: Harvard University Press, 1955), p. 18. Praise of republicanism had been expressed earlier by nonpolitical writers, notably by Ptolemy of Lucca, the continuator of St. Thomas Aquinas's *De Regimine Principum;* Ptolemy openly praised the Roman Republic and the achievements of its consuls: see Baron, *Crisis,* 1:44–46.

reestablished the government along the lines prior to 1434—testimony to the tenacity of the civic tradition. The significant addition to the government at this time was the institution of the Great Council, taken from the example of Venice. This newly established yet traditional government was itself overthrown in 1512, inaugurating a period of intense political reflection. During the years of republican government and of the Medici ascendancy, republican ideas continued to be held and occasionally voiced, true too of the brief period of resurgent republicanism in 1527-30. Thus, surveying the period of their own history which saw the successive defeat, victory, defeat, partial victory, and then ultimate extinction of the republic, the Florentines found greater relevance in the historical events in Rome that immediately preceded the end of the republic than in the admittedly greater achievements of the Emperors which brought Rome to its height of power. That this interest was shared by a number of Elizabethan Englishmen is the implication of their continued interest in dramatizations of this general subject, and of the number of translations from the classics during the same period[25] as well as books dealing with Italian affairs. In England as in Florence, many saw, for instance, in the assassination of Julius Caesar a blow struck to preserve the Roman Republic. In both Florence and England the republic Brutus stood for had many admirers; and the Florentines' admiration was reinforced by understanding the city of Florence itself to have been founded not by

---

25. On translations, see H. S. Bennett, *English Books and their Readers: 1475-1603* (2 vols.; Cambridge, England: Cambridge University Press, 1952-1965); J. G. Ebel, "A Numerical Survey of Elizabethan Translations," *The Library* 5th series 22 (1967):104-27; H. B. Lathrop, *Translations from the Classics from Caxton to Chapman* (Madison, Wisc.: University of Wisconsin Press, 1933); and Mary A. Scott, *Elizabethan Translations from the Italian* (Baltimore, Md.: Modern Language Association, 1895).

Julius Caesar, but during republican days, by veterans of Sulla's army.[26]

A man representative of intelligent and informed historicopolitical views in Florence during these years is Bernardo Rucellai (1448-1514), a Florentine aristocrat who remained devoted to the republican ideal during the times of the autocrat Lorenzo il Magnifico and Piero dei' Medici, as well as those of the democrat Savanarola. Rucellai found a place in the Medicean government, but opposed the absolutist claims advanced by the family and contributed to the house's fall in 1494. He retired from politics in 1495 when, under the direction of Savanarola, the state became a democracy; as Felix Gilbert observes, "To Rucellai the stability of an aristocratic government had seemed compatible with a somewhat privileged position for the Medici and might even have best been guaranteed by having a Medici as *primus inter pares.*"[27] Many in the group of aristocrats around the Medici, Rucellai included, habitually took Venice to be the ideal toward which Florentine government should strive: it should be mixed, a state in which the Doge represented the monarchic element, and the Senate the Aristocratic. The mass of people should of course have no role. Rucellai saw a Medici as Doge, giving stability to the state, and this view accorded with that of the majority of Florentine aristocrats after 1494.[28]

26. Cf. N. Machiavelli, *The Florentine Historie,* tr. T. B[edingfield]., (London: T.C., 1595), sig. D2ᵛ. References will be made to this edition; and *Discorsi* I.1, ed. M. Lerner (New York: Modern Library, 1940), p. 107; cf. Baron, *Crisis,* 1:52. Cf. Shakespeare's use of the associations of origin with regard to Julius Caesar's legendary building of the Tower of London: in *Richard III* it is associated with Caesar and used to further Richard's tyrannic purposes (III.i.68ff), and in *Richard II,* Richard is led to death in "Julius Caesar's ill-erected tower" (V.i.2).

27. "Bernardo Rucellai and the Orti Oricellari: a Study on the Origin of Modern Political Thought," *JWCI* 12 (1949):108.

28. Gilbert, "The Venetian Constitution in Florentine Political Thought," in *Florentine Studies,* p. 483.

Rucellai's claim to an influential place in the intellectual life of Florence lies, in major part, in the Orti Oricellari meetings he patronized in 1502-6 and again in the following decade. Although the young aristocrats who gathered together for discussions chose primarily literary and linguistic topics,[29] politics was not excluded. Rucellai himself indicates their approach in the foreword to his *De Urbe Roma* (before 1506?), using Classical and Venetian history in order to argue for aristocratic, and against democratic, government for Florence.[30] Members of his circle approached historical and political questions in the same way, although their interpretations and conclusions, with regard to Rome, Venice, and Florence, might be directly opposed to his.

It was in the Orti Oricellari that Niccolo Machiavelli had an opportunity to develop his republican views:[31] in particular, his contemporary Jacopo Nardi relates, it was for these meetings that he composed the *Discorsi*.[32] Although the full title of this work is *Discorsi sopra la prima deca di Tito Livio,* Machiavelli's interest, like that of Rucellai,[33] is in discussing the Florentine republic, which he does by placing it in the tradition of the Roman. Consequently he follows a Roman reference with one from contemporary Italy; for instance, in *Discorsi* I.7, the chapter in which he tells the Coriolanus story, Machiavelli cites Pietro Soderini's parallel experience in Florence.

---

29. See the recent studies by Armand L. De Gaetano, "G. B. Gelli and the Rebellion against Latin," *Studies in the Renaissance* 14 (1967): 131-58, and "The Florentine Academy and the Advancement of Learning through the Vernacular: the Orti Oricellari and the Sacra Accademia," *BHR* 30 (1968):19-52.

30. Gilbert, "Bernardo Rucellai," pp. 122-23 and notes.

31. J. R. Hale, *Machiavelli and Renaissance Italy* (New York: Collier, 1963), p. 149.

32. *Istorie della Città di Firenze* (Printed 1582) (Firenze, 1842), 2:85-86.

33. Gilbert, "Bernardo Rucellai," pp. 113-14, n.4, and 125.

Both the *Principe* and the *Discorsi*[34] view Italy from the standpoint of its decline into chaos and seek means of bringing it back to its former condition of virtue and preeminence. The work more directly influential in sixteenth-century European politics, the *Principe* (originally entitled *De Principatibus*[35]), is relevant to states to be governed by a monarch; restoration then should be accomplished by a prince, for the good of the state—however ambiguous that term might be.[36] The way for a prince to accomplish this end could be gradual (being permitted illegal and immoral means so long as the end were approved), or sudden:

> And as the reformation of the political condition of a state presupposes a good man, whilst the making of himself prince of a republic by violence naturally presupposes a bad one, it will consequently be exceedingly rare that a good man should be found willing to employ wicked means to become prince, even though his final object be good; or that a bad man, after having become prince, should be willing to labor for good ends, and that it should enter his mind to use for good purposes that authority which he has acquired by evil means.[37]

In the *Discorsi,* Machiavelli is concerned with republics. In this case, the people would undertake the task of reformation by themselves, and establish a government in which they would be represented; this was the situation when, led by Junius Brutus, the Romans overthrew

---

34. The dates and order of composition of these works is not yet known with certainty. Some idea of the problems involved can be got from Hans Baron, "The *Principe* and the Puzzle of the Date. . . .," *BHR* 18 (1956):405–28 and F. Chabod, *Machiavelli and the Renaissance,* tr. D. Moore (Cambridge, England: Bowes and Bowes, 1958). For the continental popularity of both works, see Adolph Gerber, *Niccolo Machiavelli: die Handschriften* (Gotha, 1912–13).

35. Machiavelli, Letter to Francesco Vettori, 10 December 1513.

36. A. H. Gilbert, *Machiavelli's "Prince" and its Forerunners* (Durham: Duke University Press, 1938), pp. 36ff, on *Prince* 6; pp. 115–16, on *Prince* 17. This phrase might mean the good of those who rule or the good of the greatest number: see Hiram Haydn, *The Counter-Renaissance* (New York: Scribner, 1950), p. 423. In a republic, the phrase refers to what English writers called "commonweale."

37. Machiavelli, *Discorsi,* I.18, p. 171.

the Tarquins. According to Machiavelli, the chances of success under these conditions would be really greater than if undertaken by a prince. In Rome, the popular reformation, strengthening the democratic elements to counter the monarchic, resulted in a well-balanced, fully mixed government; tribunes were created explicitly to give a permanent legal political existence to the people, and they accomplished the restoration of virtue and pre-eminence by bringing "the Roman republic back to its original principles" (III.1, p. 399). In Machiavelli's view, the results were good:

> Now such were the means employed at Rome; when the people wanted to obtain a law, they resorted to some of the extremes of which we have just spoken, or they refused to enroll themselves to serve in the wars, so that the Senate was obliged to satisfy them in some measure. The demands of a free people are rarely pernicious to their liberty; they are generally inspired by oppressions, experienced or apprehended; and if their fears are ill founded, resort is had to public assemblies where the mere eloquence of a single good and respectable man will make them sensible of their error. "The people," says Cicero, "although ignorant, yet are capable of appreciating the truth, and yield to it readily when it is presented to them by a man whom they esteem worthy of their confidence."
>
> (I.4, p. 120)

The common interest of these two treatises in restoring Italy to a former preeminence, and thereby correlating a particular government with the general good, suggests that the *Principe* and the *Discorsi* are not expressions of personal preferences, and therefore contradictory, but rather a convention of humanist political writing, elaborating alternative means to the same end.[38]

Machiavelli refers to classical history, characteristi-

---

38. Pointing to the seeming contradiction in liking a "popular" state, a principate, and also aristocratic Venice, Jean Bodin exclaims, "no man can judge what this wicked and inconstant man meanes"; *The Six Bookes of a Commonweale*, p. 702. See also Felix Gilbert, *Machiavelli and Guicciardini* (Princeton: Princeton University Press, 1965), p. 90.

cally, to show that the people were able to vent the hostility Coriolanus aroused in attempting to control them. The legal means were provided by the tribunes, whose institution Coriolanus vigorously opposes in Shakespeare's play. According to Machiavelli, however, they really saved the state, for, had the people killed Coriolanus as they intended, there would have occurred

> an offense of private individuals against a private individual, which kind of offenses generate fear, and fear seeks for means of defence, and for that purpose seeks partisans, and from partisans arise factions in cities, and factions cause their ruin.
>
> (I.7, p. 132)[39]

Far from being seditious, the tribunate protected both the state, by regulating the people's complaints, and the people, by providing a legal means of expression of popular wishes. In Machiavelli's own view, the Roman republic was a mixed government in which the tribunate balanced the two opposing concentrations of power, the senate and people.[40]

Basing their views on the tacit assumption that Machiavelli's *Discorsi* was not read in England (there being no published English translation before that of E. Dacres in 1636[41]), some scholars have felt that Machiavelli

39. Dionysius of Halicarnassus also discusses the summoning of Coriolanus to defend himself before the people as an important new venture and a testing of the people's rights: *Roman Antiquities* vii.21.

40. Machiavelli relied upon classical authors, but felt free to depart from them, as in this instance. In *Discorsi* I.58 he disagrees with Livy on the constancy of the people (pp. 262–65). The nature of his use of Polybius is less clear; in I.2 he follows Polybius vi closely: see *Discourses*, ed. L. J. Walker (New Haven: Yale University Press, 1950), 2:7–13. The edition of Polybius that Machiavelli might have used is not certain. P. Villari surmised that it was a Latin text: see *Niccolo Machiavelli and his Times*, trans. L. Villari (London: Kegan Paul, 1883), 3:247, 283. One such edition is Perotti's (1473). See also J. Hexter, "Seyssel, Machiavelli and Polybius vi: The Mystery of the Missing Translation," *Studies in the Renaissance* 3 (1956):75–96, and the modifications of this view in Gilbert, *Machiavelli and Guicciardini*, pp. 320–21.

41. *Machiavels discourses upon the first decade of T. Livius*, STC 17160.

and his ideas, particularly the extremist republican ideas contained in the *Discorsi,* were of marginal importance in England during the Tudor and early Stuart years.[42] However, they were more available than these men thought. In 1584 both the *Principe* and the *Discorsi* had been printed in Italian by John Wolfe (1547?-1601), a London printer who placed false information on the title page: "Palermo, appresso gli heredi d'Antoniello degli Antonielli" (STC 17159).[43] The books were bound together, and prefaced by remarks ascribed to Petruccio Ubaldini (1524?-1600?), a Florentine who lived in England. In his prefatory remarks, Ubaldini writes that from Machiavelli he learned the difference between a "principe giusto" and a tyrant, between the government of the "molti buoni" and the "poci malvagi," and, last, between a "commune ben regolato" and a "moltitudine confusa e licentiosa" (sig. *2ᵛ). Unpublished manuscripts of the *Discorsi,* perhaps made from Wolfe's edition, also circulated privately; one, by John Levett and dated 1599, has been studied by Napoleone Orsini. The prefaces point out that Machiavelli agreed with most wise men that "a bad government is to be preferred before licentiousness, yea even a very tyranny, before a popular confusion."[44] Levett possibly used the Wolfe edition, copies of which were in English libraries.[45] A recent count indicates that the *Discorsi* is extant in four

---

42. See *e.g.,* E. M. W. Tillyard, *History,* p. 21.

43. On this printer, see H. R. Hoppe, "John Wolfe, Printer and Publisher, 1579-1601," *The Library,* 4th Series 14 (1933):241-88. This supplements the earlier article of Henry Sellers, "Italian Books printed in England before 1640," *ibid.* 5 (1924):105-28. See also Adolph Gerber, "All of the five fictitious Italian editions of writings of Machiavelli and three of those of Pietro Aretino printed by John Wolfe of London (1584-88)" *MLN* 22 (1907):2-6, 129-35, 201-6. I am currently engaged on a book dealing with this printer's cultural role in late-Elizabethan England.

44. Printed in N. Orsini, *Studii sul Rinascimento italiano in Inghilterra* (Firenze: Sansoni, 1937), pp. 43-47.

45. John L. Lievsay, *The Englishman's Italian Books: 1550-1700* (Philadelphia: University of Pennsylvania Press, 1969), p. 50.

manuscript translations of the period.[46]

Explicitly, Florentine history is the subject of Machiavelli's *Historie Fiorentine* (1525), translated for English readers by T. B[edingfield]. for the London edition of 1595.[47] Book Three, chapter 1 sets forth a similar analysis of Florence in an extended comparison between it and the Roman republic. The source of political difficulty in each case was the seemingly insoluble conflict between the nobility and the people. This conflict arose, in the words of the Elizabethan translator, "through the desire of the one to command, the other, not to obey" (sig. G1^r). In each case the people determine the issue; but if their decisions led Rome to peace and civic virtue, they led Florence to dissension and civic vice. The difference lay in this: in Rome, the people wanted to share the government with the nobility and in Florence they sought to exclude the nobility from any power. It is characteristic of Machiavelli to recognize, in the contemporary world, that Venice was the preeminent Republic in Italy, and yet to deny it admiration.[48] Machiavelli's emphasis on the desirability of mixing elements is traditional, and despite his rejection of Venice as an ideal, his explicit outline for a new mixed Florentine government made up of Gonfaloniere, Senate, and Great Council is an ideal reflecting Venice.[49]

His popular bias is extremist, and this perhaps ac-

---

46. (1) Add. MS 41162, the Levett translation; (2) Harleian 7507; (3) Add. MS 4212; and (4) Hatfield 273-3; see the anonymous note "Machiavelli's *Discourses*," *N&Q*, N.S., 5 (1958):144–45. *The Prince* was also available in manuscript translations; see Hardin Craig, ed., *Machiavelli's "The Prince": an Elizabethan Translation* (Chapel Hill: University of North Carolina Press, 1944), pp. xix–xxxii.

47. In addition to the edition of 1595, the book was available in England in Wolfe's Italian edition of 1587 (STC 17161).

48. *Florentine Historie* I.28; *Discorsi* I.34.

49. "Discorso delle Cose fiorentine dopo la morte di Lorenzo," *Opere* (Milan: Feltrinelli, 1960), 2:261–77. See the qualifications further suggested by Giorgio Cadoni, "Libertà, Republica e governo misto in Machiavelli" *Rivista Internazionale di Filosofia del Diritto* 39 (1962): 462–84.

counts for his attempt to destroy the conception of aristocratic Venice as an ideal republic; the extremism is matched by the opposing monarchist attitude of Bedingfield's "address to the Reader." The application must have pleased Elizabeth's government: "optimacie," or aristocracy, and "popular governments," or democracies, are "subject to mutation, disorder, and utter ruine." This of course distorts Machiavelli's interpretation, for according to the English government which favors monarchic rule, Florence was saved when it was at last united and stabilized by the Medici. This is the view of Samuel Lewkenor's *A Discourse of Citties* (London, 1600; STC 15566), for "had not the civil discords and intestine functions of the cittizens, hindered her," Florence would have achieved greatness at an earlier date. As it is, this happened only under Cosimo dei' Medici, who strengthened the monarchic government (sig. L3^r). It comes as no surprise that Bedingfield ends his address praising Elizabeth (sig. A5^r).

Machiavelli's extremist republicanism saw and approved Roman sovereignty residing in the people protected by the tribunate; class strife was inevitable and beneficial. These views were no more generally acceptable to his own countrymen than to foreigners: his friend Francesco Guicciardini, for instance, remarked in the "Considerazioni sui *Discorsi* del Machiavelli" that the tribunes acquired their power only gradually, after their initial establishment, and did so at times by usurping power. And Guicciardini took issue with Machiavelli's interpretation that the tribunes were "uno magistrato in mezzo tra'l senato e la plebe; perchè bene erano temperamento della potenza de' nobili, ma non, e converso, della licenza della plebe."[50] As for Machiavelli's praise of civil unrest, Guicciardini observes that this is "come

50. In *Opere Inedite* I, ed. G. Canestrini (Firenze, 1857):12, on *Discorsi* I.3.

laudare in uno infermo la infermità, per la bontà del remedio che gli è stato applicato."[51] Guicciardini's distrust of the tribunate is in keeping with later, aristocratic Italian and English formulations, but did not prevent him from openly praising the mixed state (*e.g., ibid.,* pp. 15-16, on *Discorsi* I.5).

Guicciardini's responsiveness to currents of opinion in his lifetime is more sensitively and accurately chronicled in the minor works of the *Opere Inedite,* written privately and over a number of years, than in the famous *Storia d'Italia.* Since many of these *opere* remained *inedite* until the nineteenth century, there can be no question of their direct influence on other men; however, they do show the influence on Guicciardini of currents of thought available to all, for he attained his position of approving Medici rule only after traditional republicanism had proved impracticable. His essay "Del Modo di Ordinare il Governo Popolare," written in Logrogno in 1512, presents his suggestion for the best government for Florence. It corrects Machiavelli and points to the right solution to the proper mixture of the state, also advocating the establishment of a "middle link"; but for him it is to be the Senate, made up "di uomini eletti e del fiore della città," to take over the functions to be removed from the Signoria, Great Council, and Gonfaloniere. This formulation renders the state precisely as Plutarch had seen it;[52] the senate (not the tribunate) would maintain liberty because it would be a true "mezzo che regoli la ignoranzia della multitudine e ponga freno alla ambizione di uno gonfaloniere."[53]

However, the political landscape of Italy changed

---

51. *Ibid.,* p. 13, on *Discorsi* I.4.

52. See *Lives of the Noble Grecians and Romans Englished by Sir Thomas North* (1579) (London: Nutt, 1895), 1:125.

53. Francesco Guicciardini, *Dialogo e Discorsi del Reggimento di Firenze;* Vol. 7: *Francesco Guicciardini;* Vol. 140: *Scrittori d'Italia,* ed. R. Palmarocchi (Bari: Laterza, 1932), p. 227.

after 1527, the year Machiavelli died. Guicciardini served Medici interests as administrator for the Medici Pope Leo X, effective ruler of Florence for a decade after 1512, and thereafter he served another Medici, Pope Clement VII. During these years he wrote the "Dialogo del Reggimento di Firenze" (composed sometime in 1521-26), which advocates a mixed constitution in a manner more or less consistent with that outlined above, with a *consiglio* or senate of "uno temperamento tra la tirannide e licenzia populare."[54] But by this time he was thoroughly enmeshed in the conflict of loyalties between republican and Medicean rule. He declared his first duty to be to Republican Florence, but did not convince the government of that state in 1527-30; hence he was employed in state business only after the Medici restoration in 1530, at which time the majority of those overtly cherishing republican ideals submitted or went into exile.

In facing the existing political circumstances by playing a role in the Medicean government, Guicciardini was forced to modify his clear, early preference for a mixed state.[55] When Medici government or popular rule became the only clear alternatives, he opted for the former; and in the later *Storia d'Italia* (composed after 1538), he endorsed Lorenzo il Magnifico's monarchic government on the grounds of its stability. The book circulated first in manuscript and was printed at last, without the final four Books, in 1561, with a dedication to Cosimo dei' Medici. Three editions appeared in the next year, one printed by Francesco Sansovino, a popularizer of the sixteenth century who added a "Life" of the author that was itself frequently reprinted.[56] The work had a wide

54. *Ibid.*, p. 118.
55. "Considerazioni," pp. 10–12, 15, on Machiavelli's *Discorsi* I.3 and I.5.
56. On Sansovino and his role as cultural popularizer, see Paul F. Grendler, "Francesco Sansovino and Italian Popular History 1560–1600," *Studies in the Renaissance* 16 (1969) :139–80.

European currency in Latin, French, Dutch, and German.[57] In 1579 appeared an English translation from the French, dedicated to Queen Elizabeth: *The Historie of Guicciardin,* translated by Geoffrey Fenton (London: Vautrollier, 1579, STC 12458). The book was reprinted by Richard Field in 1599 and by him again, in a revised edition, in 1618.[58] Fenton accurately reproduces Guicciardini's mistrust of popular rule, but, Gottfried has shown,[59] strengthens the point by adding his opinion that government in which sovereignty is divided among many people inevitably degenerates into chaos, thus impeding action; both author and translator agree that the populace is fickle and needs to be ruled.

Thus the English translations of two major Italian documents, Machiavelli's *Istorie Fiorentine* and Guicciardini's *Storia d'Italia,* are presented to English readers from a perspective that accords with Tudor suggestions for the treatment of sixteenth-century English exigencies. This oversimplifies the positions of both authors, however; beneath the surface lie suggestions of other possibilities in government. The reflective Renaissance reader of the praise of ancient Sparta, republican Rome, and Venice, and the narration of events in Italian history contained in these works, in which each mixed government differs from the others only in details of its mixture, would not necessarily also adopt the point of view of either author or translator.

57. On the printing and translation of Guicciardini's great work, see Vincenzo Luciani, *Francesco Guicciardini e la Fortuna dell'Opera Sua,* trans. V. de Southoff (Firenze: Olschki, 1949), chapters 1 and 2.

58. STC 12459 and 12460. The other Guicciardini items in print in English were an epitome, *A Briefe Collection of the Notable Things* . . . (London: Purfoote, 1591), STC 12461, and *Two Discourses* . . . *wanting in the Thirde and Fourth Bookes* (London: Ponsonbie, 1595), STC 12462. Direct references to Guicciardini by English writers are listed by Luciani, pp. 299–304.

59. R. B. Gottfried, *Geoffrey Fenton's "Historie of Guicciardin."* Indiana University Publications, Humanities Series No. 3 (Bloomington: Indiana University Press, 1940), p. 25.

Guicciardini's views on the best government for Florence were far from unique; Felix Gilbert has found that the "Modo del Governo Veneziano" (1527-29), for instance, "is not an original work but an excerpt" of Donato Giannotti's famous *Della Repubblica de' Viniziani*.[60] Giannotti had inherited both Machiavelli's manuscript of the *Historie Fiorentine* and his position as Secretary to the *Dieci* of the city, and his approval of the Venetian political structure both in itself and as a model for Florence was lifelong. He was also familiar with Guicciardini's *Storia* in manuscript.[61] While still a young man he had written an orthodox proposal for the reformation of the government on the Venetian model, in the *Discorso sopra il fermare il Governo di Firenze* (1527), not published until 1770-89. He felt that Florence should have a mixed government in which the three elements would be divided into five branches, the Gonfaloniere, Procuratori, Senate of One Hundred, Dieci, and Consiglio Grande, the latter being the seat of ultimate authority, controlling the election of all civic officers and having final decision on all new laws other than financial.[62] This work has less political analysis—usually Giannotti's strong point—than the later and more sophisticated *Della Repubblica Fiorentina* (1531). Here Giannotti places his republican theories in historical perspective,[63] and presents a distinction between different ways of mixing the elements of the state's government.

60. "The Date of Composition of Contarini's and Giannotti's Books on Venice," *Studies in the Renaissance* 14 (1967) :181. Guicciardini's essay is printed in the Canestrini edition of *Opere Inedite* 10 (1867): 389–403.

61. Luciani, p. 61. On Giannotti's life, see Roberto Ridolfi, *Opuscoli: di Storia Letteraria e di Erudizione* (Firenze: Bibliopolis, 1942), pp. 55–164, and Randolph Starn, *Donato Giannotti and his "Epistolae"* (Geneva: Droz, 1968).

62. Reprinted in Donato Giannotti, *Opere Politiche e letterarie* ed. F-L Polidori (Firenze: Felice le Monnier, 1850), 1:3–15; cf. Cecil Roth, *The Last Florentine Republic* (London: Methuen, 1925), p. 94.

63. Baron, 1:372 and 2:631.

From a conventional outline of the simple states and their perversions,[64] Giannotti proceeds to stress that tyranny may arise from division and weakness quite as much as from corruption of a ruler. When the leader of a victorious faction becomes master of all, as was the case at Rome with Marius and Sulla and at Florence with Cosimo dei' Medici, some men, like Scipio Africanus, nobly chose self-exile. Giannotti contrasts Scipio Africanus with Coriolanus and others like him, "li quali, per occupare la commune libertà" (p. 73) basely led armies of strangers to the very gates of their homeland.

Giannotti's interest, in this work, is less with individual acts than with the condition of the government; in states like Rome and Florence, each element is as powerful as each other one, each balancing the other precariously. This situation results, in his view, in perpetual opposition, for "l'una non veniva avere rispetto all'altra, estimando potere quanto quella" (I. 164). The result is civil discord, a condition leading to ruin (p. 163). This is Polybius's view, and Giannotti observes with disapproval precisely what Polybius had praised about Rome, that it would be understood by a foreigner to be a monarchy, aristocracy, or democracy, depending on where he focused his examination.[65]

Greater stability would be provided by the second kind of mixture, in which one element is stronger than the others: "balance" thus yields to imbalance, or true "mixture." An example of this form was Rome "innanzi a' Tarquinii," at the time of the Tarquins, when it was ruled by the combination of people, the Senate and King. The Senate and people depended more upon the king than he on them, however, a situation from which civil concord naturally resulted; and Giannotti points out that

---

64. Giannotti refers to Polybius, with whom he was clearly familiar, in 1 :74.
65. Cf. Polybius vi.11, trans. W. R. Paton. Loeb Classical Library (Cambridge, Mass.: Harvard University Press, 1954), 3 :295–97.

hardly any civil disorder followed the overthrow of the Tarquins (pp. 164-65). This interpretation of true mixture, with people, nobles, and king functioning within the context of the notion of "commonwealth" and leaning toward kingship, resembles the English formulation of limitations placed on absolute monarchy represented by the term "King-in-parliament."

Guicciardini and Giannotti present strikingly similar attitudes toward the right government for Florence: a republic based on the model of Venice that would take popular interests into account although sovereignty would lie with the aristocracy. The fullest analytical study of Venetian government is the *Della Repubblica de' Viniziani,* written with encouragement from Bembo, widely circulated when composed in 1525-27, and printed in 1540.[66] It restates the familiar analysis of the Venetian state, and stresses particularly how the constitution protects the people from the powerful few by scrupulous observance of impartial laws; implicitly, those concerned with legal judgment fulfill the function of the classical tribunes. Like Thucydides and Aristotle,[67] Giannotti sees the mixed state as combining oligarchic and democratic elements.

The books we have been considering, by Giannotti, Guicciardini, and Machiavelli, are listed in catalogues of sixteenth-century libraries in England: the 1542 edition of Giannotti appears in the catalogue of Sir Edward Coke's library, along with three Italian editions of the *Principe* (1537, 1541, and 1584) and two of the *Dis-*

---

66. On Bembo, see William J. Bouwsma, *Venice and the Defense of Republican Liberty* (Berkeley: University of California Press, 1968), p. 159; on the date of composition, see Gilbert, "The Date . . . ," p. 182.

67. In *Della Repubblica de' Viniziani,* Giannotti cites three stages in the development of the Consiglio grande: first, Venice was ruled by Consuls, then by tribunes. Since the latter formed a "concilio . . . molto temerario," it was replaced by the rule of Doges, the superciliousness of whom gave rise to the grand council in ca. A.D. 1175. See Giannotti, 2:41 ff.

corsi (1537 and 1584; the 1584 editions are the work of the English printer John Wolfe). Although the library was catalogued only in 1634, Coke's large number of Italian books (18 percent of the total) were for the most part acquired from his second wife, who had inherited them from her first husband, Sir Christopher Hatton, who had died in 1591.[68] The Lumley library, catalogued in 1609, contained similar Italian books, many of them acquired in the previous century: an incomplete edition of Guicciardini's *Storia,* in the Florentine edition of 1561 (No. 1130), and a complete copy of Fenton's 1579 translation (No. 1137); also Machiavelli's *Discorsi* (1543 ed., No. 1347) and a Contarini (ed. of Basle, 1544 or 1547, or one of Venice, 1592, No. 1169).[69]

These records represent a continuity of interest in Italian books from Elizabethan to Jacobean times. But the meaning of the availability of these books can be more richly illustrated by following out the suggestions of the nature of Giannotti's study of Venice. It is a humanist dialogue introducing, in a Paduan setting, men famous in real life: Pietro Bembo, "la cui fama, per le sue virtù per tutto risuona," and Leonico Tomeo, "della filosofia greca e latina grandissimo dottore" (p. 9), works of whom are also recorded in the Lumley catalogue (Nos. 92, 1365, 1418; 1348). The ensuing conversation, between Trifone Gabriello and Giovanni Borgherini, takes place at Bembo's house in Padua. Bembo and Leonico, one recalls, were both tutors to Reginald Pole, at the time of the dialogue's composition actually resident in that city, and they drew many other men

68. Lievsay, pp. 48–49, and *A Catalogue of the Library of Sir Edward Coke,* ed. W. O. Hassall. Yale Law Library Publications No. 12 (New Haven: Yale University Press, 1950).

69. *The Lumley Library: the Catalogue of 1609,* ed. Sears Jayne and F. R. Johnson (London: British Museum, 1956).

thither as well. In addition, Padua had a university that was a center attracting, because of its quality and location within the tolerant Veneto, teachers and students of many different beliefs and from many different countries, notably Germany and England. While Bembo lived there, his liberal Catholic influence encouraged the continued free play of ideas; in this atmosphere Pole came into contact with a number of men from different countries holding a variety of political and religious beliefs.

During his first (1521-26) and second (1532-36) periods of residence at Padua, Pole formulated political beliefs which made residence in England under Henry VIII impossible. His convictions made him receptive to Catholic reformist theology, which at first met with the Church's support. Indeed Pope Paul III himself recognized the need for reform within the Church, and in 1536 called a preliminary council, chaired by Gasparo Cardinal Contarini, which counted Pole, and perhaps Piermartire Vermiglio,[70] among its members. The commission's report, *Consilium delectorum cardinalium et aliorum praelatorium de emendanda ecclesia,* not only encouraged reformation, but was conciliatory toward the Protestants. It received wide circulation, particularly among the Northern Protestants in Strassburg.[71]

The year 1536 marks the high tide of reformist Catholic thought in Italy, for in that year it also found expression in Bernardino Ochino's Lenten sermons in Naples, unrecorded yet apparently influential upon, as influenced by, Juan de Valdès. The latter's views were effectively dispersed in Italy in the *Trattato Utilissimo del Beneficio di Giesù Christo Crocifisso* (1543), a work condemned by the Church but approved by Ochino,

---

70. Philip McNair, *Peter Martyr in Italy* (Oxford: at the Clarendon Press, 1967), pp. 133–38.

71. Frederick C. Church, *The Italian Reformers: 1534–64* (New York: Columbia University Press, 1932), p. 23.

Vermiglio, Pole,[72] and Contarini; but the *Beneficio,* long thought to be the Valdès-inspired Reformist Catholic work of the otherwise obscure Benedetto da Mantova, has now been shown to be a compilation of "passages from Protestant writers, especially Jean Calvin and Martin Bucer."[73] Its fame spread to England, when the English branch of the humanist-reformist movement found it palatable. It was translated into English in 1548 by Edward Courtenay, Earl of Devonshire and cousin to Pole, and, McConika reports, was found suitable for the education of the future Edward VI; the copy in the Cambridge University Library bears the signature and annotations of the young prince.[74]

The ideas shared by Contarini and Pole on such matters as justification by faith and denial of original sin after baptism, strikingly similar to Luther's ideas, grew from topics of discussion in intellectual circles that included Englishmen, Germans, and Italians, many of the last republican exiles from Florence and Rome after 1527-30. At this time such views could be held in good conscience by men professing themselves Roman Catholics. But at the Ratisbon Conference in 1541, Contarini failed to effect a reconciliation between Protestants and Catholics. This was a momentous failure signaling intransigence on both sides; thereafter the Catholic Church relinquished a conciliar approach; under Paul III, Cardinal Caraffa reorganized the Inquisition (1542). Caraffa, who became Pope Paul IV in 1555, distrusted Pole and Contarini, and the Jesuits made certain at the Coun-

---

72. This work was the subject of conversations in Pole's circle at Viterbo; see *ibid.,* p. 47.

73. Tommaso Bozza, *"Il Beneficio di Cristo" e la Istituzione della Religione cristiana di Calvino* (Rome: privately printed, 1961); I have not seen this essay, and rely on the summaries in Delio Cantimari, "Il Mestiere dello Storico," *Itinerarî* 8 (Genova, 1961) and McNair, pp. 47ff.

74. James K. McConika, *English Humanists and Reformation Politics* (Oxford: at the Clarendon Press, 1965), pp. 5–6.

cil of Trent that conciliation of the Protestants was condemned as a policy.

Contarini died in 1542; Pole remained within the
Church but had difficulties with Pope Paul IV, who re-
pudiated his policies in reclaiming England to Catholicism under Queen Mary. Other men found the Church
too narrow, however. Some of them, all over Italy, most
receptive to reformist ideas, suffered the political consequences of their religious beliefs. At first they were
forced to move to republican Venice, and when Venice
ceased to be a haven, they moved on, to Switzerland and
even to Poland. Many left the Church entirely. While
on the Continent, they suffered because they never fully
accepted Lutheran or Calvinist doctrine; a few, like the
Beneficio, found their way to England, where they were
welcomed by Archbishop Cranmer, who was attempting
to "mediate between the different branches of the reformed community."[75] The exiles found in the English
religion and government a middle way between the excesses of Catholicism and of Puritanism.

For our purposes, a brief look at the careers of three
men, Piermartire Vermiglio, Bernardino Ochino, and
Pierpaolo Vergerio, will illustrate the interconnections
of some of the men and topics we have been concerned
with. Ochino (1487-1564) escaped from the Inquisition
and Italy after conferring with Vermiglio and the dying
Contarini in 1542. He moved to Switzerland, and from
thence migrated to England with Vermiglio at the in-
vitation of Cranmer in 1547. He was given a prebend
at Canterbury in 1548, and wrote *A Tragoedie or Dialogue of the Unjuste Usurped Primacie of the Bishop of
Rome* (1549, STC 188770-71),[76] translated into En-

---

75. *Ibid.,* p. 249.

76. The work was entered in the *Stationers' Register* to Robert
Waldegrave on 11 September 1587, perhaps for a contemplated re-
printing (Arber 2:475).

glish by John Ponet. Vermiglio (1500-62), meanwhile, filled a vacant canonry at Christchurch, Oxford. After Bucer's death in 1551, Cranmer worked particularly closely with him in revising ecclesiastical laws for the Edwardian church. Both Ochino and Vermiglio knew Ponet, and both fled when Mary acceded to the throne. Vermiglio was joined, after he arrived in Strassburg, by a number of English exiles, including Ponet. The English exiles regarded themselves as the hope of the Church of England; one means of actualizing this hope lay in propaganda.[77] The Venetian ambassador to England during these years, Giovanni Michiel, bears witness to their activities; on 11 November, 1555, he wrote, "It is understood that wherever they go, whether to Italy, Germany, or France, they licentiously disseminate many things against the English government and the present religion."[78]

The failings of the Roman Church were under attack by Italians and other continentals as well as by English exiles; and the religious concern was not divorced from historical and political dimensions. For instance, the high number of editions of Guicciardini's *Storia* that issued, after 1561, from Venetian, German, and English presses is largely owing to the author's anti-clericalism.[79] Further reading in the first volume of the *Opere Inedite* yields the following from the "Ricordi Politici e Civili": "Il grado che ho avuto con più pontefici, mi ha necessitato a amare per il particolare mio la grandezza loro; e se non fussi questo rispetto, arei amato Martino Lutero quanto me medesimo" (p. 87). This note of dissatisfaction and flirting with Protestantism became more potent in the decades after Guicciardini's death. One of the most voci-

---

77. C. H. Garrett, *The Marian Exiles* (Cambridge, England: at the University Press, 1936), *passim*.

78. Great Britain, Public Record Office, *Calendar of State Papers, Venetian, 1555–56,* No. 274.

79. Gottfried, pp. 20ff.

ferous critics was Pierpaolo Vergerio (1498-1565), a lawyer in Bologna who turned to the Church after the death of his wife Diana Contarini in 1527; in 1536 he became Bishop of Capodistria, and, a propagandist by nature, promulgated within his diocese essentially Protestant doctrine. In 1549 he left Italy to avoid prosecution, and corresponded with Richard Morysine, the English ambassador to Vienna. After Bucer's death in 1551, the government of Edward VI offered him a position as pastor of the Italian Church in London, along with a professorship at Cambridge. He declined in order to remain on the Continent, where he engaged in polemics against the Council of Trent and political manipulations of the Pope and Emperor; a reformist Catholic and antityrannic sympathizer, he, like others on the continent, joined forces with the English exiles in combating the Roman Church. Vergerio was the editor of the Protestant-sponsored reissue of Pole, entitled the *Pro Ecclesiasticae Unitatis Defensione* ([W. Rihelius: Argentorati] 1555).

Particularly in Florence, republican political sympathies had been strengthened during the successive crises of the late fifteenth and early sixteenth centuries, and many Italians looked back, during those years, to Roman history to find an analogous conflict between liberty and tyranny. They saw, after 1530, the effective political victory through the land of the forces of Spain; imperial influence in temporal matters extended to the Papacy as well, and Italian religious conformists found their efforts similarly thwarted from the 1540s onward. Men of either or both republican political and reformist Catholic persuasions made individual adjustments to their predicaments; those Catholics who, not yet absorbed into Protestantism, made their way to England, found there a congenial atmosphere of religious reform and mixed-state government. After Mary's accession, however, they and the Englishmen who followed them back to the Continent were subjected to relentless Catholic pressure which forced them to espouse religious and political extremes. Those who returned to England under Elizabeth found that although their anti-Catholic views were appreciated, their positive religious ones were accepted only with caution, and because of the shortage of manpower faced by Archbishop Parker.[80] Certainly their drastic anti-monarchic views were rejected. However, we have already seen in the case of the Marian exile John Ponet to what extent such political expressions were really extremist formulations of the acceptable ideal of mixed government so long familiar to native English and Italian political thought.

It has been suggested that John Ponet learned of Italy and Italian customs, particularly the habit of using Venice as the ideal of the mixed state, from Piermartire Vermiglio and Bernardino Ochino.[81] But the information and the convention were quite generally available to educated Englishmen of his time.[82] One of the most popular sixteenth-century books to focus on the politics of the subject was Cardinal Contarini's modified humanist *laudatio*,[83] referred to by Sidney in his 1573 letter to Hubert Languet quoted earlier in this chapter. The book was frequently reprinted on the Continent, and, translated by Sir Lewes Lewkenor (later to be named Master of Ceremonies by King James I), was printed in London by John Windet as *The Common Wealth and Government of Venice* (STC 5642). Less a work of political analysis than Giannotti's dialogue, the book is

80. This subject has been studied in a London University thesis by J. I. Daeley, "The Episcopal Administration of Matthew Parker, Archbishop of Canterbury, 1559–75," reported in London University, *Bulletin of the Institute of Historical Research* 40 (1967):228–31.

81. W. S. Hudson, *John Ponet* (Chicago: University of Chicago Press, [1942]), p. 177.

82. Z. S. Fink, *The Classical Republicans,* pp. 41–45.

83. F. Gilbert, *Macchiavelli and Guicciardini,* p. 91, n. 57.

an advertisement for an ideal state as seen by a liberal Catholic whose reformist views made him praise the climate that nurtured them. Lewkenor draws attention to Contarini's idealizing presentation of the city's government as a mixture of Prince, Senators, and Great Council:[84] people can see

> in the person of the Venetian prince . . . a straunge and un-usuall form of a most excellent Monarchie. Then what more perfect and lively pattern of a well ordered Aristocraticall government [can they see] then that of their councell of Pregati or Senators . . . ? . . . Lastly if they desire to see a most rare and matchlesse president of a Democrasie or popular estate, let them behold their great Councell.
>
> (sigs. A2^{r-v})

This follows Polybius quite closely, but ignores Giannotti's distinction between kinds of mixture. Contarini stresses the unity of the mixed government (sigs. C3^{r-v}); although the Great Council is the ground of all authority (sig. A2^{r-v}), it is balanced by the aristocracy, for the Senate and *Dieci* "do represent the state of the nobility, and are (as it were) the meane or middle, which reconcileth and bindeth together the two extremes" (sig. K1^{r}). Again, this view corresponds to tradition, especially the views of Polybius and Plutarch, and it might also accord with formulations of the English state.

Dedicatory sonnets were prefixed to Lewkenor's translation, and the authors praise Venice in high terms. Edmund Spenser, for instance, remarks that Venice is distinguished by her "policie of right" (sig. A3^{v}). Sir John Harington praises the republican Venice for being "for freedome, emulous to ancient Rome,/ Famous for counsell much, and much for armes" (sig. A4^{r}).[85] It is

---

84. Lewkenor was himself widely read in history and politics; his translation includes extracts from a variety of Italian writers, including Giannotti and the popularizer Sansovino. See Fink, p. 42.

85. Harington showed a republican sympathy in his reference to Marcus Brutus as "the stout Roman that kild *Caesar* for his tyranny" (*Orlando Furioso* (London: Field, 1591), Table).

not only like Rome, however: according to I[ohn] Ashley, geographical parallelism enforces an identity with England:

> Fayer mayden towne . . .
> Now I prognosticate thy ruinous case,
> When thou shalt from thy Adriatique seas,
> View in this Ocean Isle thy painted face,
> In these pure colours coyest eyes to please,
> Then gazing in thy shadowes peereles eye,
> Enamor'd like *Narcissus* thou shalt die.
>
> (sig. *3ᵛ) [86]

Englishmen had long been impressed by Venice; they were struck by her longevity, which they attributed to her constitution and rule by law, just as Polybius had attributed the longevity and success of Rome to its mixed constitution. They were also struck by similarities between Venice and Rome and Venice and England. A major distinguishing characteristic of the Roman Republic was, of course, its tribunate, the element that countered aggressive acts, whether by monarchic or aristocratic elements, that aimed at control of the "commonweale." This office had its parallel in Venice and England. In Venice, laws existed to fulfill this function; Contarini, recognizing that they had to be defended and enforced, makes explicit the implication of Giannotti's analysis and sees that the function of one group of magistrates, the *avvocatori* or advocators, is

> to defend lawes pure and inviolate . . . so that their authority and power is much like unto that of the Tribunes of the Romaine people, but that they were to defend the liberty of the people, and ours onely the force of the lawes.
>
> (sig. M3ʳ)

---

86. On Polybius's geographical parallelism see P. Pédech, *La Méthode historique de Polybe* (Paris: Société d'Editions "les belles lettres," 1964), chapter 9.

Lewkenor's Contarini presented to English readers and to English dramatists a Venice ideal by virtue of its perfect system of justice. In 1596-98, for instance, Shakespeare wrote *The Merchant of Venice,* concerned in part with the administration of justice in that city. The action of IV.i takes place in a courtroom presided over by the Doge and "magnificoes," or Senators, acting as judges; as the New Arden editor rightly points out,[87] this detail is anachronistic. In this scene, Portia utters the conventional view of Venetian justice with epigrammatic force:

> There is no power in Venice
> Can alter a decree established.
>
> (IV.i.218–19)[88]

Although this remark may be slightly ironic, it is with propriety that Portia, who is from Belmont, achieves true justice in Venice.

A few years after the appearance of Lewkenor's translation, Ben Jonson wrote *Volpone* (1605-6), like Shakespeare's a play concerned with Venetian justice.[89] Jonson shows greater familiarity with the myth of Venice: in IV.i, Sir Politic Would-be tells Peregrine "some few particulars . . . / . . . fit to be knowne/ Of your crude traveller." He stresses the city's freedom of thought:

> for your religion, professe none;
> But wonder, at the diversitie of all;
> And, for your part, protest, were there no other
> But simply the lawes o'th' land, you could content you:
> NIC: MACHIAVEL and Monsieur BODINE, both
> Were of this minde.
>
> (ll. 22–27)

---

87. John Russell Brown, ed., *The Merchant of Venice* by William Shakespeare ("The Arden Shakespeare": Cambridge, Mass.: Harvard University Press, 1955), p. 103.

88. Cf. III.iii.26–31.

89. R. H. Perkinson, "*Volpone* and the Reputation of Venetian Justice," *MLR* 35 (1940): 11–18.

Sir Politic speaks as an accomplished traveler; he claims to have been taken for a citizen of Venice because

> I had read CONTARENE, tooke me a house,
> Dealt with my *Jewes*, to furnish it.
>   (ll. 40–41)

And in the courtroom scenes of Act Five, judgment and sentencing are performed by four *Avocatore,* protectors of justice and implicitly approved neo-Roman tribunes. Although Shakespeare's own use of Contarini is not clear, at least one critic has thought that he used it in writing *Othello* (1604).[90] Ben Jonson and Shakespeare, like Sidney before them, made literary use of the mixed governments of foreign states, and expected their audiences and readers to be familiar with them.

The Italian traditions of mixed government, from which Machiavelli's extremism was only a momentary departure, encompassed a variety of mixtures that suited a variety of immediate political situations during the sixteenth century. Venice was an ideal, and after 1530 the only major Italian example. Italian discussions and analyses of it were of a state identified by Englishmen with freedom and religious resistance to the Pope and Spain; further, it had a form of government different from England's, yet still analogous to it. In the 1580s Sidney's *Arcadia* shows a sophisticated awareness of various forms of government; and Fulke Greville (1554-1628) demonstrates the continuity of such awareness into the Jacobean age in the biography he wrote of Sidney and in a verse essay, "A Treatise of Monarchy," both of which were printed only years after their author's death, in 1652 and 1670 respectively.[91]

---

90. Kenneth Muir, "Shakespeare and Lewkenor," *RES* 7 (1956):182–83.

91. The "Treatise" is reprinted in *"The Remains": being Poems of*

In the *Life of Sir Philip Sidney,* Greville looks back with admiration on Elizabethan days and contrasts them with contemporary Jacobean ones.[92] To enforce his judgments, he minimizes Elizabeth's absolutism and understands her to have been a constitutional monarch. He approves of what has been understood to have been Sidney's ideal for England, "a mixed government, based on carefully circumscribed rights and obligations of the various estates . . . administered jointly by a beneficent, patriarchal monarch and a virtuous aristocracy."[93]

For Greville, Elizabeth was a strong monarch who preserved a monarchy-weighted balance among three elements of the state:

> . . . she preserv'd her state above the affronts of Nobility, or people; and according to birth right, still became a soveraigne Judge over any dutifull, or encroaching petitions of Nobles, or Commons.[94]

This is contrasted immediately to the rule of "some moderne Princes," presumably referring to James. The contrast is extended by praise of Elizabeth's distribution of offices among many people, who could thus freely balance each other; by contrast, the modern prince's unjust and partial rule will lead to "the slavish liberties of Transcendancy" (p. 196).

Monarchy and Religion, ed. G. A. Wilkes (Oxford: Oxford University Press, 1965). Greville knew Bodin and Buchanan's *De Jure Regni;* and H. N. Maclean, "Fulke Greville: Kingship and Sovereignty," *HLQ* 16 (1952–53): 258, decides that Greville "evolved a doctrine of sovereignty which contained important elements from both sides."

92. Cf. *Nugae Antiquae,* rev. ed. (London: Dodsley, 1779), 2: 274–75, letter of Lord Thomas Howard to Sir John Harington, 1611: "You have lived to see the trim of old times, and what passed in the Queens days: These thinges are no more the same; your Queen did talk of her subjects love and good affections, and in good truth she aimed well; our King talketh of his Subjects fear and subjection. . . ." See also MacLean, pp. 266, 271.

93. Fritz Caspari, *Humanism and the Social Order in Tudor England* (Chicago: University of Chicago Press, 1954), p. 172. Cf. *Life,* pp. 187–89, 192.

94. *Life,* p. 175.

In Greville's view, a strong monarchy would confirm the people's liberty, for that can be assured only by a stable hierarchy which in turn can only be assured by monarchy.[95] Any change at all from this is bad; ordered hierarchy is implicitly associated with Eden and the Golden Age:

> all fundamentall changes (especially of Religion) in Princes would be found (as she [Elizabeth] conceived) the true discipline of Atheisme amongst her Subjects; all sacrifices, obedience excepted, being but deare-bought knowledges of the Serpent, to expulse Kings, and People once again out of Mediocrity, that reciprocall Paradise of mutuall humane duties.
>
> (*Life,* p. 180)

Change, he goes on to assert, would lead to a "wilderness of ignorance, and violence of will" (pp. 180-81, 193).

Greville turned to Rome quite incidentally in Sonnet 30 of *Caelica,* in order to praise the republic; but he omits the tribunate and points to its later failure:

> *Rome,* while thy Senate gouernours did choose,
> Your souldiers florish'd, Citizens were free,
> Thy State by Change of *Consuls* did not loose,
> They honour'd were that serv'd or ruled thee:
>
> But after thy proud Legions gave thee Lawes,
> That their bought voices Empire did bestow,
> Worthinesse no more was of election cause,
> Authority her owners did not know.

Distrust in republicanism is more fully treated in the "Treatise of Monarchy," in which he discusses government with relation to Rome, "for all free states a glass"

---

95. Chorus Quartus of Greville's *Alaham* presents the people's view of the right relations between monarch and subjects: the people must be ruled well and firmly. The chorus advises, "Princes descend not, keep your selves above," (*Poems and Dramas of Fulke Greville,* 2 vols., ed. G. Bullough [Edinburgh: Oliver and Boyd, 1939]: 2: 204).

(stanza 304). The overthrow of the Tarquins which made Rome a republic inevitably led to the establishment of Empire (stanza 587) because of the confusion of a government "waveringe, never fixt" brought on by the "manie-headed powre":

> Thus sicke, and fullie ripe for cure, or death,
> *Rome* did enforce a *Caesar* of her owne
> To loose his honor, or to breake his faith;
> Her State alike beinge each way overthrowne:
>   Wherin yet he that brought back Monarchie
>   Err'd less, then he who sett the people free.
>   (stanza 591)

Although in this stanza Greville renders the ambiguity of Caesar's position (1. 3), he goes on to formulate his clear preference by regarding the Empire as a reestablishment of the monarchy, and a return to ordered and better government. The inevitability of the process is confirmed by Greville's refusal to see the fully developed Republic as anything but a democracy. That the alternatives presented are only monarchy and democracy, disregarding the possibilities inherent in the idea of mixture, both expresses the practical English distrust of an equally mixed government and dictates which form is to be approved. *Coriolanus* casts its political problems in the same light.

Practical distrust is elaborated in section 15 of the "Treatise," which compares aristocracy with monarchy and democracy "jointlie." Greville begins this section by acknowledging that "our bookes be fill'd with praise/ Of good mens virtues, freedomes popular," praise which includes the Roman republic, but argues that close study will show that no enduring state has ever been democratic or aristocratic. The reason is that consolidation is inevitable: such states degenerate into "a servile Oligarchall Tyrannie" (stanza 642). Although this might seem at first to agree with orthodox Elizabethan expressions, it actually leads to a recognition of his breadth of reference and his sense of England as a "free state": for Greville very deliberately held a middle path between absolutism on the one hand and medieval constitutionalism, which he saw as democracy, on the other. He goes on to cite Rome and Venice:

> So that such onlie have escap'd mischance,
> As luckilie, by publique opposition,
> To ballance Consulls, Tribunes did advance,
> Or by a more refined composition,
>   Have rais'd (like *Venice*) some well-bounded Duke,
>   Their selfe-growne Senators to overlooke.
>   (stanza 643)

Although Greville's interpretation is certainly not a Venetian's, in according Venice an advanced government in which the limited-monarchic element controls the aristocratic Greville presents his idea of the mixed state of Venice in terms of his idealistic image of England.

Greville and many other Englishmen looked on Venice with limited approval, and, we shall see, were sympathetic when the city was placed under Papal interdict in 1606-7, an event Greville refers to in *Monarchy,* stanza 214. But when it came to overt comparison with their own government, these same Englishmen preferred England. Sidney had remarked, in a letter of 1579 to his brother Robert, that although Venetians might have good laws and customs,

> wee can hardly proporcion [them] to our selves, because they are quite of a contrarie goverment, there is little there but tyranous oppression, & servile yeilding to them, that have little or noe rule over them.[96]

This negative judgment reflects the English preoccupa-

---

96. Sidney, *Works* 3: 127.

tion with tyranny, rather than Sidney's disapproval of all mixed governments. This blend of theoretical approval and disapproval of individual instances of practice is also expressed by the young Francis Bacon, who observed in 1589 that

> it may be, in civil states, a republic is a better policy than a kingdom: yet God forbid that lawful kingdoms should be tied to innovate and make alteration. . . . Neither yet do I admit that their form (though it were possible and convenient) is better than ours, if some abuses were taken away.[97]

In England there was no question of electing a monarch for a lifetime, and some Englishmen disapproved of some details of Venetian administration; but the difference between such reservations and acceptable mixed-state views is really not great.

English sixteenth-century writers show familiarity with, and at least limited approval of, mixed government, and clearly expected readers to be similarly familiar with it. They might know of it from native studies of England and its own government, the fruit of the "Historical Revolution."[98] Or they might have learned of it from a variety of studies relating to Italy, classical as well as contemporary, to which they were led by sympathy with the religious reformation and antipathy for papal and Imperial politics. The traditional, native view of England as a mixed government occupied a middle position between tyranny and democratic chaos in an age in which each of the two extreme positions grew stronger. Similarly, the congenial reception given to the Italian religious exiles before Mary's accession marked a middle

97. *The Works of Francis Bacon 8,* ed. J. Spedding *et al.,* (London, 1862): 85. Bacon admitted several forms of government to be valid, as Allen points out in *English Political Thought: 1603–1660* (London: Methuen, 1938), 1: 54–55.

98. See F. Smith Fussner, *The Historical Revolution* (New York: Columbia University Press, 1962), *passim.*

path that the Church of England sought to maintain in the face of the polarization of the field into post-Tridentine Catholicism and equally militant Puritanism, a division which carried with it political implications. King James inherited these antagonisms with the English Crown; during his reign, he increased the tension of the discord, which ultimately took the greater part of the seventeenth century to work itself out. We must now turn to the uses that this Anglo-Italian mixture of related ideas was put to, in the Jacobean years to 1611, in order to complete the study of the intellectual context of Shakespeare's *Coriolanus*.

5
Jacobean Applications

James and the Prerogative of Parliament

Under the Tudors, the view of England as *"dominium politicum et regale"* was subordinated to a new claim of royal absolutism that stressed unquestioning obedience to the reigning monarch. The immoderate views of extremist Catholics and Protestants were prominent criticisms of this principle in Elizabeth's day. Temperate formulations of limitation, like the mixed state views of Sir Thomas Smith, were relatively rare, but were not prosecuted as disloyal; however, they became difficult to hold in the new Jacobean world after 1603. Inheriting many constitutional situations that Elizabeth had been content to leave unresolved, James promoted the polarization of political issues at about the time that Shakespeare's *Coriolanus* appeared.

This tense but potentially rich political atmosphere had been long growing. In the years immediately following Queen Mary's death, many of the exiles returned to England to begin pressing upon Elizabeth's government

their religious and political arguments for the limitation
of royal prerogative by Puritan[1] advisors. They did so
in books, sermons, and in the House of Commons; they
were answered by books, sermons, and Crown-inspired
parliamentary machinations. These men demanded that
political or ecclesiastical advisors handle matters of state,
normally considered royal prerogative, including

> Church, where by the constitutional theory of the Reformation
> the Queen's supremacy was part of the royal prerogative; . . .
> questions of high policy, such as the succession; and . . . the
> royal administration—the Exchequer, purveyors, licenses, mo-
> nopolies, and such-like grants by royal letters-patent.[2]

This attempt to establish for itself an acknowledged
legal role as counterbalance and limitation on royal
power was urged by a Commons that became, during
Elizabeth's reign, more educated and consequently more
aware of historical precedent.[3] In 1563, some 139 out of
the 420 members had been to Oxford, Cambridge, or
one of the Inns of Court; by 1593, the number was more

1. This inclusive term came into use in England in 1567–68; it
includes Episcopal, Presbyterian, and Congregational Puritans. See M.
M. Knappen, *Tudor Puritanism* (Chicago: University of Chicago Press,
1939), which cites, among the "common denominator principles," "a
passionate love of civic freedom and moral earnestness," pp. 488–89.

2. J. E. Neale, *Elizabeth I and her Parliaments: 1559–1581* (London:
Cape, 1953), p. 189.

3. The process by which the House of Commons achieved the right
of the initiative in legislation has been studied by several twentieth-
century historians. In addition to the book cited in the previous note,
there is also, by the same author, *Elizabeth I and her Parliaments:
1584–1601* (London: Cape, 1957); *The Elizabethan House of Commons*
(London: Cape, 1949); and the earlier article "Peter Wentworth,"
EHR 39 (1924): 36–54 and 175–205. The following books and articles
have materially contributed to the knowledge of the period: Wallace
Notestein, "The Winning of the Initiative by the House of Commons."
British Academy Lecture (London: Oxford University Press, 1924);
D. H. Willson, "The Earl of Salisbury and the 'Court' Party in
Parliament, 1604–10," *AHR* 36 (1931): 274–94; W. M. Wallace, *Sir
Edwin Sandys and the First Parliament of James I* (Philadelphia:
University of Pennsylvania, 1940); and G. L. Mosse, *The Struggle
for Sovereignty in England* (East Lansing: Michigan State College
Press, 1950).

than half.[4] Similarly, by the latter date, some 43% of Commons had had specifically legal training.[5] This change in education manifested itself in a tendency toward independence backed by a knowledge of precedent extending to pre-Tudor times. Both their study of English legal traditions and their religious predispositions encouraged in Members of the House of Commons a sympathy with the idea of restraint on monarchic power.

To accomplish its goals, Commons had to safeguard and extend its traditional liberties,[6] which, however, often clashed with royal prerogative. Commons set up a committee of grievances in 1571; it grew in power and scope over the years until it became a standing committee, one of several that came to devote themselves to

> the painstaking collection of grievances from all sources, to the sifting of them, and to an elaborate statement of them in documentary form. The whole membership of the House was engaged in gathering the case against the government.[7]

Clearly this became a case of Parliament's establishing an agency directly counter to the interests of royal power; from the royal point of view, the agency was seditious.

However, the Members of Commons who took part in these activities regarded themselves as part of the government, and assumed a public identity by virtue of their parliamentary office. The most notorious among them, Peter Wentworth (1523-97), gave a famous speech in 1576 in which he based his arguments squarely on medieval precedent, remarking, in Sir Simonds D'Ewes report,

---

4. Neale, *Commons,* pp. 307–8, puts the figure at 54%.
5. *Ibid.*
6. Simonds D'Ewes, *A Compleat Journal of . . . the House of Lords and House of Commons throughout the whole Reign of Queen Elizabeth* (London: J. S[tarkey]., 1708), pp. 42–43, gives an account of the Speaker's formal petitioning of the rights of Commons.
7. Notestein, p. 32.

that "the King ought not to be under man, but under God
and the Law, because the Law maketh him a King." On
this occasion Wentworth said further that "free Speech
and Conscience" in Commons are granted "by a special
Law, as that without the which the Prince and State
cannot be preserved or maintained." He was swiftly examined by a committee that included the entire Privy
Council. Asked for his sources of information regarding
certain rumors about the Queen, Wentworth refused to
answer, saying,

> I am now no private Person, I am a publick, and a Councellor
> to the whole State in that place where it is lawful for me to
> speak my mind freely, and not for you as Councellors to call
> me to account for any thing that I do speak in the House.[8]

He claimed for himself a public position in fact analogous to the countermagistracy of the classical tribunes.
That England had no such officially recognized position
is made clear by Wentworth's repeated jailings despite
parliamentary immunity, and by his death in the Tower
at the age of 75. The pressure he applied was felt to be
seditious.

Political action in the Elizabethan House of Commons
was only one means, and belief in its effectiveness as a
corrective to an imperfect monarch was not universal.
The Inns of Court tragedy *Ferrex and Porrex, or Gorboduc* (1561) reflects diverging audience views on this
matter. Trusted counsellors, anxious to please Gorboduc,
allow the division of Britain, which causes civil discord;
under such circumstances, only Parliament could undertake the reunification of the kingdom, for "Parliament
is the law of the land, the great middle force that alone
can forestall anarchy and feudalism."[9] There will be no
peace until

---

8. D'Ewes, pp. 238, 241.
9. David M. Bevington, *Tudor Drama and Politics* (Cambridge,
Mass: Harvard University Press, 1968), p. 146.

> by common counsel of you all
> In Parliament the regall diademe
> Be set in certaine place of governaunce.
>
> (V.ii.157–59)

This view is expressed by Arostus and corresponds to Thomas Norton's known support of the practical wisdom of allowing Parliament to decide the succession and future of the realm after a monarch's death. Opposed to Arostus is Eubulus, who voices Thomas Sackville's more "conservative and nationalistic, neither Catholic nor Puritan" attitude:[10]

> Alas, in Parliament what hope can be,
> When is of Parliament no hope at all?
> Which, though it be assembled by consent,
> Yet is not likely with consent to end,
> While eche one for himselfe, or for his frend,
> Against his foe, shall travaile what he may.
>
> (V.ii.253–58)

It is Norton, the translator of Calvin's *Institutes* (definitive version, 1559), who reflects the theologian's emphasis on Parliament.[11]

Prominent among the English Puritan divines advocating the strict limitation of royal will was Thomas Cartwright (1535-1603), Lady Margaret Professor of Divinity at Cambridge.[12] He lectured[13] and developed

---

10. *Ibid.*, p. 143.

11. Cf. the discussion of Ponet in Chapter 3 above. See S. F. Johnson, "Early Elizabethan Tragedies of the Inns of Court" (Ph.D. dissertation, Harvard University, 1947), 1: 60–64, on Norton's translation of Calvin and on his religious and political ideas; Norton's parliamentary career is also considered, pp. 71–81.

12. Cartwright is chiefly remembered for a Cambridge University debate of 1564, in which he took the negative side of the topic "Monarchia est optimus status Reipublicae"; his speech is reprinted in A. F. Scott-Pearson, *Thomas Cartwright and Elizabethan Puritanism: 1535–1603* (Cambridge, England: Cambridge University Press, 1925), pp. 419–20. This is a standard debate topic, however (see, *e.g.*, Erasmus, *De Copia* II, "Ratio colligendi exempla": "Potior monarchia, an democratia"), and need not reflect any debater's personal view. Rather,

ideas that were considered seditious to the integrity of the monarchic state. His political views, virtually identical to Wentworth's, were similarly the subject of a governmental enquiry, in 1591. According to the 1606 account written by Matthew Sutcliffe, Dean of Exeter, Cartwright was subsequently asked whether he swore

> truely in the Starre-chamber, when he affirmed on his oth, that he never affirmed or allowed that in every monarchy there ought to be certain magistrates like to the Spartaine Ephori, with authoritie to controll and depose the king, and to proceed further against him.[14]

Cartwright admitted the charge "where the lawes of the lande doo establish such an authoritie as the Ephori of Lacedaemonia had,"[15] but otherwise denied it. No matter: the government's clear hostility precluded admission of the office's role as a healthy balance existing for the stability of the state. Rather, the government's question associates "certain magistrates" with the ancient Ephorate (itself traditionally the analogue of the Roman tribunate[16]) and the two with revolutionary tendencies. The question thus stresses the office's destructive antagonism; in Archbishop John Whitgift's words, with which

it reflects a vital Elizabethan interest in this continuing topic. The debate occurs in a context more relevant for Shakespeare in Montaigne, who here is probably relying on his extensive reading of Plutarch: "I have started a hundred quarrels in defense of Pompey for the cause of Brutus," *Essays* III.9, here quoted from *Complete Works of Montaigne,* ed. D. M. Frame (Stanford: Stanford University Press, 1958), p. 763.

13. Notably on Acts 1:15; see Scott-Pearson, p. 26.

14. Quoted in Scott-Pearson, p. 334, from Matthew Sutcliffe, *Examination and Confrontation on a Scurrilous Treatise . . . published by M. Kellison* (London, 1606), STC 23464.

15. Cartwright, *A Briefe Apologie against M. Sutcliffe* ([Middelburg,] 1596), STC 4706, sig. C1ᵛ, quoted in *Cartwrightiana,* ed. A. Peel and L. H. Carlson (London: Allen and Unwin, 1951). p. 4.

16. This identification is made explicit by Jean Bodin, *Six Bookes of a Commonweale,* trans. R. Knolles (London, 1606), ed. K. D. McRae (Cambridge, Mass.: Harvard University Press, 1962), p. 187.

Elizabeth and James agreed,[17] the Puritan-tribune goals
were "a democratical ataxy, yea, an ochlocracy."[18] Those
who accepted this Crown view associated the Puritans
with those in classical civilizations who, in terms of English monarchy, were mutinous.[19] Thus English Puritan
extremists were also as dangerous to the government as
the foreign Roman Catholics, whose efforts closely parallel theirs.

The Roman Catholic Counter-Reformation had been
active throughout Elizabeth's reign; she herself had been
excommunicated in 1570 and the crowns of Europe in-
vited by the Pope to move against the heretic nation.
In 1588 Spain attempted to do just this. Thus Puritans
and Papists were a common threat[20] that attempted to
deny temporal sovereignty to the monarch in England.
James I, who nearly lost his life in a plot within two
years of his accession, took over this view and referred
to Jesuits simply as "nothing but *Puritan-papists*."[21]

James held simple and strong political views which he
expressed, before acceding to the English throne, in *The
Trew Law of Free Monarchs: or, the Reciprock and
Mutuall Dueties betwixt a free King, and his naturall
Subjects* (1598). Here he approves of monarchy as a

17. Letter of July 6, 1590, in *The Letters of Queen Elizabeth,* ed.
G. B. Harrison (London: Cassell, 1935), pp. 203–4.
18. John Strype, *Life and Acts of John Whitgift* (Oxford: at the
Clarendon Press, 1822), 2: 159. On Polybius's invention of the term
"ochlocracy" see K. Von Fritz, *The Theory of the Mixed Contitution
in Antiquity* (New York: Columbia University Press 1954), p. 44. The
term became the perverse counterpart of "democracy" when that came
to have a favorable connotation: see P. Pédech, *La Méthode historique
de Polybe* (Paris: Société d'Editions "Les belles letters," 1964), p. 318.
19. W. G. Zeeveld, *Foundations of Tudor Policy* (Cambridge, Mass.:
Harvard University Press, 1948), p. 333.
20. See Patrick McGrath, *Papists and Puritans under Elizabeth*
(London: Blandford, 1967), *passim*.
21. James I, "A Premonition" (1609), *Political Works of James I,*
ed. C. H. McIlwain (Cambridge, Mass.: Harvard University Press,
1918), p. 126. All references in this chapter to James's writings will
be to this edition.

reflection of divine unity, and illustrates it with the Scottish king Fergus, who, "a wise king comming in among barbares, first established the estate and forme of governement, and thereafter made lawes by himselfe, and his successours according thereto" (p. 62). Conquest, to be distinguished from usurpation, allows a king and his descendants to rule over land absolutely, by analogy to the ownership of private property:

> the King is over-Lord of the whole land: so is he Master over every person that inhabiteth the same, having power over the life and death of every one of them.
>
> (p. 63)

William the Conqueror became king in this way,[22] and, like all kings, instituted law for the benefit of his new subjects; law, therefore is *lex regis* (p. 62). The king exists prior to his subjects, and is "above the law, as both the author and giver of strength thereto"; however, as a matter of good will, the King may decide to adhere to the law (p. 63).

Like the Elizabethan government, James was interested in civil obedience, and effectively summarizes:

> The duetie, and alleageance of the people to their lawfull king, their obedience, I say, ought to be to him, as to Gods Lieutenant in earth, obeying his commands in all thing, except directly against God, as the commands of Gods Minister, acknowledging him a Judge set by GOD over them, having power to judge them, but to be judged onely by God, whom to onely hee must give count of his judgement; fearing him as their Judge, loving him as their father; praying for him as their protectour; for his continuance, if he be good; for his amendement, if he be wicked; following and obeying his lawfull commands, eschewing and flying his fury in his unlawfull, without resistance, but by sobbes and teares to God.
>
> (p. 61)

---

22. Cf. Bodin, p. 203.

Although James might modify his absolutist views by conceding to practice the notion of good will, his understanding of kingship is basically different from that inherited from the English Middle Ages. Rather, his is a "Roman conception of a king *legibus solutus,* placed at a distance so immeasurably above his *subditi* that he can in no way be bound by earthly law to the performance of any duties to them."[23]

James's view, really not compatible with educated moderate opinion of the time, precipitated disagreement. Almost simultaneous with their joy at receiving a royal heir who was both male and non-Catholic, the members of the House of Commons drew up the *Apologie of the House of Commons* (1604), a set of principles in opposition to those of James. This document says in part:

> The prerogatives of Princes may easily, and do daily, grow. The Privileges of the Subject are for the most part at an ever-lasting stand. . . . It will appear by examination of truth and right, that your majesty should be misinformed, if any man should deliver, that the kings of England have any absolute power in themselves, either to alter religion . . . or to make any laws concerning the same, otherwise than as in temporal causes, by consent of parliament. . . . The voice of the people, in the things of their knowledge, is said to be as the voice of God.[24]

The disagreement on principles was extended to practice in the first Jacobean Parliament.

James was less adequately equipped than Elizabeth

---

23. McIlwain, p. xlii.

24. "Apology of the House of Commons, made to the King touching their Privileges" (1604), in W. Cobbett, ed., *The Parliamentary History of England* (London, 1806), 1: 1034, 1038–39, 1042. The spirit behind this document indicates that D. H. Willson's generalization, "before 1603 the Crown had controlled the Commons" (*Parliamentary Diary of Robert Bowyer: 1606–07* (Minneapolis: University of Minnesota Press, 1931), p. xviii) is only superficially accurate. Neale's two volumes of Elizabethan Parliaments have exhaustively shown the frequently stormy relations between Crown and Commons during Elizabeth's reign.

had been to deal with this difficulty. For passage through
Commons of matters she favored, she had relied on her
manner of presentation; James was unable to do so.
Elizabeth's word had usually been conveyed to Parliament by a member of the Privy Council; James failed
to keep this impressive distance. Elizabeth had been,
whenever possible, brief and decisive; James relinquished
both the air of mystery and decision by meddling, reminding, and urging, causing Commons in particular to
regard his words with less than former awe. Elizabeth
had kept some of her Privy Councillors in Commons to
exert a measurable influence on its decisions;[25] James
kept few of his there, for when a man was considered
able, he was put on a special committee or made a peer.[26]
Those who did remain lacked sufficient tact and ability
to be effective. James looked to Sir Robert Cecil (1563-
1612), the Earl of Salisbury, to mediate between himself
and Commons, but Cecil, a major link between the Tudor
and Stuart governments, was unsuccessful in carrying the
tradition of the Privy Council's domination of Commons
into the new age.

By about 1610 the Crown-Parliament opposition had
been clearly drawn up. Wallace Notestein has shown
that by this time, when the Speaker of the House of
Commons (selected by the Crown and expected to advance the royal viewpoint), attempted to perform this
task in the committees and subcommittees where business
was effectually handled, he could be told that in his direction of proceedings he was a servant of Commons. In
such a situation, if the Privy Council hoped to control
Parliament, it could do so only by cementing the House
of Lords in its traditional alliance with the Crown; how-

---

25. Four in 1593; three in 1597; five in 1601. See Neale, *Commons*,
p. 308.
26. In 1606–7 only two members of the Privy Council were in Commons; see W. M. Wallace, p. 22.

ever, the Peers were disturbed by James's practice of raising money by giving patents and monopolies and by laying impositions. Further, they were aggravated by his creation of new peers who had no English political experience.[27] The elder Peers, who disliked Scots habits and the idea of Scots power,[28] refused to support James's ideals, particularly that of unifying Britain. James alienated both Commons and a significant section of the nobility, which thus relinquished its mediating role.

James's first Parliament began with the presentation of abuses;[29] the difficulty encountered by Crown supporters set the tone for the future.[30] The second session, which reopened on January 21, 1606,[31] virtually began with similar complaints over purveyance, a matter of royal prerogative that had within it the whole question of the nature of English government.[32] It is particularly instructive for a study of Shakespeare's *Coriolanus* to notice the kind of language used to carry on this disagreement. Bowyer records that on February 11 the King sent a message that there would be redress of grievances, but, as Cecil wrote on the 15th,

[The King] willed you to shewe your greavaunces, yet he is not ignorant how dangerous a thing it is to sommon subjects

---

27. Commons was annoyed by James's grants to favorites; but the Peers were annoyed by his alienation of one-fourth of the royal estates to other Peers. The latter acts, during 1603–28, coincided with the observable loss in royal prestige and power due to the corrupt administration and the discontent of the nobles over courtly promotions; see L. Stone, *The Crisis of the Aristocracy* (Oxford: at the Clarendon Press, 1965), pp. 487–88, 493–95, and summary, 500–501.

28. See James's 1607 disclaimer to both Houses in *Works,* pp. 294–95.

29. Wallace, p. 25.

30. On Francis Bacon's role in the first session, see Joel J. Epstein, "Francis Bacon: Mediator in the Parliament of 1604," *The Historian* 30 (1968) : 219–37.

31. It had been opened on November 5, but was prorogued on the 9th because of the Gunpowder Plot.

32. W. G. Zeeveld, *"Coriolanus* and Jacobean Politics," *MLR* 57 (1962) :325ff.

to complaine but thinking that there was none among you that woulde take on them to be Tribunes of the people: and the King namely spake of the abuse of Purveyors.

(p. 42)

These words were repeated to Parliament, except for words "to this effect viz. that the Lords did not expect anie to speake as the Tribunes of the people" (p. 46). Perhaps because the analogy would have been received as needlessly provocative, the report omitted James's identification of the outspoken popular leaders in Commons with the revolutionary Roman tribunate. But James's placing of the contemporary political situation in a Roman setting with an anti-tribune bias is clear and was picked up in the report by Sir Edward Hoby.[33]

James had used the analogy with the same bias in a speech delivered to Parliament in 1605, after the discovery of the Gunpowder Plot. He referred to his recent salvation as analogous to the saving of Rome from Hannibal by Scipio Africanus, and cast a wry look at ungrateful magistrates who complained; Scipio, who had been accused

by the *Tribunes* of the People of *Rome* for mispending and wasting in his *Punick* warres the Cities Treasure, even upon the sudden brake out with that diversion of them from that matter, . . . [saying] it was fitter for them all, leaving other matters, to runne to the Temple to praise God for that so great delivery.

(p. 284)[34]

In the session of Parliament which convened in November 1606, James spoke again, referring to "tribunes of the people whose mouths could not be stopped, either from the matters of the Puritans, or of the purveyance," and demanded that "if any such plebeian tribunes should

---

33. Quoted *ibid.*, p. 328.
34. Cf. Plutarch, *Scipio Africanus,* in 6: 428-29, and Heywood's citation, in chapter 2 above, n. 31.

incur any offence . . . Commons would correct them
for it."[35]

Speaking in the same year against the king's right to
lay impositions without the assent of Parliament, the
"tribune"[36] Sir Henry Yelverton (1566-1629) cited
Livy, Bracton, and Fortescue, all sources sympathetic to
the mixed state. Yelverton made several points relying
on received English tradition and classical precedent:

> 1. It is against the naturall frame and constitution of the
> policie of this kingdome, which is *jus publicum regni,* and so
> subverteth the fundamentall law of the realme, and induceth
> a new forme of state and government. . . . 4. It is against the
> practice and action of our common-wealth, *contra morem ma-*
> *jorum;* and this is the modestest rule to limit both king's pre-
> rogatives, and subjects liberties.

The *morem majorum,* a balance of king and people, is
represented in government by king-in-Parliament. Re-
hearsing the "two-fold power" of the king,

> the one in parliament, as he is assisted with the consent of the
> whole state; the other out of parliament, as he is sole, and
> singular, guided merely by his own will,

Yelverton went on to show the former to be supreme.
To do so, he relied on precedent:

> Can any man give me a reason, why the king can only in
> parliament make lawes? No man ever read any law whereby
> it was so ordained; and yet no man ever read that any king
> practised the contrary. Therefore it is the originall right of
> the kingdome, and the very natural constitution of our state
> and policy, being one of the highest rights of soveraigne power.

Citing with approval Sir John Fortescue to the effect
that "England . . . is *principatus mixtus et politicus,*"

35. Quoted in Cobbett, pp. 1071–72.
36. Bowyer, p. 123, n. 1; Zeeveld, *Foundations,* p. 328.

Yelverton concluded that "the king hath his soveraign power in parliament, assisted and strengthened with the consent of the whole kingdom."[37] As he said in 1607, Members of Parliament "were not bound to the commaundements of the kinge," and he went on to repeat "that old point of tying allegeance to the lawe and crowne, not to the persone of the king."[38]

The temperance achieved by the unified yet mixed rule of King-in-Parliament ideally allowed divergent elements to express themselves; but this balance was destroyed by the inflexibility and extremism of both Crown and Commons. At best, this was a dangerous situation; it was even more dangerous for the nation at large, for one of the sides believed the other to be seditious and destructive, threatening England with "ochlocracy." James attempted to solve the difficulty, not by attempting balance, relying on the moderate peerage, but by asserting, over and over again, his conception of divine-right rule. Consequently the disaffected nobility tended to take sides rather than attempt to transcend and heal division; as the "Special Observations" attributed to Lord Ellesmere (d. 1617) observe,

> The popular state ever since the beginning of his Majesty's gracious and sweet government hath grown big and audacious, and in every session of parliament swelled more and more.[39]

This tense atmosphere encouraged, perhaps even forced, men in court circles to rethink and reassess their conception of the nature of English government.[40]

One of those who addressed himself to this problem

---

37. The foregoing quotations appear in *A Complete Collection of State Trials,* ed. T. B. Howell (London, 1816), 2: 481, 482, 483, 485–86.

38. Quoted in Bowyer, p. 377.

39. Quoted by P. Williams, review of *Proceedings in Parliament, 1610,* ed. by E. R. Foster. 2 vols. (New Haven: Yale University Press, 1966), in *Renaissance Quarterly* 21 (1968): 482.

40. H. N. Maclean, "Fulke Greville: Kingship and Sovereignty," *HLQ* 16 (1952–53): 266, makes this point with reference to Greville.

was Sir Walter Ralegh (1552-1618). Ralegh's political writings were, with the exception of the passages of *The History of the World,* all printed posthumously, and seem at first to be entirely miscellaneous and derivative. Recent studies have made their essential coherence readily discernible, however: his thought is representative of traditional English mixed-state attitudes, which he clung to in the face of Jacobean autocracy. Two works on politics have been studied in particular, in an attempt to analyze Ralegh's political thinking. These are *The Prince, or Maxims of State,* first printed in London in 1642, and *The Cabinet-Council,* first printed from a manuscript supplied by John Milton, in London in 1658. Both of these works are fundamentally collections of political commonplaces derived from Machiavelli and Guicciardini primarily, rather than systematic discourses,[41] and are rejected from the Ralegh canon by prominent modern scholars.[42]

Discussion of his political views must therefore be based on the *History of the World* (1614) and the dialogue, *Prerogative of Parliaments* (1615),[43] along with incidental observations scattered elsewhere. The *History* shows a particular orientation toward politics, concen-

---

41. J. W. Allen, *English Political Thought 1603–60* (London: Methuen, 1938), 1: 65, seeks to treat them in this way. Their anthological nature has, however, been recognized. V. Luciani, "Ralegh's Cabinet-Council and Guicciardini's Aphorisms," *SP* 46 (1949): 20–30, discusses the collector's reliance on a gathering of political commonplaces from Aristotle, Plato, Livy, and Guicciardini made by Francesco Sansovino (1521–83), entitled *Concetti Politici* (1578), a partial translation of which, by R. Hitchcock and entitled *The Quintessence of Wit,* was printed in England in 1590 (STC 21744). On Sansovino's role as popularizer of Italian Renaissance historical knowledge, see chapter 4 above, n. 58.

Chapter 26 of the *Cabinet-Council* is derived from Machiavelli's *Discorsi:* see N. Kempner, *Raleghs Staatstheoretische Schriften* (Leipsic: Tauchnitz, 1928), pp. 102–28.

42. Pierre Lefranc, *Sir Walter Ralegh: Ecrivain* (Paris: Armand Colin, 1968), pp. 67–70, rejects Ralegh's authorship of *Maxims;* Lefranc, p. 64, and E. A. Strathmann, "A Note on the Ralegh Canon," *TLS,* 13 April, 1956, p. 228, both reject his authorship of *The Cabinet-Council.*

43. Lefranc, p. 196.

trating less on theory than on the documentation of the relations between the monarchs and their subjects. Ralegh's *History* shares with the work of other English writers an anti-tyrannic attitude; it is clearly expressed in the Preface, in which rulers are judged and Henry VIII called a "merciless Prince."[44] Elsewhere, limits on monarchs' powers are suggested (II.339-52) and the overthrows of tyrants are narrated at length (VI.50-75). The *History* is known to have displeased James I, who remarked on "Sir Walter Ralegh's description of the kings he hates, of whom he speaketh but evil."[45]

According to Ralegh's account of the Coriolanus story, the people of Rome "instigated by some desperate bank-routs, thinking themselves wrongfully oppressed by the Senate and consuls," rose against authority; mention is made of the role of the tribunate. Menenius Agrippa's "discreet allusion of the inconvenience in the head and belly's discord to that present occasion" calmed the people.[46] Ralegh omits the members that rebel, and makes the discord exist between the head, or monarchic element, and the belly, or aristocratic element of the state, in accordance with his interest in contemporary England, discussed at length in the *Prerogative*.[47]

According to Ben Jonson, "the best wits of England were Employed for making of [Ralegh's] *Historie*,"[48] and while in the Tower Ralegh had used the library of

44. *The Works of Sir Walter Raleigh* (Oxford: at the Clarendon Press, 1829), 2: viii–xxx, xvi–xvii. References will be made to this edition, cited by volume and page number.

45. Letter to Sir Robert Carr, quoted in John Racin, Jr., "The Early Editions of Sir Walter Ralegh's *The History of the World*," SB 17 (1964): 204.

46. *Works,* 5:531.

47. By contrast, Shakespeare's formulation of the fable in *Coriolanus* places the strife between the belly and the other members; this is in accordance with his accurate presentation of the aristocratic Roman government existing at the time that the tribunate was instituted. See below, chapter 6.

48. *Ben Jonson* 1, ed. C. H. Herford and P. Simpson (Oxford: at the Clarendon Press, 1925) :138.

the Italian scholar Henry Percy, Ninth Earl of North-umberland ("The Wizard Earl").[49] The *History* shows evidence of acquaintance with sophisticated political thought,[50] and in the later *Prerogative* Ralegh brings historical enquiry to bear on the situation in his own country. This essay, in dialogue form, seems to have been widely circulated in manuscript upon its completion; it was printed only in 1628, appearing with fictitious places of origin indicated on the title pages (STC 20648, 48a, and 50). The work remained popular, appearing in 1640, 1661, and in eight editions of *The Remains* between 1657 and 1726.[51]

After a prefatory address to James, a Justice of the Peace and a Councillor discuss the proper relations between an English King and Parliament. The Justice, who seems to express Ralegh's views, says that on the one hand, the King is above his subjects and cannot be called in question by them; on the other, however, by the common law of the land the King's power is limited with respect to his relations with his subjects. The Justice shows the wisdom of kings since the time of Henry I (1068-1135) in consulting Parliament. Like Polybius and Machiavelli, Ralegh clearly recognizes that the state consists of three elements—King, nobility, and Commons;[52] as a practical matter, it is necessary for the King to join with one or the other element to limit the power of the third.[53] Ralegh argues that the King should ally himself with the people,[54] thus accepting the results of Tudor efforts to secure the throne by systematically weakening the English aristocracy. The immediate problem,

49. M. C. Bradbrook, *The School of Night* (Cambridge, England: Cambridge University Press, 1936), p. 72.
50. Cf. Ralegh, 2: 347–52 (which mentions Charron), with *Of Wisdom,* trans. S. Lennard (London, 1608), p. 168. STC 5051.
51. Lefranc, p. 204.
52. *Works,* 8: 159–60, 215–16.
53. *Ibid.,* pp. 159–60, 182–83.
54. Cf. Machiavelli's views, above, chapter 4.

which Ralegh thus addresses to James in a formulation strikingly parallel to that of *Coriolanus,* is the reconcilement of the monarchic and popular elements of the state.[55]

The date of composition places the essay immediately after the "Addled Parliament" of 1614, at which James's demands for money and his prerogatives were again met by Commons' demands for its rights. As is well known, James dissolved the Parliament after two months, during which nothing important had been accomplished, and refused to call another for seven years. Ralegh's work analyzes the historical balance between respect for the King's rights and for the subjects' from a point of view very relevant to the circumstances surrounding the period of its composition. He argues that the King should call another Parliament,[56] for that way wisdom lies; the parliamentary deadlock had occurred over a nation in serious financial trouble, and the solution is to listen for wisdom from any sources. The traditional view of Ralegh was written at a time when the government of England was being, and would for a short while continue to be, directed by a conservative, Protestant group headed by the Secretary of State, Sir Ralph Winwood (1563?-1617), William Herbert, third Earl of Pembroke (1580-1630), and the Archbishop of Canterbury, George Abbot (1562-1633).[57]

To effect a reconciliation between King and Commons, Ralegh depended on the aristocracy to assume the role of mediator, and be a truly good councillor. However, the Justice's interlocutor, ironically an official Councillor, is intent on guarding the Councillors' privilege:

Hereof you may assure yourself, that we will never allow of

55. Ralegh, *Works,* 8:211–12.
56. *Ibid.,* pp. 216–17.
57. G. P. V. Akrigg, *Jacobean Pageant* (Cambridge, Mass.: Harvard University Press, 1962), p. 328.

any invention, how profitable soever, unless it proceed, or seem
to proceed, from ourselves.

(p. 218)

With this remark, and with veiled threats, the Councillor
parts from the Justice of the Peace, who speaks for the
importance of Parliament and the roles within it of
Commons, Lords, and King, and for the continued existence of traditional mixed government.

In an age of Jacobean would-be autocracy, the *Prerogative* points to the temperate mixed-state tradition,
and catches the note of loyalty to government by King-in-
Parliament. Ralegh's mixed-state preferences are not
precisely those of Sidney and Greville, yet all three in
effect endorse "royal, mixed government":

> It hath been observed also, that since these troubles from
> the barons, the kings of England, to lessen the power of the
> nobility, and balance them, have yielded to the growing great-
> ness and privileges of the commons; and what effect that will
> have, time can only shew. Politicians do affirm, that nobility
> preserves liberty longer than the commons, and for instance
> say, Solon's popular state came far short of Lycurgus's by
> mixed government; for the popular state of Athens soon fell,
> whilst the royal, mixed government of Sparta stood a mighty
> time; by the nobility Sparta and Venice enjoyed their freedom
> longer than Rome.[58]

James I and Venice

King James I found it necessary to assert his temporal rights not only against dissent at home, but also
against Roman Catholics on the Continent: both denied

58. "A Discourse of War in General" (1614–16), 8: 296. Cf. Machiavelli, *Discorsi,* I. 2 and I. 5, ed. Lerner, pp. 114–15, 121; the parallels are mentioned in Lefranc, pp. 625–26, no. 36; Ralegh mentions
Machiavelli and Guicciardini in this essay, p. 266. On Ralegh and
Guicciardini, see Lefranc, pp. 636–37.

his pretensions to absolute power, and in addition the latter attacked him as a heretic king against whom it would be meritorious to take arms. The most notorious example of what the English conceived of as yet another Roman Catholic attempt at tyrannicide was the gunpowder plot, scheduled for November 5, 1605; it remained a live issue for fully five years afterwards.[59] Thereafter James became uncompromising in his opposition to Papal secular claims, and pressed forward an Oath of Allegiance requiring those under indictment for recusancy to affirm him to be King, denying authority to the Pope's contrary view and the alleged right of subjects to take action against a ruler. Striking directly at the Pope, the Oath provoked replies from papal advocates. Chief among them was Cardinal Bellarmine (1542-1621), whose support of papal claims was based more on theological considerations than on political ones.[60] Bellarmine was a formidable opponent, and in the ensuing quarrel James found it advisable to encourage and reward support for his position. Just as he imported the famous Continental scholar Isaac Casaubon (1559-1614) to help in composing replies to attacks from abroad,[61] so James solicited support within England for his theories of kingship.

Very shortly James was brought into direct conflict with the Pope, for Paul V issued, on September 22, 1606,

59. B. N. De Luna, *Jonson's Romish Plot* (Oxford: at the Clarendon Press, 1967), pp. 40–41, 66.

60. He felt that the unified rule of Christendom by the Pope reflected the structure of reality, and that this took precedence over incidental and theoretical approval of mixed constitutions in secular governments. See William J. Bouwsma, *Venice and the Defense of Republican Liberty* (Berkeley: University of California Press, 1968), pp. 319–22. Bouwsma's summary of Roman Catholic monarchist arguments should be compared with the "Elizabethan World Picture" arguments above, chapter 1; that differing, republican arguments were cogent and acceptable to many is further proof that the equation "order = absolute monarchy" cannot be presupposed of Shakespeare's plays.

61. Summarized by D. H. Willson, *King James VI and I* (London: Cape, 1956), pp. 230–31.

a bull against the Oath, which had been taken by many English Roman Catholics.[62] He reissued the bull on August 23 of the following year; James countered with the *Apologie for the Oath of Allegiance* (1607), asserting that the Oath was in the first place purely a civil matter; the validity of such a distinction was an embattled topic, however. James reissued the *Apologie* in 1609, with additions that were calculated to be polemical in the extreme—in fact calling the Pope Antichrist—and made sure that the volume was circulated through the Courts of Europe. At home, James helped to support his case by finding as many anti-papal Catholics as he could to share his view openly.[63] While this was going on, he became involved in an analogous dispute between Pope Paul V and the Republic of Venice over papal rights in temporal matters. This dispute of 1606-7, and England's near-involvement in it, were widely known and acclaimed by anti-papal forces.

The position of independence from Rome that Venice had practiced during the sixteenth century clashed with the new Church policies of Paul V. The immediate cause of disagreement concerned Venice's custom of trying clergy in civil courts; the Pope objected both to this and to a series of measures that sharply limited the Church's local ownership of real estate. When Venice remained unmoved by two papal briefs, the Pope issued, on April 17, 1606, a bull of Interdict and Excommunication against the entire city. The city replied that the charges were unjust, and held the bull "not only for unjust and unlawfull, but also for annulled and of no value, and so without force, frustrated, and unlawfully thundered."[64]

---

62. De Luna, p. 42; see also McIlwain, pp. lxxii–lxxiii.
63. McIlwain, *ibid.*
64. Leonardo Donato (Donà), Doge of Venice, *protesta* of May 6, 1606, translated in the anonymous *Declaration of the Variance betweene the Pope, and the Segniory of Venice* (s. 1., 1606), sig. C3r. (STC 19482.)

Venice took steps to assure that the clergy in the city would respond to the autonomy of the state, and expelled the Jesuits, many of whom took up the pen to support the Pope.

As a further slap to papal authority, Venice elected her own Theological Counsellor, the friar Paolo Sarpi (1552-1623), who encouraged many men, including Casaubon,[65] to write in defense of the Republic. To Rome, such behavior was heretical, and Sarpi was blamed for having provoked the interdict. The reasons for this are less his role as Counsellor or his personal beliefs than a long-standing papalist feeling that he and his associates represented a freedom of thought that was dangerous and ought to be condemned, that they "inherited the poison of Luther, the atheism of M. Spirone of Padua, and the impiety of Marsilio of Padua."[66] Although this charge is formulated with the clarity of Counter-Reformation intransigence, it is true that in its independent attitude the Republic relied on, and further developed, "those tendencies in Italian Evangelism, long kept alive in Venice, which had so frightened the leaders of the early Counter Reformation some seven decades earlier."[67] Not surprisingly, the Venetians were during this time interested and sympathetic students of the fall of the Florentine Republic.[68] The issue at hand, between a Venice that Rome associated with Calvin and Luther, and a Rome that Europe generally found to be unnecessarily rigid, not to say intransigent, concerned the Pope's claim to temporal power, claims many imagined were being implemented by the Jesuits. Sarpi bluntly termed

---

65. Sarpi later encouraged Casaubon to edit Polybius as a stroke in defense of human liberty: see his letter to Leschassier dated May 13, 1610.

66. Quoted in Bouwsma, p. 366.

67. *Ibid.,* p. 452.

68. *Ibid.,* pp. xiii, 168, 557, etc.

the Pope's action a plea for "absolute monarchy,"[69] and Sir Henry Wotton (1568-1639), the English ambassador to Venice after 1604, understood the Interdict on Venice and the Gunpowder Plot in England to be linked Jesuit plots to gain control of Europe.[70]

Protestant countries followed events closely. By June, 1606, Wotton had apprised James I of the situation, and had declared to the Venetian ambassador to England that James sympathized with the Republic. Sarpi recorded later that Wotton further proposed, "as for him selfe, a League with his King, and other *Princes* his friends."[71] Sarpi was told that when in August Venice requested assurance of English support, James, then in the company of King Christian IV of Denmark, replied that he would be "ingratefull and unjust" if he failed to support the Republic.[72]

James's support was of a cause kindred to his own, although he clearly distinguished between the free monarchy of the English King and

> such sort of governors, as the dukes of *Venice* are, whose Aristocratick and limited government, is nothing like to free Monarchies; although the malice of some writers hath not beene ashamed to mis-know any difference to be betwixt them.[73]

In October, Venice asked for concrete help, but by that time James and his advisors had had second thoughts, confirming Sarpi's accurate assessment of the English king

---

69. *History of the Quarrels of Pope Paul V. with the State of Venice,* trans. C. P[otter]. (London, 1626), sig. A1ᵛ (STC 21766). Sarpi goes on to remark that Pope Paul wanted a "Spirituall and Temporall Monarchie of all the world" (sig. B1ʳ).

70. Logan Pearsall Smith, *The Life and Letters of Sir Henry Wotton* (Oxford: at the Clarendon Press, 1907), 1:80.

71. Sarpi, *Quarrels,* sig. Z4ʳ⁻ᵛ.

72. *Ibid.,* sig. Aa4ᵛ. While Christian IV was in England, Shakespeare was writing *Macbeth:* see H. N. Paul, *The Royal Play of "Macbeth"* (New York: Macmillan, 1950).

73. James I, *Political Works,* p. 64.

as a talker rather than a doer.[74] It was the maneuvering of the French King Henri IV that brought Pope Paul, by the Spring of 1607, to realize he "had weakened his power by exceeding it";[75] he revoked the interdict, after which Venice revoked her edicts.

Although these dramatic events—which suggested for the space of a few months a possible alliance of England and Venice in a common cause against the Papacy and its secular arm, Austro-Spanish military forces—came to nothing, they received publicity in England. One anonymous work stresses the parallelism between this situation and several in England's past. In *A Declaration of the Variance betweene the Pope, and the Segniory of Venice* (1606, STC 19482), the author prays that God "will blesse this the *Venetians* encounter of the Romish pride, with the like success, which it pleased him to give to the like adventure, in the time of King Henry VIII when he revived the question of the Popes Pontifical decrees, and did eject his false and ill-gotten Supremacie" (sig. A4ʳ). Despite the very real dangers the Republic will face,[76] the author can see some hope of success, for England is an example to her: English history had demonstrated, over many years, "that the Pope had no right in this kingdome to order, governe, command, or censure any causes of persons, Civill or Ecclesiasticall" (sig. G4ʳ). And he proceeds to list significant moments, during the reigns of several of England's kings, when this principle was tested, and then further states that these records can be verified because they have been collected by Sir Edward Coke (sig. G4ᵛ).

Two tracts by Sarpi were also made available to En-

---

74. See John L. Lievsay, "Paolo Sarpi's Appraisal of James I," *Essays in History and Literature presented . . . to Stanley Pargellis* (Chicago: The Newberry Library, 1965), pp. 109–17.
75. Izaac Walton, "The Life of Sir Henry Wotton" (1651), *The Lives* (New York: Scott-Thaw, 1903), p. 105.
76. The work brings events up to June, 1606. See sig. F4ʳ.

glish readers during these years.[77] In particular, *A Full and Satisfactorie Answer made to the late Unadvised Bull* (1606, STC 21759) is a reply to the Pope and a defense, complete with historical precedent, of Venice's policy of subordinating ecclesiastical affairs to those of the state. Sarpi stood by the view

> that *God* hath established two Governments in the World, the one Spirituall, and the other Temporall, each of them being supreme and independent upon the other.[78]

This argument on secular autonomy and the whole issue of the essential nature of government were popularized in England. Venice's position that its secular government derived from God was parallel to England's insistence on the supremacy of the state, and drew the same counter-argument from Rome, preeminently from the Jesuit Bellarmine.[79]

Sarpi and other participants and observers particularly stressed the disruptive role of Jesuits in terms that would have met with England's, and James's, approval:

> Nor doe they only act but teach *Sedition;* give rules of disloyalty, perjury, and parricide; make their Disciples beleeve that *Rebellion* is a vertue, and the murthering of a *Prince* a merit; that a *Clarke* cannot be a *traitor,* because he is no Subject; and that a King ought not to raigne or live if he serve not the *Pope,* who hath . . . all Power in Heaven and Earth.[80]

---

77. Sarpi's major work, the *Historie of the Councel of Trent,* was not completed until 1616; it was smuggled out of Italy and printed, with a dedication to James I, in London in Italian (1619, STC 21760) and Latin (1620, STC 21764), and was then reprinted four times in England during the course of the century.

78. *Quarrels,* sigs. Dd1ᵛ–2ʳ; see the entire summary, sigs. Dd1ᵛ–Ee1ᵛ. The quoted passage appears *verbatim* in a *consulto* of 1608, quoted Bouwsma, p. 540. The other work, aimed at James's antagonist, is *An Apologie . . . unto Cardinall Bellarmine* (1607, STC 21757).

79. Bouwsma, pp. 432–37.

80. *Quarrels,* sig. A2ᵛ.

The Jesuit dislike of Venice and the distinction between that city and other states, mentioned by James in a quotation cited above, is also singled out by Sarpi: the Jesuits "praised *Monarchy,* and blamed an *Aristocratie,* with certaine Maximes very contrary to the Government and Institution of the Republique."[81]

Despite James's lack of action, the anti-papal position of both states suggested other areas of agreement between England and Venice. James emerged from the crisis as the only European Prince clearly to support the Republic against the Pope; and the Venetian state emerged a state to some extent similar to England and opposed to papal oppression. After the Interdict was lifted, Wotton, who had long been in favor of a militant Protestant league, continued to involve himself in a possible general religious reform in Venice. Hoping to attack the papacy by seducing Venice from Roman Catholicism, he worked on a plan to encourage Italian states against the Pope, to smuggle in anti-papal books, and to convert prominent Venetians to form a single Protestant congregation.[82]

Such hopes were illusory. Luther had expressed them in 1528 and Ochino in 1542, but by and large sixteenth-century Italian converts tended to be Catholics whose Evangelical position made them unacceptable to Counter-Reformation Catholicism; Sarpi for one clearly distinguished this position from Protestantism.[83] But, according to Wotton, Sarpi himself further formulated a vast plan according to which James would make himself head

81. *Ibid.,* sig. T1[v]. The author of *A Declaration* mentions Venice's strength in defense and attributes this to the "Senatoriall government" of that state (sig. G2[r]); England is similarly strong in its government by a mixture of Parliament, Sovereign and Counsellors (sig. I1[v]).

82. This was hardly realistic. Listing the possible outcomes of the quarrel, *A Declaration* hopes for a negotiated peace, but indicates the probability of schism since neither party will be moderate (sig. G1[r]). In this event Venice would have become Greek rather than Roman Catholic—however, not Protestant (sig. D2[v]-3[r]).

83. See Bouwsma, p. 583.

of an international Protestant Union to defeat the papacy and liberate Italy.[84] In any case, the plan came to nothing since James was unwilling, although he did subsequently offer Sarpi asylum in England.

The political crisis with the Pope was pursued by the Venetian nobles for a while, but the movement died out after 1610. In that year Henri IV was assassinated (an event also linked to the Gunpowder Plot by some writers in England,[85] and thereafter Venice, responding to a changed European climate, became less independent. But for some four years, during James's early reign and the composition of Shakespeare's *Coriolanus,* these events revived awareness of the long history and peculiar mixed government of Venice, the story of which had been told to Jonson and Shakespeare by Contarini; it also formulated with renewed urgency questions about the essentially civil nature of human existence and the meaning and importance of law. These matters were in the forefront of current concerns, both on the Continent and in England, for some years following 1606.

James and His Supporters

One of the major sources for English assertions of the royal prerogative against rival claims of Puritans and Papists was the political thought of Jean Bodin (1530-96), whose *Six Livres de la République* (1576) was translated into English by Richard Knolles in 1606.[86] In this translation, "commonweale" is defined as a "lawfull government of many families, and of that which unto them in common belongeth, with a puissant sov-

---

84. Smith, 1: 90–98.
85. De Luna, pp. 34, 40.
86. Gabriel Harvey mentions that Bodin's book was read by English scholars as early as 1581. See *Gabriel Harvey's Marginalia,* ed. G. C. Moore Smith (Stratford: Shakespeare Head Press, 1913), p. 79.

ereigntie" (p. 1). Bodin sets out to reinterpret the "divers formes of Commonweales" (p. iii), particularly examining Sparta, Rome, and Venice, and dismisses the existence of a state ruled by a mixed government. For him, Rome after the expulsion of the kings became essentially popular,[87] albeit with an aristocratic government (pp. 199, 246, 249). Because the Senate did not have the power to make laws alone (p. 157), which is the first and most important mark of sovereignty (p. 162), Rome could not be called an aristocratic state. Rather, with the establishment of the tribunate, the people got sovereignty (p. 246); the tribunes, "keepers of the libertie of the people" (p. 274), could veto political decisions that worked against the people's interest. Bodin thus sees the tribunate as a counter-magistracy that, like the ephors, could be used to prevent kings from "the exercising of tyranny" (p. 187). The office itself is not disapproved, only the excesses attendant upon popular states, which tend to "advance the most vitious and unworthy men to offices and dignities" (p. 703). Thus the tribunes "oftentimes . . . toke upon them more than belonged to their place, or than was by law permitted them, oftentimes propounding their edicts and prohibitions" (pp. 302-3). Bodin is further critical of the popular state:

> I have discoursed here of the more at large, to shew the inconveniences which follow a Popular estate, to the end I might reduce them to reason which seeke to withdraw the subject from the obedience of their naturall prince, through a false hope of libertie, in framing of Popular states: the which in effect is nothing else, but the most pernitious tyranny that can be imagined, if it bee not governed by wise and vertuous men.
> (p. 708)

He also argues against monarchic states which attempt

---

87. Guicciardini disagreed; in the "Considerazioni sui *Discorsi* del Machiavelli [I.6]," he observes, "il governo di Roma era misto, non plebeo," *Opere Inedite* 1 (Firenze, 1857): 16.

to deny the laws of God and nature (pp. 92, 104-6) as a limitation on the king's power, and supports as best the "royal monarchy" (p. 720). The royal monarch

> or King, is he which placed in soveraigntie yeeldeth himselfe as obedient unto the lawes of nature as he desireth his subjects to be towards him selfe, leaving unto every man his naturall libertie, and the proprietie of his owne goods.
>
> (p. 204)[88]

In England, Bodin's precise formulations of traditional politics, fitting the French political situation, became slurred over in new, English applications. In particular, Bodin's emphasis on laws "of God and nature" clearly limited royal power and coincided with native English political theories.[89] In fact Yelverton, in a passage cited above, identified sovereignty with the power of making laws and demonstrated that in England the king-in-parliament was superior to the king alone, who could not make law alone. According to this thoroughly traditional view, sovereignty really resided in Parliament.

To argue against this notion of limitation, it was necessary for royalists to play down what Bodin had implied, in his definition of the state, by the adjective "lawfull," potentially a danger to a theory of divine-right monarchy.[90] James is known to have approved of the bias of some of these new arguments. One such work is Pierre Charron's *De la Sagesse* (1601), translated

---

88. Contrast James's beliefs, presented above, in the present chapter. Bodin argued against the papal assertion of temporal sovereignty (p. 146), and his arguments were used by others against the Pope; see G. L. Mosse, "The Influence of Jean Bodin's *République* on English Political Thought," *Mediaevalia et Humanistica* 5 (1948):80.

89. Bodin's political views changed between 1566 and 1576, causing him to stress the power of the king at the later date; see Beatrice Reynolds, *Proponents of Limited Monarchy in Sixteenth Century France: Francis Hotman and Jean Bodin* (New York: Columbia University Press, 1931), pp. 177–86.

90. See Mosse, pp. 77–82.

into English by Samson Lennard in 1608.[91] This book, which reflects French emphasis on strong national monarchy, coincides at several points with James's beliefs. Like James, Charron insisted on the king's right to make law without the consent of the governed and on his freedom from external restraints. Charron defined sovereignty as

> a perpetuall and absolute power, without constraint either of time or condition. It consisteth in a power to give lawes to all in general, and to every one in particular, without the consent of any other.
>
> (sig. N7ᵛ)

Not only are the words of kings greater than law; except that they are "inforced in their proceedings by a thousand considerations and respects, whereby many times they must captivate their designments, desires, and wills" (sig. O2ʳ), kings are not bound to such private virtues as truth and honesty. More refined than ordinary people, kings show, in their independence, almost heroic qualities: "the ordinarie maners of great personages are, untamed pride, . . . violence too licentious, . . . suspition, jealousie, . . . whereby it falleth out that they are many time in alarum and feare" (sig. N8ʳ).[92] However, like James, Charron recognized the danger of tyranny, and he placed great emphasis on monarchs' voluntary self-restraint in the interests of peaceful living. Since a strong ruler needs both good will and authority (sigs. Bb5ᵛ-6ʳ), he should not exert that power which is virtually absolute (sig. Ii7ʳ); although he is above law, he should still observe it. But under no condition has anyone the right

---

91. Pierre Charron, *Of Wisdome,* trans. S. Lennard (London [1608]), (S.R. 17 July 1606).

92. Coriolanus shares some of these qualities; Bodin treats them ironically when, for instance, speaking of the "best king" he excludes "one as is accomplished with all heroicall vertues . . . which in the fables of the Auncient worthies, were propounded with more magnificence than truth. . . . such as never was, nor ever shall be" (p. 211).

to question royal authority. Bodin and Charron are not the only authors with these biases to be printed in English in the years immediately preceding the composition of *Coriolanus*. Together they present to any reader a range of views that form sufficient background to make *Coriolanus* immediately relevant to its audience; this is especially true of the extreme, anti-popular opinions of Coriolanus himself.

In 1606 appeared another book, in part derived from Bodin, that repeated many of James's views on monarchy. This is *A Comparative Discourse of the Bodies Natural and Politique* (STC 11188), by Edward Forset.[93] Like Bodin's *République*,[94] the *Comparative Discourse* refers to the body-state analogy, a version of which was used by Menenius (sig. #4^r), and places the fable in a political, rather than purely rhetorical,[95] context. Forset supports James's views: the king is both the head and the heart of the state (sigs. E1^v-2^r) and precedes the people in existence. Although the people might at times elect a king, they are in reality secondary to a divinely ordered event. Again like James, Forset felt that sovereignty, embodied in the king, cherishes the commonwealth as the soul cherishes the body, or as parts of the body the source of their strength:

> There is not in the Commonwealth, any the least synew for mocion, the least vaine for norishment, the least spirite for life and action, the least strength for defence, or offence, the least member for use and benefit, which is not replenished with this power, and sucketh from this overflowing cesterne, all his subsistance and performance.
>
> (sig. C3^r)

Forset goes on to imply that the sovereign has the right

93. Forset is studied in J. W. Allen, *English Political Thought: 1603–60* (London: Methuen, 1938), 1: 76–84.

94. See, *e.g.,* pp. 53, 531, 708.

95. Kenneth Muir, "Menenius' Fable," *N&Q* 198 (1953): 240–42.

of absolute power, but, as if in recognition of James's parliamentary difficulties, he modifies this view in practice: sovereigns who govern most prudently will make law only with "consultation and consent" of some assembly—clearly the English Parliament. The good of the commonwealth is the aim of the sovereign, although as Forset formulates it the role of every part of the body politic is to make happy the soul of the sovereign:

> the Princes contentment must be the hapinesse of the Subject, and the subjects welfare the securitie of the Prince: And so shall the Commonwealth be compleatly blessed.
>
> (sig. N4ᵛ)

Forset's book not only supports James's position; its contents closely parallel the interests of Shakespeare's *Coriolanus,* a play in which the ideal relationship of the members of the state is disrupted. Charron had written that kings' behavior is characterized by heroic excesses; Forset, realizing the practical consequences of such excesses, mentions that "discontentednesse" in subjects would cause the "universall ruine" of all (sig. I4ʳ). Forset explicitly supports the Union of Britain (sigs. Iiᵛ-2ʳ), and, in expanding the body-state analogy, cites the commonplace parallel of magistrates and doctors (sigs. L1ʳ-2ʳ), thus suggesting the noticeable strain of disease imagery in the play.[96] In different ways, all of these topics occur in *Coriolanus.*

The publication of the translations by Knolles and Lennard and of the book by Forset took place between 1606 and 1608, making them approximately contemporaneous with the composition of *Coriolanus* and with James's assertions against his first Parliament and against papal interference in temporal matters. The

---

96. Maurice Charney, *Shakespeare's Roman Plays* (Cambridge, Mass.: Harvard University Press, 1961), pp. 157–63. Charney also observes, "After *Hamlet, Coriolanus* has the largest number of disease images in Shakespeare," p. 237, n. 11.

books were political formulations designed for English readers; the last two were pleasing to James because they endorsed his well-known divine-right theories. In these cases, the men responsible were close to Court circles. Lennard, a friend of Sir Philip Sidney, was patronized by Prince Henry and by William Herbert, Earl of Pembroke, one of those to whom Shakespeare's Folio was dedicated in 1623. Forset was a Justice of the Peace involved in examining the Gunpowder Plot conspirators, perhaps the same Forset (or Fauset) who secretly recorded conversations between Garnet and Hall.[97] James granted Forset a manor in Tyburn in 1611, probably as a reward for faithful support.[98]

In England, the argument between royal absolutism and strictly limited monarchy had reached a new stage with the accession of James. The division worsened as a result of each side insisting immoderately on its extremist view in the face of an opposition no less extreme. Once belief in a unified King-in-Parliament was effectively destroyed, Plutarch's vision of the noble Senate as mediating between the monarchic and popular elements became a possible hope. But rather than seek to rule by soliciting the support of a moderate nobility, James asserted his royal prerogative against his Roman Catholic and Puritan enemies. This policy led, in the former case, to a renewed acquaintance with the ancient republican state of Venice and to a possible coalition with it against the Pope. Although Englishmen would have supported such an alliance, the very popularity of Venice, so frequently cited as analogous to Rome and, in a variety of ways, to England, would have countered his royalist arguments. At home, James rewarded the expression in court circles of views modifying French political theory sufficiently to make it coincide with his own.

---

97. De Luna, pp. 276–77, makes this suggestion.
98. Mosse, p. 79.

Shakespeare, the dramatist of the King's Men who had already deliberately written plays that spoke to James's interests, had in the court climate itself not only the subject of a political drama but also a clear indication of the treatment he ought to give it. A work of literature seeking to represent such a situation and address its audience's political concerns would require the flexibility afforded by Rome rather than the narrow orthodoxy required of a monarchist English dramatic setting. Even to the unconcerned or unintelligent members of the *Coriolanus* audience, the debilitating results on the state of dissension within would be quite clear. However, Shakespeare relied on the more cultivated to use their knowledge of a wide range of political opinion, made possible by contact with the classics and with Italy, to consider the dramatized situation and the normative standards for civic virtue which the play proposes. If honored, they would yield continued honorable political and moral existence.

6

A Reading of *Coriolanus* (1608-11)

In the interaction between the literary works studied above and the climates of opinion in England and on the Continent subsequently sketched was the opportunity for the composition of a play that would be both a self-sufficient work of art and a reflection of the cross-currents of ideas urgent in European Counter-Reformation civilization. Further, specific conflicts are an underlying and continuous element that must be recognized for an appreciation of the nature of Shakespeare's achievement; there was a Jacobean parallel to the Roman political situation of *Coriolanus*. Some areas of the relationship between the play and its time may be apparent from suggestions already made; however, it remains to attempt a close reading of the whole play to bring out its biases and the fullness of its scope. Thus the reader may find it useful to have a text beside him while reading the following pages.[1]

Act One places the action specifically in time and

1. References are to *Coriolanus*, ed. John Dover Wilson. The New Shakespeare (Cambridge, Eng.: Cambridge University Press, 1960).

place; it introduces the heroism of Caius Marcius, the political climate of civil dissension, and the newly established tribunate. It should be clear from earlier chapters that no predictions can be made as to Renaissance treatment of these elements; although the often-quoted Elizabethan writer William Fulbecke, for instance, termed pre-Imperial Rome a time of "continuall factions," even he did not really condemn it entirely, as we have seen.[2] However, the story Shakespeare chose to dramatize was considered to be, even in monarchist eyes, the single instance of failure, that is, of actual armed strife, in this early period of Rome's history.[3] The note of failure is strengthened in its initial suggestiveness by an unchangeable part of the story: the inference from *Titus Andronicus* IV.iv.67-68[4] is that the audience of the play knew from the start at least that Coriolanus marched in revenge against his own country with foreign troops.

Act One

Coriolanus opens with civil insurrection: the Roman mob seeks relief from famine, for which it blames the patricians. Chief among these is Caius Marcius, soon to be surnamed "Coriolanus," whom the mob calls "proud" (I.i.33) yet admits is deserving of thanks for protecting Rome (ll. 36-39). Any sympathy that might be aroused by the people's famine is promptly qualified by the First Citizen's remark "Let us kill him, and we'll have corn at our own price" (ll. 10-11), which illustrates the limitation of awareness of political realities under which the

---

2. *Historicall Collection of Continuall Factions* (London: Ponsonby, 1601), sigs. B2ᵛ-3ʳ (this work was originally written in 1584). STC 11412. Quoted above, chapter 1.
3. *Shakespeare's Appian*, ed. E. Schanzer (Liverpool: Liverpool University Press, 1956), p. 5.
4. See above, chapter 2.

people operate; sympathy is further modified by the humor of First Citizen's subsequent remarks (ll. 15-24).[5] A characteristically ambiguous picture of Caius Marcius emerges from this initial discussion; the people's divided view of his pride or love of country establishes a nonheroic and civilian point of reference. It is in this context that Menenius Agrippa, seeking to modify the anger of the people, tells the famous Fable of the Belly and Members; Marcius is set aside for the moment from the immediate concern, which now centers on the civilian commonwealth.

The version of the ancient body analogy that Menenius tells is that the members accused the belly of merely "cupboarding the viand" (l. 99), or hoarding the nourishment, without taking an active part in the activities of the body, whereas the other members were "mutually participate" (l. 102). The belly's answer argues for interdependence, each according to its appointed function; the belly distributes the food to each other member, and keeps only the "bran" for itself. After a series of generally benign interchanges, Menenius makes the application:

> The senators of Rome are this good Belly,
> And you the mutinous members: for examine
> Their counsels and their cares, digest things rightly
> Touching the weal o'th' common, you shall find
> No public benefit which you receive
> But it proceeds or comes from them to you,
> And no way from yourselves.
>
> (ll. 147–53)

As he thus applies it, the body-state analogy endorses the absolute rule of the patrician Senate, that is, the existing form of government in Rome following the ex-

---

5. T. W. Baldwin, *The Organization and Personnel of the Shakespearean Company* (Princeton: Princeton University Press, 1927), p. 241, suggests that First Citizen is a role in Robert Armin's line.

pulsion of the kings. This accounts for Menenius's selection of the "Belly" as ruler, rather than the "Head," which was the common choice of those discussing monarchy. Shakespeare's modification of the fable points clearly to the *status quo* of the aristocratic government of Rome: Menenius's plea is for the continuance of traditional government.

Versions of Menenius's fable were often told in conjunction with the Coriolanus story, one of the historical events in which it was used in an attempt to quiet rebellion. It is cited both by Shakespeare's sources[6] and Elizabethans as an example of the effective public use of rhetoric which enforced obedience to political order.[7] In 1598, King James I had used the body-state analogy to argue for the primacy of the "head" or "Prince":

> As the discourse and direction flowes from the head, and the execution according thereunto belongs to the rest of the members, every one according to their office: so it is betwixt a wise Prince, and his people. As the judgement comming from the head may not onely imploy the members, every one in their owne office, as long as they are able for it; but likewise in case any of them be affected with any infirmitie must care and provide for their remedy, in-case it be curable, and if otherwise, gar cut them off for feare of infecting of the rest: even so is it betwixt the Prince, and his people. And as there is ever hope of curing any diseased member by the direction of the head, as long as it is whole; but by the contrary, if it be troubled, all the members are partakers of that paine, so is it betwixt the Prince and his people.[8]

6. Plutarch's *Coriolanus*, Livy's *Ab Urbe Condita* ii; see also Dionysius of Halicarnassus, *Roman Antiquities* vi, which, although not a direct "source," merits lengthy discussion in G. Bullough, *Narrative and Dramatic Sources of Shakespeare* 5 (London: Routlege, 1964): 462–73.

7. Significant literary uses in English occur in Edmund Spenser, *Faerie Queene* (1596), IV.2.2.7, *The Poetical Works of Edmund Spenser*, ed. J. C. Smith (Oxford: at the Clarendon Press, 1909), 2.19, and Sir Philip Sidney, *Apologie for Poetrie* (1595), *The Complete Works of Sir Philip Sidney*, ed. A. Feuillerat (Cambridge, Eng.: at the University Press, 1912–26), 3:21.

8. James I, "The Trew Law of Free Monarchies," *Political Works*

The political possibilities held out include only, on the one hand, rule by the "Belly," an aristocracy of which the regal equivalent, the consul, is a part, or, on the other hand, rule by the "Members," the common people, that is to say, democracy. This is an initial limitation deliberately imposed by the author: Shakespeare thus avoids suggesting the fully developed mixed government that Polybius described in Rome, that Italian theorists described in Italy—and that English theorists described in England. The action of *Coriolanus* takes place at a time of crisis, in the clash between only two opposing extremes.

The subject of Roman politics is not allowed to remain static with the application of this fable; the private counterpart to public concerns now appears as Menenius quiets the people. Caius Marcius himself enters, promptly striking a new tone of sternness:

> What's the matter, you dissentious rogues
> That, rubbing the poor itch of your opinion,
> Make yourselves scabs?
>
> (I.i.163–65)

This tone has proved to be a stumbling block for twen-

---

of James I, ed. C. H. McIlwain (Cambridge, Mass.: Harvard University Press, 1918), p. 65. That James's application of the fable was eccentric is shown by the study of P. Archambault, "The Analogy of the 'Body' in Renaissance Political Literature," *BHR* 29 (1967):21–53. Although to this study it might be added that republican views rejected the organic metaphor because it allowed the state to be a reality transcending its parts (see *Coriolanus* I.i.65–71) whereas they saw it as only the sum of those parts, yet, generally, writers using the body analogy were, as Archambault states, "concerned . . . with limiting, by an appeal to forces within or without the Prince, the absolute, arbitrary power of rule" (p. 52). One relevant example is Sir Walter Ralegh, who gave James an opposing but equally commonplace answer: "Shall the head yield to the feet? Certainly it ought, where they are grieved; for wisdom will rather regard the commodity, than object the disgrace; seeing if the feet lie in fetters, the head cannot be freed, and where the feet feel but their own pains, the head doth not only suffer by participation, but withal by consideration of the evil." *The Works of Sir Walter Raleigh* (Oxford: at the Clarendon Press, 1829), 8:155.

tieth-century critics, for by and large they have allowed
it to determine their condemning response to the character.[9] For one thing, often no distinction is made between
Marcius and the Marcius who is later absorbed into the
public name Coriolanus. Hence he has been charged with
self-centered pride[10] resulting from childish stubbornness[11] and with radical deficiency as a human being;[12]
his refusal to change has been related to the fact that
Coriolanus is a simple, limited hero never given an "in-
side" to be torn apart by doubt.[13]

Others have tried to account for, indeed to justify,
Coriolanus's disagreeable qualities. Eugene Waith has
argued that it is inappropriate to see the play's action
in the conventional terms of approval and disapproval;
if the audience is to react at all appropriately to what is
presented, it ought to overlook the impulse to disapprove,
and respond to heroism with *admiratio,* wonder, a response covering a range of emotions from awe to aston-
ishment.[14] Such a view presupposes a positive dramatic
presentation of the hero's major quality, which Waith,
following Werner Jaeger, terms *areté,* or *virtus,* valor

---

9. Two exceptions are: H. M. Richmond, *Shakespeare's Political
Plays* (New York: Random House, 1967), which refers to the confrontation of the people by Coriolanus as "the confrontation of the mediocre
by the true norm of civic responsibility," p. 223; and H. Oliver, "Coriolanus as Tragic Hero," *SQ* 10 (1959):53–60.

10. M. W. MacCallum, *Shakespeare's Roman Plays and their Background* (London: Macmillan, 1910), pp. 598, 602.

11. E. Honig, *"Sejanus* and *Coriolanus:* a Study in Alienation," *MLQ*
12 (1951):408, 421.

12. W. Farnham, *Shakespeare's Tragic Frontier* (Berkeley: University of California Press, 1950), p. 263.

13. A. C. Bradley, *"Coriolanus"* ("British Academy Lecture"); London and New York: Oxford University Press, 1912), pp. 5ff; M. Proser,
The Heroic Image in Five Shakespearean Tragedies (Princeton:
Princeton University Press, 1965), pp. 138–44; also W. Rosen, *Shakespeare and the Craft of Tragedy* (Cambridge, Mass.: Harvard University Press, 1960), pp. 187, 206.

14. Eugene Waith, *The Herculean Hero in Marlowe, Chapman,
Shakespeare and Dryden* (London: Chatto and Windus, 1962), p. 38;
see also J. V. Cunningham, *Woe or Wonder* ([Denver,] University of
Denver Press, [1951]), pp. 62–105.

(*Cor.* II.ii.82-83). However, can one accurately speak of Coriolanus's "aspiration . . . towards that ideal and supra-personal sphere, in which alone he can have real value"?[15] The question of the hero's nobility is not simple: strength, fortitude, constancy,[16] and self-assurance he has, but self-centeredness can only with difficulty be called acceptable "devotion to his integrity,"[17] noble in a character who is so clearly involved in the life of his country.

Nevertheless, the play is, as Waith points out, the "impossibility . . . of reliving a myth";[18] Coriolanus does not live in "social ether,"[19] and criticism must take into consideration the social and political demands placed upon him. Clearly there is a tension between him and others; Maurice Charney has written that "the essence of the tragedy lies in the grinding and pull of the public and private motives, choices, and abilities."[20] The play

---

15. Werner Jaeger, *Paideia* 1 (New York: Oxford University Press, 1939), p. 8.

16. Rosen, pp. 163, 201; for a simplistic approach, see C. B. Watson, *Shakespeare and the Renaissance Concept of Honor* (Princeton: Princeton University Press, 1960), p. 258, and, for a corrective, Norman Rabkin, *Shakespeare and the Common Understanding* (New York: Free Press, 1967), p. 12. The presence of the Roman commonwealth thus makes ironic such a quality as Coriolanus's heroic constancy, which of course was uncritically extolled by classical and Christian stoicism and its latter-day adherents, for example Guillaume Du Vair's *Philosophie Morale des Stoiques* (1585; London ed. 1598, STC 7374) and Justus Lipsius's *De Constantia* (1584; London ed. 1595, STC 15695).

17. In addition to Waith, p. 24, see Irving Ribner, "Tragedy of Coriolanus," *ES* 34 (1953):1–9.

18. Waith, p. 138.

19. Northrop Frye, *Anatomy of Criticism* (Princeton: Princeton University Press, 1957), p. 284.

20. *Shakespeare's Roman Plays* (Cambridge, Mass.: Harvard University Press, 1961), p. 217. But he goes on to mislead; there is, he adds, "some common ground between Shakespeare's English and Roman history plays, for both offer a sort of case-book of illustrations for Elizabethan political theory." The following specifically accept *Coriolanus* as reflecting predictable Elizabethan political views. Oliver, p. 57; O. J. Campbell, *Shakespeare's Satire* (Oxford: Oxford University Press, 1943), p. 203, and Reuben Brower, *Coriolanus* by William Shakespeare. Signet classic Shakespeare (New York: New American Library, 1966), p. xlix.

itself prevents the critic from seeing in Coriolanus an ideal representation of the patrician class or of the noble Roman or English soldier: qualities which in other contexts (or, more accurately, in the absence of them) might be extolled must here be condemned. The unswerving personal pursuit of honor and valor is dangerous to society; the point is made eloquently by the Venetian Doge Leonardo Donà, in the passage that serves as epigraph to this book.[21]

Instead, therefore, of propagandistic illustration of foregone conclusions, the audience should expect the long process of weighing opposing claims, complicated by changing dramatic situations. With reference to the speech with which this short digression began, there is no overwhelming reason to convict Marcius at this early moment of inhuman hatred: in *2 Henry VI*, for instance, Sir Humphrey Stafford uses similar terms which are approved in the context of the Cade rebellion:

> Rebellions hinds, the filth and scum of Kent,
> Mark'd for the gallows! Lay your weapons down;
> Home to your cottages; foresake this groom.
>
> (IV.ii.130–32)

In the Roman play, the effect of the speech is not to alienate Marcius from the audience's sympathy; rather, it demonstrates the disparity of attitudes toward the common people existing within the aristocracy. Menenius, and presumably other patricians like him, will cajole the people, but Marcius will not. Immediately recognizable as an aristocratic extremist, he attacks the people for their chronic discontent and uncertainty:

> He that trusts to you,
> Where he should find you lions, finds you hares;

---

21. I have translated Donà's speech from *Paolo V e La Republica Veneta*, ed. Enrico Cornet (Vienna: Tendler, 1859), pp. 297–98. For the context in which Donà spoke, see William J. Bouwsma, *Venice and the Defense of Republican Liberty* (Berkeley: University of California Press, 1968), pp. 410–11.

Where foxes, geese: you are no surer, no,
Than is the coal of fire upon the ice,
Or hailstone in the sun.

(ll. 169–73)

The controlling body-state analogy makes clear Coriolanus's meaning: the government of Rome must be unified and autocratic, a reflection of his personal constancy. However, the presence of a powerful social context indicates that the value of constancy, in its private and public aspects, is to be tested: in this way Shakespeare makes a Renaissance commonplace take on intensely dramatic life.

Before the audience can take in Coriolanus's speeches, it learns that the cowardly people who tell tales and gossip are represented elsewhere by the "other troop." Despite that it too is criticized for sighing "forth proverbs" (l. 204), it has managed to extract from the patricians the constitutional establishment of popular magistrates, the tribunes.

This momentous event, presenting Rome's government as changing, occurs offstage, thus keeping the immediate action and characters directly before the audience.[22] The establishment of the tribunate, a major republican victory praised by many on the Continent in the Renaissance and still in the Counter-Reformation,[23] and that mirrored the goals of some of the representatives to England's House of Commons, is undercut in this way: it is associated with innovation and insurrection. Although this change made Rome's a mixed government, the politics of the event are interpreted for the audience, by means of this indirect presentation, as the prospect of popular sovereignty. Although ordinarily the new state would have been seen by some members of the

---

22. Cf. the discussion of *Julius Caesar,* above, chapter 2.
23. See Jean Bodin, *Six Bookes of the Commonweale,* trans. R. Knolles (1606), ed. K. D. McRae (Cambridge, Mass.: Harvard University Press, 1962), p. 246.

audience as a parallel to Jacobean England, it could not, in this instance and in this manipulated staging, be approved by any but the most militant of extremists in the audience. No doubt the latter would have argued against the presentation, and insisted that both Rome and England had mixed governments; but Shakespeare's play does not admit this possibility into the action. Of all the available possibilities of presenting this political situation, Shakespeare chooses one consonant with King James's royalist view of it as a rivalry between absolute monarchy and democracy, between rule and misrule, between order and chaos. James had firm objections to democracy, and in discussing the troubled politics of Scotland in his childhood, he had put the problem in a similar way. In *Basilikon Doron,* he observed that certain "fierie spirited men in the ministerie," seeking to establish a democracy,

> gote such a guyding of the people at that time of confusion, as finding the guste of government sweete, they begouth to fantasie to themselves, a Democratick forme of government: and having (by the iniquity of time) bene over-well baited upon the wracke, . . . setled themselves so faste upon that imagined Democracie, as they fed themselves with the hope to become *Tribuni plebis.*[24]

Onstage, the voicing of opposing reactions to the new tribunate underlines the differences between the parties: Marcius refers to the tribunes as existing simply "to defend their vulgar wisdoms" (l. 214), yet the people are made so exceedingly happy that they "threw their

24. James VI, *Basilikon Doron of James VI,* 1, ed. James Craigie (Edinburgh: for the Scottish Text Society, 3rd Series, 1944) :75. I shall quote from the 1603 text in this edition, which provides three texts, with full notes and commentary. There is a marginal note to this passage, which reads, "Suche were the Demagogi at Athens"; since the governments of Rome, Sparta and Athens were commonly identified, the mixed state might be easily associated with democracy. See also K. Von Fritz, *The Theory of the Mixed Constitution in Antiquity* (New York: Columbia University Press, 1954), p. 7.

caps/ As they would hang them on the horns o'th'
moon,/ Shouting their emulation" (I.i.211-13). This
joy measures the importance of the event, the change in
government allowing the plebeians a legal role in the
state's affairs rivaling that of the aristocrats. Marcius
objects to the tribunate on the grounds that it will "in
time/ Win upon power and throw forth greater themes/
For insurrection's arguing" (ll. 218-20). After this
abstract objection, both practical and theoretical politics
are held in abeyance while the Roman heroes rally to
meet the Volscian threat and exit to defeat it during the
rest of Act One. When they leave the stage, two of the
five tribunes (the only two the audience ever sees) remain to reflect on Marcius.

The first scene thus ends as it began, with popular
commentary directed at Marcius: this technique of
"commonweale" framing of heroism will be characteristic of the play.[25] The point of reference throughout is
the civilian state of Rome; Marcius's military heroism
is admitted, but it is his civilian behavior that is discussed
and subjected to some consideration. The elements in
the presentation of the mob itself that mitigated the
acceptability of its comments on Marcius are removed
in the case of the tribunes; the latter, by contrast to their
constituency, are not stupid and do not vacillate. They
are adroit politicians.

They agree that since Marcius wants to gain fame, he

---

25. Cf. Samuel Daniel's *Civil Wars,* Book 8 of which was added in
1609; stanza 7 similarly frames heroic action:

> But, here no *Cato* with a Senate stood
> For Common-wealth: nor here were any sought
> T'emancipate the State, for publique good;
> But onely, headlong, for their faction wrought.
> Here, every man runs-on to spend his bloud,
> To get but what he had already got.
> For, whether *Pompey,* or a *Caesar* wonne,
> Their state was ever sure to be all one.

The Civil Wars, ed. L. Michel (New Haven: Yale University Press,
1958), p. 267.

is wise to be second in command:[26] for if things go ill in the wars, the people will be disposed to wish that he had commanded, and if things go well, the people will thank him (ll. 262-75). They charge that he has plotted to gain fame by means characteristic of civilian politics; by means, that is, which are political and distinctly unheroic. This ascription of deliberate insidiousness to Marcius contradicts the audience's impression of him: such duplicity seems impossible in the blunt early-Roman hero. However the suggestion lingers, reflecting on the speakers as well as on Marcius; it lingers in the audience's mind, reminding it, during the battle scenes, that this is what Marcius will return to.

The events of the following two scenes present aspects of the heroic side of the total action. Aufidius is established as Marcius's antagonist (I.i.227-35; I.ii.12, 34-36) in an honorable and heroic engagement; and the qualities observed in Marcius are shown to exist in his mother Volumnia and his son, whose aggressive warlike behavior proceeds like his father's, with success and disregard for the value of the thing captured (and destroyed):[27] young Marcius tears the "gilded butterfly" apart in "one on's father's moods" (I.iii.67).

Although this formulation must provoke audience disapproval of the elder Marcius, the note of irony directed at the heroic world in Valeria's rendering of the Penelope story (ll. 83-85) remains, on the whole, muted during the subsequent battle scenes. In these actions, Marcius exercises virtues of rough, early-Roman military behav-

---

26. P. A. Jorgensen, *Shakespeare's Military World* (Berkeley: University of California Press, 1956), pp. 38–43, 50–54, discusses contemporary attitudes toward divided command, and analyzes the two instances of it in *Coriolanus:* the partnerships of Coriolanus and Cominius and later with Aufidius. Cf. the remarks of the tribunes, I.i.260–71 with those of the Lieutenant, IV.vii.12–16.

27. Coriolanus's heroic self-concern has been noticed by several critics, who generally condemn it: see G. W. Knight, *The Imperial Theme* (London: Oxford University Press, 1931), p. 161; M. Proser, p. 147, and D. A. Traversi, *"Coriolanus," Scrutiny* 6 (1937):51–53.

ior that successfully defeats the enemy and enables him to capture the enemy city Corioli singlehandedly. Rome's common soldiers show themselves in battle to be as unheroic and irresponsible as they are in peacetime (I.iv. 29 SD; I. v). As in Plutarch, so in the play Marcius's victorious bravery is solitary, in contrast with the modest success of the troops under Cominius (I.vi.1-9). As in Menenius's handling of the people, Cominius's compromise is a practical, but entirely less noble, solution to human difficulties. Compromise led to the establishment of tribunes, danger to the established state; and compromise on the battlefield would certainly not have won the war, particularly against an army led by Marcius's worthy antagonist Aufidius.

By I.ix Rome has won its military victory, and the play prepares to direct the audience's attention back to the city. Cominius, the first in command and historically the reigning Consul,[28] looks forward to bearing the news of victory and of Marcius's bravery to Rome—that is, transporting them to a civilian climate. While still in a military environment, Marcius is inclined to reject praise, saying that he has done what he could for his country (ll. 15-19); he also refuses to accept special awards for his services. On this apparent virtue Cominius comments:

> Too modest are you;
> More cruel to your good report than grateful
> To us that give you truly. By your patience,
> If 'gainst yourself you be incensed, we'll put you
> (Like one that means his proper harm) in manacles,
> Then reason safely with you.
>
> (I.ix.53–58)

He proceeds to honor Marcius with the additional name

---

28. Plutarch, *Coriolanus* 8, *Plutarch's Lives of the Noble Grecians and Romans Englished by Sir Thomas North* (1579). Tudor Translations (London: Nutt, 1895), 2:150.

"Coriolanus" (ll. 58-66), by which the hero is hereafter called, except by his enemies. Whether Coriolanus likes it or not, his military actions will be brought into the Forum. The subjection of military victory to civilian reward, begun here, is paralleled even in the heroic plane by Aufidius, who adopts villainous "policy":

> Mine emulation
> Hath not that honour in't it had; for where
> I thought to crush him in an equal force,
> True sword to sword, I'll potch at him some way,
> Or wrath or craft may get him.
>
> (I.x.12–16)

Specific plans are for the moment not formulated; Aufidius remains for some time a vague threat. When he reappears, his antagonism will be acted out in politics.

Act Two

At the beginning of Act Two, the tribunes are speaking with Menenius about the outcome of the war and Coriolanus's possible success. Although Menenius's part in this conversation is comic,[29] much of what he says is quite serious. He tells the two tribunes that despite their age, they are not wise, and that they are "a brace of unmeriting, proud, violent, testy magistrates (alias fools) as any in Rome" (ll. 42-44).[30] In answer to countercriticism, he replies that "What I think I utter, and spend my malice in my breath" (ll. 52-53), a moderate straightforwardness that is in marked contrast to the tribunes. He significantly mentions that they are not "Lycurguses" (l. 54), referring to the esteemed Spar-

---

29. O. J. Campbell, p. 204.
30. Wilson's editorial note (p. 173, note to l. 43) on this remark juxtaposes the English gentry's attitude toward London Justices of the Peace.

tan law-giver, whose biography Plutarch wrote and who was a standard of political wisdom.[31] Menenius further criticizes these magistrates for being unable to solve petty problems: they leave controversies "the more entangled by [their] hearing." (1. 76). In this important interchange, Menenius's moderation encourages belief, and the succeeding action of the play makes more serious his suggestions that the tribunes are "unmeriting, proud, violent."

According to the stage directions, the tribunes now stand "aside," both enacting the alienation of one major section of Rome from the heroic business of the patricians and also contributing to framing that action by their later comments. The mother and wife of Coriolanus, accompanied by Valeria,[32] enter with good news of the Roman victory. Entering in a grand triumphant procession between Cominius and the silent Titus Lartius, Coriolanus kneels before his mother (1. 167SD). Volumnia, who has darkly mentioned that her son will "stand for his place" (1. 147), once again suggests that "one thing" still lacks (1. 198); but Coriolanus seems to disclaim interest in it. When the procession leaves, the tribunes once again step forward.

The tribunes now for the first time make clear plans for the future, at the same time revealing themselves. So far, the audience has heard of their potential evil only from patrician lips; but now the tribunes begin to conform to royalist expectations of "Tribunes of the people." The names of the two tribunes are Junius Brutus and Sicinius Velutus. The first was also the name of the republican hero[33] who led the overthrow of the kings in Rome; as such Shakespeare had presented him in *Lucrece,* and mentioned him in *Julius Caesar* as an

---

31. He was an *approved* "innovating wealsman" (Wilson, p. 173). Wilson suggests that Shakespeare knew Plutarch's *Lycurgus.*
32. On Valeria, see above, chapter 2, n. 19.
33. Plutarch, *Publicola* 1, in 1:249–50.

ancestor to Marcus Brutus. On the Continent, the name was linked to later anti-monarchist formulations: "Junius Brutus" is, for instance, the pseudonym of the author of an important and influential tract in French Protestant political theory, the *Vindiciae contra Tyrannos* (1579),[34] usually attributed to Sidney's friend Hubert Languet, to Philippe de Duplessis-Mornay, or, by some, to François Hotman, Theodore de Bèze, or even Robert Parsons. The anonymous tract was widely known, and was especially dear to foes of tyranny; such men almost deified Brutus and certainly glorified the revolt against the Tarquins.[35] Like most of the Huguenot tracts,[36] the *Vindiciae* is not fully republican, but rather anti-monarchist in the sense that it wishes to replace government-by-royal-sovereignty with government by some form of popular sovereignty. The author's single reference to England, knowledge of which he in all likelihood derived from John Knox and Christopher Goodman, is to say "in the kingdom of England and Scotland the sovereignty seems to be in the Parliament. . . . The authority of this assembly has been so sacred and inviolable, that the king dare not abrogate or alter what had been there once decreed."[37] This formulation, in a widely read work, of a delicate point of contemporary controversy would have made the *Vindiciae* and the very name Junius Brutus unpalatable to King James.

A related negative association of Junius Brutus is with the action of another man, reported in detail by Dionysius of Halicarnassus. At the time of the secession of the common people, a vain, pretentious, but shrewd man

34. An English translation of chapter 4 appeared in Hubert Languet's *A Short Apology for Christian Soldiers* (1588), STC 15207. Latin editions appeared in 1579 and 1580.

35. H. Laski, ed., *Vindiciae contra Tyrannos: a Defense of Liberty against Tyrants* (London: Bell, 1924), p. 23.

36. The exception is La Boétie's *Discours sur la Servitude Volontaire, ou Contr'un* (ca. 1548; reprinted 1576).

37. *Vindiciae,* p. 134.

named Lucius Junius, who added the surname Brutus
for the sake of its popular appeal, acted as spokesman
for the people. This Brutus demanded popular magistrates, because he

> feared the time to come and the tyrannical men who might
> one day if occasion offered, again attempt to make the people
> feel their resentment for what they had done. There was one
> safeguard only, he said, for any who were afraid of their
> superiors, and that was for them to be convinced that those
> who desired to injure them had not the power to do so; for
> as long as there was the power to do evil, evil men would
> never lack the will.[38]

Dionysius's account contains two elements of relevance
to *Coriolanus*. First, a tribune named Lucius Junius Brutus craftily takes the name of the leader of the rebellion
against the Tarquins; but that hero later became not a
tribune, but a consul. The false Brutus appropriates the
name for the popularity and the associations of freedom
that attach to it. Second, the plebeians' view is that the
patricians are an evil force alien to their interests, against
whom they must defend themselves; the official government is not at all an agency of the whole community.

Such are the immediate associations of the Brutus
who describes to his colleague and the play's audience
the popular reception of the hero. Sicinius concludes that
Coriolanus will be consul, within the Roman republic
analogous to kingship; this is the fitting reward for the
military leader, what Volumnia had referred to earlier,
and what Coriolanus had seemed to disclaim interest in.
But one detail is missing: in order to make clearer the
opposition between an extremist among aristocrats and
extremist leaders among the people, Shakespeare does
not mention the fact that Rome normally had a second

---

38. Dionysius of Halicarnassus, *Roman Antiquities* vi.87. Loeb Classical Library (Cambridge, Mass.: Harvard University Press, 1937), in
4:115. On Renaissance school-use of Dionysius, see above, chapter 2,
n. 57.

consul, of equal power, who acted as a check to the first. This distortion of history makes the parallel to English kingship more pointed.

Coriolanus is endorsed by the Senate to be a candidate for the consulate, and must be approved by the people. The tribunes see a threat of an anti-plebeian monarchist government; for good reason Brutus remarks "then our office may/ During his power go sleep" (ll. 219-20). They consider their situation politically, noting (the adverb will be of great significance) that Coriolanus "cannot temp'rately transport his honours" (l. 221) and that the people, being indeed as unstable as Coriolanus indicated, forget their dislikes:

> Doubt not
> The commoners, for whom we stand, but they
> Upon their ancient malice will forget
> With the least cause these his new honours.
> (ll. 223-26)

They report, to the audience, that Coriolanus once swore that he would not appear before the people in the "napless vesture of humility" (l. 231); they decide this attitude will be "to him . . . / A sure destruction" (ll. 239-40). Brutus summarizes the uncompromising rivalry clearly, in the same way Coriolanus does later: "So it must fall out/ To him or our authorities" (ll. 240-41).

The tribunes plan to act surreptitiously, to "suggest" (l. 242) Coriolanus's hatred and the prospect of oppression to the people; this, Sicinius adds, should be suggested—the repetition enforces the duplicity—at a time when "his soaring insolence/ Shall touch" them (ll. 251-52). The contrast between the great, unwavering and therefore predictable Coriolanus and the petty, politically effective, and crafty tribunes is unmistakable.

The presentation of the now-evil tribunes who continue

to demonstrate their evil through the rest of the play corresponds to King James's view of his opponents in the House of Commons. As a reigning monarch, James was none too happy about a functioning Parliament. Publicly, he acknowledged that its purpose was to make good laws; privately, he understood the tradition of calling Parliament in England, at least occasionally, and appreciated the revenue he got from it. Otherwise it was

> the in-justest judgement-seate that may be, being abused to mens particulars: irrevocable decreits against particulare parties being given therin under colour of generall lawes, & ofttimes th' Estates not knowing themselves whome therby they hurt.[39]

In another passage attributing the decay of the Roman Catholic church to "Pride, Ambition, and Avarice," he discussed the extremity of the opposition, the Scottish reformation,

> wherein many things were inordinatly done by a populare tumult & rebellion, of such as blindly were doing the work of God, but clogged with their owne passions and particular respects, as well appeared by the destruction of our policie; and not proceeding from the Princes ordour.[40]

This passage bears the marginal note: "The occasion of the Tribunat of some Puritanes." Similarly, the Roman commonwealth, which ought to glorify and be glorified by the heroic action, is in the hands of the "evil tribunes" who do not react as their constituency does; rather, motivated perhaps according to Menenius's suggestion, by pride, they actively seek control of the state. In his contemporary and Crown-approved book, Edward Forset had observed that, as disease in an important part of the body is most serious, just so is the case of men in important places:

39. *Basilikon Doron,* p. 61.
40. *Ibid.,* p. 75.

Factious, (besides their withdrawing of their faith, alleageance, and former good services) they doe not only seduce the unskilfull and unruly Commons, but also traine on with their suggestion of colourable causes, some officers of publique trust (as parts of the reasonable power) to adhere unto them in their misconceiving adventures, till all be endaungered by such mutinous confusion.[41]

The application to tribunes who become evil is clear.[42]

Act Two, scene two also frames the centrally placed heroic celebrations with civilian assessments. The scene begins with a reasonable conversation on Coriolanus between two anonymous Officers.[43] Following immediately upon the tribunes' planning, this discussion modifies, by means of the impartial assessment of choral characters, the terms in which the tribunes saw him; at the same time it stresses the knowledge that the context in which Coriolanus exists is now civilian. The discussion also extends more seriously the play's first interchange on Coriolanus; in reply to the Second Officer's report that Coriolanus will probably be elected, winning against two unnamed opponents (l. 3), First Officer says that Coriolanus is "vengeance proud." His interlocutor prefers to call this "his noble carelessness," and says that no matter what, Coriolanus has "deserved worthily of his country" (l. 23); whatever one may think further about him, "for their [the people's] tongues to be silent and not

41. *A Comparative Discourse of the Bodies Natural and Politique* (London, 1606), sigs. L4^v–M1^r. STC 11188.

42. Harry Levin, ed., *Coriolanus* by William Shakespeare ("Pelican Shakespeare"; Baltimore: Penguin, 1956), p. 21, observes that "interpretation has varied between the extremes of left and right," and that Shakespeare's treatment of the multitude "is anti-demagogic rather than anti-democratic." However, in the early seventeenth century the two were not so neatly separable.

43. The scene with the officers is drawn from Plutarch's *Comparison* between Alcibiades and Coriolanus: see G. Bullough, 5:482. These officers, Harley Granville-Barker pertinently observes, are not plebeian, but "of a definite dignity, the equivalent, possibly, in Shakespeare's mind, to officers of Parliament, who may bring to their covenanted respect for its members, Lords or Commons, a very critical private view of their individual worth." *Prefaces to Shakespeare* (Princeton: Princeton University Press, 1951), 2:207 n.

confess so much were a kind of ingrateful injury" (ll. 29-30). First Officer ends the discussion by agreeing that he is "a worthy man" (l. 33), a phrase Menenius repeats immediately after Cominius's speech of praise.

When the two Officers leave the stage, the business of the Senate begins. The occasion is a formal public recognition of Coriolanus's greatness, expressed by means of an oration in his praise. Before Cominius can begin, a Senator, in calling for attention, asks that the tribunes listen and approve what follows. Brutus adds to Sicinius's reply that they will be happy to do so if only Coriolanus will remember "a kinder value of the people than/ He hath hereto prized them at" (ll. 57-58). Ignoring the suggestion that Coriolanus should value the people more naturally, Menenius answers

> He loves your people;
> But tie him not to be their bedfellow.
> (ll. 62–63)

This divergence of attitudes introduces the speech. After Coriolanus leaves the stage, his heroic traits and lineage are set forth by Cominius, who establishes immediately his standard of behavior: "valour" (l. 82). He illustrates it by referring to Coriolanus's fighting, at the age of sixteen, for the overthrow of the tyrannic Tarquins and in his later battles, most recently culminating in his single-handed capture of Corioli. The emphasis falls so heavily on heroic valor that it assimilates the man to it:

> His sword, death's stamp,
> Where it did mark, it took; from face to foot
> He was a thing of blood, whose every motion
> Was timed with dying cries. Alone he ent'red
> The mortal gate of th' city, which he painted
> With shunless destiny; aidless came off,
> And with a sudden re-enforcement struck
> Corioli like a planet.
> (ll. 105–12
> 108–15)

Menenius responds to this with "worthy man!" (l. 120), and the Senate agrees to support Coriolanus for the consulate. He must, however, "speak to the people" (l. 133). The tribunes notice that he promptly seeks to avoid this, to adhere to tradition and ignore the recent innovation. Menenius appeals to moderation and warns Coriolanus against insisting on the point; but the tribunes' presence reminds the audience that they are still watching for a time when "his soaring insolence/ Shall touch the people" (II.i.251).

The heroism of the *laus* is presented after a conversation that took Coriolanus into account in the social situation in Rome; as soon as it is over, that social reference returns immediately. Framed in this way, there is little reason for the audience to have hopes that could fully echo those of the Senators as they leave: "To Coriolanus come all joy and honour!" (l. 152). But, as if to insure a sense of foreboding for the future of the hero, the two tribunes are once more left alone on the stage; they almost immediately exit to report the Senate's proceedings to the awaiting people. Yet their few lines indicate that they know Coriolanus's "intent," that he will "use" the people he despises. Whatever action Coriolanus decides upon, the tribunes will be there to oppose him.

Act Two scene three proceeds in a manner analogous to that of the preceding scene: an initial discussion between men, in this case plebeians, is followed by action involving Coriolanus; after this the tribunes speak to the people. In this scene too, the final action undercuts the apparent success of the preceding.

The opening conversation concerns the approval that Coriolanus seeks. Third Citizen says that Coriolanus has done great deeds for Rome; Rome must accept them, for to do otherwise would be "ingrateful," and "ingratitude is monstrous" (ll. 10, 9).[44] There follows some comedy on the people's lack of constancy, aimed at lightening the serious tone of the preceding scenes and, no doubt, at the amusement of the gentlemen in the play's audience.

Upon entering, Coriolanus parodies the normal expectation, so that his companion, Menenius, must caution him to speak to the people temperately.[45] Unexpectedly, he does; or so at least it seems to the people. Third Citizen tells him that the "price" of the consulship is "to ask it kindly" (l. 73). Like Menenius in the preceding scene, Coriolanus ignores this suggestion of "nature," and equates the votes, or "voices," with "alms." Third Citizen senses that this unnatural indifference is "something odd" (l. 82). What characterizes Coriolanus in this scene, as elsewhere, is straightforward honesty:

> I will, sir, flatter my sworn brother, the people, to earn a dearer estimation of them; 'tis a condition they account gentle: and since the wisdom of their choice is rather to have my hat than my heart, I will practise the insinuating nod, and be off to them most counterfeitly; that is, sir, I will counterfeit the bewitchment of some popular man, and give it bountiful to the desirers. Therefore, beseech you I may be consul.
> (ll. 94–102)

Coriolanus merely lists his actions, proceeding from specific references, "wounds two dozen odd; battles thrice six," to the more generalized notion of service, "Done

44. This remark of course recalls the two Officers (II.ii.29–30); it is also ironic, for Rome was associated with ingratitude. See above, chapter 2, and below in chapter 6.

45. Plutarch contains nothing of Coriolanus's extreme dislike of seeking the people's votes; there may be in this characteristic a reflection of James's well-known dislike of crowds of commoners. See *The Time Triumphant,* by Gilbert Dugdale (London, 1604), sig. B2 (STC 7292), cited by J. W. Lever, ed., *Measure for Measure* by William Shakespeare. Arden Shakespeare (Cambridge, Mass.: Harvard University Press, 1965), p. xxxiv.

many things, some less, some more" (ll. 127-29). He knows that the people do not care about his actions, his bravery, or his heroism; they want to be appealed to, to be assured that he has performed deeds—it hardly matters which—for their approval. Coriolanus puts the matter in terms they will readily understand: "Indeed, I would be consul" (l. 130). Coriolanus has not bent to flatter the people; audience approval of such rectitude is qualified, however, by his intransigent tone. Yet because he has said what is expected and wanted, and because he goes through the ritual of appeal, the people approve the Senate's choice.

The tribunes enter to tell him, as well as the audience (which need not know more about Roman election procedures than the play tells it) that the last step will be Coriolanus's "approbation" in the Senate House (ll. 142-44), at which the people must be present. The last part of the third scene is entirely popular. The people return, having perceived that Coriolanus's indifference mocks them. When several have spoken in this vein, the tribunes intensify the popular discontent; referring to their instructions (ll. 176-77, 190), they tell the people,

> You should have said
> That as his worthy deeds did claim no less
> Than what he stood for, so his gracious nature
> Would think upon you for your voices, and
> Translate his malice toward you into love,
> Standing your friendly lord.
>
> (ll. 184–89)

This would have resulted either in extracting a promise to be honored, or in provoking his "choler" (l. 197), and so providing an excuse for not electing him.

The people are moved, and decide that "he's not confirmed," for the ceremonies of installation have yet to be performed. Nothing is made of the doubtful legality of this point and the tribunes thereupon direct the action of the crowd: the people are to warn other people of Coriolanus's tyrannic intentions, and in discussion, are to decide to revoke their approval. Further, the consuls protect themselves against charges of sedition by inviting the people to lay the blame for the election on them: the tribunes mask their villainy by seeming loyal. The people, now in a frenzy, rush off the stage; Brutus and Sicinius remain for a moment to remark that they will watch for their opportunity. The last lines make absolutely clear the process by which this result will be arrived at:

> And this shall seem, as partly 'tis, their own,
> Which we have goaded onward.
>   (ll. 261–62)

The tribunes are evil leaders—really misleaders—of the people, dramatic parallels of King James's Puritan antagonists who sought "to become *Tribuni plebis:* and so in a populare government by leading the people by the nose, to beare the sway of all the rule."[46] Audience reservations about Coriolanus's excesses are subordinated at this point to disapproval of tribune demagogues.

Act Two closes a large segment of the play's action. Heroism and politics, the extremes of Coriolanus and the tribunes, have been presented, scrutinized, and found wanting. Where is the political and moral standard?

Act Three

External danger to Rome is mentioned in the first line and provides an ominous backdrop against which succeeding events unfold. The tribunes enter and, in report-

---

46. *Basilikon Doron*, p. 75.

ing that the people are now incensed against him, give Coriolanus fuel for further expressions of disapproval of the role of the common people in government. In the following dialogue, Coriolanus extracts from the tribunes the information that the new development is a rethinking of matters already decided—his "mocking" of the people, which was at first passed over, and his refusal to agree to a free distribution of corn, a matter which had been "known before" (l. 46). Coriolanus therefore accuses the tribunes of double-dealing (l. 48); the temperate Cominius remarks that "the people are abused" (l. 57), although he tactfully refrains from saying by whom.

In a series of speeches (ll. 64-170) Coriolanus develops his view of the political situation in which this is all happening; some members of Shakespeare's audience may have had sympathy with it, but also great reservations, since it precludes any possibility of unifying the state. Coriolanus's argument develops from the tribunes' accusation that he finds the people "time-pleasers, flatterers, foes to nobleness" (l. 45). He replies by repeating a speech the audience has not heard before: in "soothing" the people, the nobility are nourishing "the cockle of rebellion, insolence, sedition" (l. 70). Despite two pleas by Menenius (ll. 63, 74), each reinforced by First Senator (ll. 64, 75), he goes on to say that, as he has protected Rome from her enemies, so he will protect her from a new enemy he likens to a disease:

> As for my country I have shed my blood,
> Not fearing outward force, so shall my lungs
> Coin words till their decay against those measles,
> Which we disdain should tetter us, yet sought
> The very way to catch them.
>
> (ll. 76–80)

The inflexible terms in which Coriolanus expresses his

argument were elicited by the extremity of the tribunes; but in any case they should have been disapproved, at least in theory, by King James, who had in earlier times written of propriety in a king's language:

> Remember also, to put a difference betwixt your forme of language in reasoning, and your pronouncing of sentences, or declaratour of your wil in judgement, or anie other waies in the points of your office. For in the former case, ye must reason pleasantlie and pacientlie, not like a king, but like a private man and a scholer: otherwaies, your impacience of contradiction will be interpreted to be for lacke of reason on your parte. Where in the pointes of your office, ye should ripelie advise indeede, before ye give forth your sentence: but fra it be given forth, the suffering of any contradiction, diminisheth the Majestie of your authoritie, and maketh the processes endlesse. The like forme would also be observed by all your inferiour judges and Magistrates.[47]

But Coriolanus is unable to work for peaceful relations and is cast in the pattern of a military hero who is an inept ruler in the civilian politics of the state—a pattern Shakespeare had employed in the tyrant Macbeth.

These words further aggravate the situation, and Sicinius concludes that Coriolanus's

>   is a mind
> That shall remain a poison where it is,
> Not poison any further.
>
>   (ll. 86–88)

Coriolanus is incensed by the presumptuousness of the tribune's "absolute 'shall'" and expands his argument along the lines earlier suggested by Menenius (II.i.42-44): the new officers will be proud and usurp dignities not suiting their office, dignities they will take away from the Senate. For him there is no possibility that both groups can wield power; "you are plebeians,/ If they

47. *Ibid.*, p. 183.

be senators" (ll. 101-2). The people will always elect

> such a one as he, who puts his "shall,"
> His popular "shall," against a graver bench
> Than ever frowned in Greece. By Jove himself,
> It makes the consuls base! and my soul aches
> To know, when two authorities are up,
> Neither supreme, how soon confusion
> May enter 'twixt the gap of both and take
> The one by th' other.
>
> (III.i.105-12)

Suggested by "Greece" and recalling Menenius's mention of Lycurgus (II.i.54), Coriolanus contrasts government in that country, where "the people had more absolute power" (ll. 115-16), to government in Rome; bowing to the people, Greece had "nourished disobedience, fed/ The ruin of the state." Similarly, for Rome to give the people corn would result in allowing "the crows to peck the eagles" (l. 139), that is, the obliteration of qualitative superiority.

Coriolanus's concluding speeches expand the concern with Rome's immediate situation to include general speculation applicable to other governments as well.

> This double worship,
> Where one part does disdain with cause, the other
> Insult without all reason; where gentry, title, wisdom,
> Cannot conclude but by the yea and no
> Of general ignorance—it must omit
> Real necessities, and give way the while
> To unstable slightness. Purpose so barred, it follows
> Nothing is done to purpose.
>
> (ll. 142-49)

The Senate, clearly, ought to abolish the tribunate; as it was granted "in a rebellion," so it should be abandoned "in a better hour" (l. 168).[48]

---

48. At l. 174, Sicinius terms Coriolanus a "traitorous innovator." The word "innovator" appears here for the only time in Shakespeare,

When the people enter, the tribunes "kindle" a fire which threatens, a senator points out, "to unbuild the city," to "lay the city flat" (ll. 197, 203). The tribunes' real threat of chaos is clear,[49] and the counter-charge, that the "people are the city," (l. 199) attractive as it may be to some members of a twentieth-century audience, is an example of the kind of thinking that will lead to destruction: such a city would be no more stable than the unstable people. Buildings and cities are characteristic images in a play in which political and social organization are so fundamental;[50] "Rome" gives its name not only to a city but to a nation as well, and the destruction foreseen is also national. The state —any state—in existence allows order and civilization; once it is destroyed, men "would feed on one another" (I.i.187).

After the people reaffirm their confidence in the tribunes (ll. 200-201), the latter, as intransigent as Coriolanus, call for his death. At this point the role of the patricians emerges with clarity: they must attempt to temper both sides. Menenius is drowned out: the result is violence, in which the people and tribunes are "beat in" (228 S D). This is the turning point: after this moment the play ceases to reflect contemporary politics. Although the English king faced a popular opposition in his lifetime, the confrontation did not proceed to the extremes now to be dramatized. The play becomes a warning to the audience of the possible, indeed the prob-

---

in a charge which is clearly a psychological projection on the part of the speaker. The word "innovation" occurs three times in Shakespeare, each time with clear disapproval: *1 Henry IV*, V.i.78; *Hamlet*, II.ii.347; and *Othello*, II.iii.42.

49. This evocation of chaos contrasts to Coriolanus's (III.ii.1–6), which is self-referent and more customary for Shakespearean tragic heroes: see E. A. M. Colman, "The End of Coriolanus," *ELH* 34 (1967):13.

50. This is in contrast to plays with Christian settings, where images of chaos and disruption are drawn from the universe at large, often with biblical overtones (*e.g.*, *2 Henry VI*, V.ii.40–45) but not to pagan Roman plays like *Julius Caesar* and *Antony and Cleopatra*.

able, consequences of the patrician failure to achieve balance. In the aftermath, the patricians call for radically modified tactics. Coriolanus must depart; force is of no use, Cominius sees, for "now 'tis odds beyond arithmetic" (l. 244). Menenius underlines this assessment by his accurate observing that Coriolanus's unbending "nature is too noble for the world" (l. 254).

The people reenter, reiterating the charge that Coriolanus is a traitor. With sickening irony, the tribunes justly appeal to law: Coriolanus "hath resisted law,/ And therefore law shall scorn him further trial/ Than the severity of the public power." They deny him the title Consul (ll. 278-79) and deny the validity of the election he has just gone through. Menenius meets them with temperate replies that Rome should show gratitude to Coriolanus, arguments that the tribunes dismiss as "clean kam" (l. 302). However, Menenius succeeds once again in quieting the crowd, referring to the dangers of not proceeding "by process," which would otherwise result in civil dissension that would "sack great Rome with Romans" (l. 314). The scene ends by the people's partly agreeing to refrain from violence while Menenius will bring Coriolanus to answer the charges against him, which is "the human way" of resolving the difficulty for the moment. The difficulty of getting Coriolanus to admit the necessary modifications, and then the impossibility of his putting his admission into action, concerns the rest of Act Three.

Scene one has presented the early stages of chaos. The only hope for Rome is that moderation will be possible, and it is precisely the possibility of modifying Coriolanus that scene two takes up. This Shakespearean addition to Plutarch's account examines the possibility of achieving the necessary compromise by presenting the attempts of the patricians to prevail on Coriolanus to moderate his extreme opinions. Although they find him injudicious,

Volumnia, the anonymous "Noble" of the first lines, and Menenius essentially agree with him:

> *Volumnia:* Pray be counselled:
> I have a heart as little apt as yours,
> But yet a brain that leads my use of anger
> To better vantage.

> *Menenius:* Well said, noble woman!
> Before he should thus stoop to th' herd—but that
> The violent fit o' th' time craves it as physic
> For the whole state—I would put mine armour on,
> Which I can scarcely bear.
>
> (III.ii.28–35)

Volumnia argues that he should adopt "policy" (l. 48), and her advice takes on an authority greater than her personal, maternal pleading:

> I am in this,
> Your wife, your son, these senators, the nobles.
>
> (ll. 64–65)

She goes on to instruct him how to appeal to the people; an opportunity to do so immediately presents itself when Cominius appears and allows that such action may be the solution to the nobility's difficulties.

Just as Coriolanus maintained an absolute public position and ignored the temperate nobility, so there is no temperance within him: he cannot achieve the middle position, between regal and popular behavior, which James felt was important:

> Be not over sparing in your courtesies; for that will be imputed to in-civility & arrogancie: nor yet over prodigal in jowking or nodding at every step; for that forme of being populare, becommeth better aspiring *Absalons,* then lawfull Kings.[51]

---

51. *Basilikon Doron,* p. 181. *Richard II,* a play of English kingship much concerned with Bolingbroke's claim to the throne, allows that

Only by making Temperance queen of the other virtues can one be a good ruler: Temperance is a "wise moderation" which should govern "not onely in all your affections and passions, but even in your moste vertuous actions."[52] But for Coriolanus, the adoption of "policy" would involve organic changes within him. His "throat of war" must be turned into "a pipe/ Small as an eunuch or the virgin voice/ That babies lulls asleep," and his face must take on the characteristics of a knave, a schoolboy; his knees must bend like those of a beggar (ll. 112-17). He wavers and decides only when Volumnia confronts him, contrasting the "valiantness" (l. 129) he has inherited from her with his "pride" (l. 130) which prevents him from acting as he should. When Coriolanus leaves, intending to act "mildly" rather than "kindly," the audience is left hoping that the compromise planned might work, but at the same time doubting both its ultimate morality and Coriolanus's ability to be mild.[53]

Scene three begins and ends with the tribunes on stage; first, Brutus announces the charges to be made against Coriolanus: "he affects/ Tyrannical power" and, if he evades this charge, "the spoil got on the Antiates/ Was ne'er distributed." (ll. 1-5). The tribunes are bringing all conceivable charges against him, and their admission that such a blunt warrior might "evade" the first is tantamount to admitting it to be trumped up. If all else fails, they plan to anger Coriolanus, for "being once

---

appeal to the populace may be either flattering or sincere (I.iv.20ff). Bolingbroke goes into exile bearing his "fortune/ As 'twere to banish their [the people's] affects with him," an ambiguous statement, as M. M. Mahood has pointed out in *Shakespeare's Word-Play* (London: Methuen, 1957), p. 79. However, *Coriolanus* is about the people's right to political expression; although the concern here is deeper than in the earlier play, there is no ambiguity in the choice Coriolanus must make: either he must flatter or he must seek to dispossess the people of their political power.

52. *Basilikon Doron*, pp. 137-39.

53. This scene, in which Volumnia persuades Coriolanus to agree to a trial by the people, is, as Bullough has pointed out (5:485), a parallel to Menenius's calming of the tribunes' rage.

chafed, he cannot/ Be reined again to temperance" (ll. 27-28).

Coriolanus is the only patrician who cannot respond to the ideal of Temperance, which is the more important not only because of its place in the Greco-Roman and Christian traditions, but also because King James so strongly urged it. According to his precepts, a king

> cannot be thought worthie to rule and command others, that cannot rule and dantone his owne proper affections and unreasonable appetites.[54]

For a King,

> any sinne that ye committe . . . [is] an exemplare sinne, & therefore drawing with it the whole multitude to be guiltie of the same.[55]

Coriolanus is manipulated and the result is fully anticipated by an audience which has recently seen the action of III.i and knows the extremity to which the intemperate Coriolanus is easily pushed. Coriolanus enters to a caution from Menenius, "Calmly, I beseech you" (l. 31), and a prayer for Rome's safety, for justice administered by "worthy men," love, and peace (ll. 33-37). He interrupts Menenius's persuasive argument and asks why, "being passed for consul with full voice" (l. 59), he must see the honor removed from him in the same hour. The personal reference is typical; although the question is about the change in the people's understanding that has led to the present situation, it is presented in terms of himself. The charge of seeking to be tyrant is begun by Sicinius in line 63, and the scene ends at line 143 with Coriolanus's banishment imposed; thus quickly are the results brought about by the tribunes' charge, thus quick is Coriolanus's reaction.

---

54. *Basilikon Doron,* p. 25. Temperance had been alluded to by the tribunes also, who associated its lack with ultimate failure in II.i.221–23.
55. *Ibid.,* p. 27.

Coriolanus's objections to the existing state are directed at the tribunate, which is here included in "all seasoned office" (l. 64),—ironically, for a Jacobean court audience, and for any audience remembering the establishment of the tribunate in I.i. The word "traitor" ignites Coriolanus's temper, and by line 75 the people are crying "To th' rock, to th' rock with him." The tribunes are careful to formulate Coriolanus's offenses in legal terms (ll. 77-82) and, in banishing him, insist on their legal right:

> In the name o' th' people,
> And in the power of us the tribunes, we,
> Even from this instant, banish him our city,
> In peril of precipitation
> From off the rock Tarpeian, never more
> To enter our Rome gates. I' th' people's name,
> I say it shall be so.
>
> (ll. 99–105)

At this moment Cominius interjects the major speech which evokes social and emotional positives. He treasures his country's good:

> I have been consul, and can show for Rome
> Her enemies' marks upon me. I do love
> My country's good with a respect more tender,
> More holy and profound, than mine own life,
> My dear wife's estimate, her womb's increase
> And treasure of my loins; then if I would
> Speak that—
>
> (ll. 110–16)

Like all appeals by the aristocracy, his words are interrupted by the extremist exponents of action, in this case the tribunes, who change the sentence to banishment.[56]

---

56. Presumably to avoid the danger of civil war fought between patricians and plebeians, the sentence is changed from the death penalty to banishment; when the latter is proposed, it recalls Sicinius's observation that "to eject him hence/ Were but our danger, and to keep him here/ Our certain death" (III.i.285-87).

The placing of the patrician Cominius's appeal to Temperance indicates that Coriolanus and the tribunes are at opposite extremes, just as they were in the play's first scene. The speech, an evocation of the grounds of a mean course, establishes poetically a norm which is not given a practical role in the play. The scene ends with Coriolanus's speech banishing "you," the tribune-led people, and "despising/ For you the city," which he leaves a prey to foreign invasion.

Act Four

To enforce a sense of Coriolanus's isolation (present since his victory in Corioli), Shakespeare modified Plutarch's account and has the hero leave Rome alone. The presentation of a Rome not restored to health by his banishment shows that no cure has been effected, and that some further action on his part is inevitable. The point is made clear by Volumnia's taunting of the tribunes in scene two: she continues the internal division of Rome by speaking like Coriolanus (cf. III.iii.89-90, IV.ii.50-51). In Menenius's view she too is extreme, and he cautions her, significantly, much as he cautioned her son, with "peace, peace" (ll. 12, 29).

Rome continues to be divided and weak: this condition is made common public knowledge by the interchange between "a Roman and a Volsce" (IV.iii.1 SD) which reports that the nobility of Rome may disestablish the tribunate. The division of the "people against the senators, patricians, and nobles," is to be taken advantage of by the Volscians, who hope to "come upon them in the heat of their division" (ll. 18-19).

The presence of the antagonistic Volscians is a constant threat to Rome. Since, later in history, Rome extended its boundaries and unified the peninsula, the threat is ultimately the result of division, when geography and language suggested the possibility of union.[57] James was of course in favor of the unification of Britain, and the play's action corresponds to his remarks on the subject. Unification

> may easilie be done betwixt these two nations, beeing both but one Ile of *Britaine,* and alreadie joyned in unitie of Religion, & language. So that even as in the times of our ancestors, the long warres and many bloodie battels betwixt these two countries, bred a naturall and haereditarie hatred in every of them, against the other: the uniting and welding of them heerafter in one, by all sort of friendship, commerce, and alliance: will by the contrary, produce and maintaine a naturall & inseparable unitie of love amongst them.[58]

But at this moment, Coriolanus's defection to the Volscians is, in the terms of the play, defection to an enemy power. The decision has been considered to be inadequately motivated but it is elaborately explained and accounted for in public terms in discussion with Aufidius. Coriolanus will join Aufidius "in mere spite,/ To be full quit of those my banishers" (IV.v.85-86), and asks only that Aufidius take advantage of this opportunity and turn it to his own account in helping Coriolanus fight against his "cank'red country" (l. 94). Aufidius agrees to do so; and Coriolanus is made the deciding factor in this attack on Rome, since Aufidius was prepared only to march "against your territories,/ Though not for Rome itself" (ll. 137-38). Coriolanus is cast, then, in the role of a leader who marches on his own country in

---

57. Granville-Barker stresses the "dramatic effect" of dressing adversaries distinctly (p. 155 n.). But a Jacobean audience aware of James's interest in unifying Britain would regard the clash of English and Scots troops from a point of view rather different from that from which they regarded the Egyptian-Roman clash in *Antony*. Knowledge of later Roman history would tend to make the situation in *Coriolanus* closer to those in *Macbeth* and *King Lear* than to those in the later tragedy.

58. *Basilikon Doron,* p. 201; cf. the "Speech of 1607," *Political Works,* ed. McIlwain, pp. 292-98.

revenge, leading enemy troops, and seeking its destruction.

Because the banishment of Coriolanus leads so directly into his subsequent actions, it is necessary to attempt to see the ways Shakespeare's audience might have understood it. Coriolanus is the monarch, or more properly the monarch-analogue, forced into exile; the exile itself does not necessarily cause the audience to accept his guilt or to judge him guilty of high treason. Indeed, in Shakespeare generally, banishment from Rome illustrates Rome's "ingratitude" to the individual for loyal service. The standard Shakespearean adjective is "ingrateful," and it recurs, after the Elizabethan *Titus Andronicus* (V.i.12), with noticeable frequency in plays of the early Jacobean years: in *Coriolanus* (II.ii.30, II.iii.10) *Timon of Athens* (IV.ii.45, IV.iii.194) and *King Lear* (II.iv. 165, III.ii.9). The noun "ingratitude" appears more frequently; a related use is that of Sextus Pompeius, speaking of his father, Caesar's antagonist (*Antony and Cleopatra* II.vi.22).[59] In all these cases, the individual considers himself to be acted upon unjustly by the state;[60] and the audience's view would correspond to choric Third Citizen's "ingratitude is monstrous," to which he added, ominously, "for the multitude to be ingrateful, were to make a monster of the multitude" (II.iii.9-11). But the multitude is a "Hydra" (III.i.93).

59. Cf. *Julius Caesar* I.i.37–60, which ends with this word with reference to the elder Pompey. The word "ungrateful" also occurs in Shakespeare: *MND* III.ii.195; *Richard III,* II.ii.91; *Cor.* IV.v.133; *Titus* IV.i.111 and IV.iii.17, *Timon* III.ii.80.

60. See *e.g.,* Appian, p. 5: *"Coriolanus, . . . being unjustly banished,* fled to the *Volscians,* and made warre against his countrey." This does not necessarily mean that the individual does not contribute to the situation: for instance, Coriolanus, who, F. Chappell has shown, is akin to Cato the Elder, differs from him in that Cato secured his personal safety by practicing oratory, allowing him to counter the impeachment of enemies. See Chappell, "Shakespeare's *Coriolanus* and Plutarch's *Life of Cato,*" *Renaissance Papers* (Southeastern Renaissance Conference, 1962), pp. 9–16, and Plutarch, *Cato the Elder* 2, 4, in III.4, 6–7. See also the sensitive article by Peter F. Neumeyer, "Ingratitude is Monstrous," *CE* 26 (1964):192–98.

The exiled man has two courses of action. If he places "commonweale" above all, he will accept his fate, like Scipio Africanus.[61] If he does not, he may decide to right his wrong by revenge. Several of Plutarch's subjects face crises of loyalty. In Shakespeare's *Coriolanus,* the occurrence of the name Cotus (IV.v.3-4) has been thought to reflect reading of Plutarch's *Agesilaus,* in which that hero changes allies repeatedly without adverse comment by the author.[62] Other Plutarchan examples include Themistocles and Camillus, Cimon, Pelopidas, Aristides and Metellus;[63] notable among those who marched against their homelands in revenge are Julius Caesar, Marius, and Sulla.[64]

Shakespeare's own work provides numerous examples of such a pattern. In *2 Henry VI* (ca. 1591) the Duke of York, who was sent to Ireland to pacify an uprising (III.i.304-14) returns at the head of an invading Irish army to depose Henry. His purpose is to usurp the throne; he dissembles to Buckingham, saying that he has come "to remove proud Somerset from the King" (V.i. 2, 36), that is, he masks personal ambition by a seeming loyalty to "commonweale" concerns. In *King John* (ca. 1596),[65] the English nobles Pembroke, Salisbury, and Bigot revolt from John's apparently tyrannical rule to join the French Dauphin's impending invasion of England. Although at first treated as traitors, they are accorded a sense of the enormity of their action, which they attribute to "the infection of the time" (V.ii.20).

---

61. See above, chapter 2, n. 31.
62. *Agesilaus* 8–10, in 4:167–70; on Shakespeare's knowledge of this, see Bullough 5:489.
63. *Camillus* 12, in 1:334; *Pericles* 9, in 2:125; *Pelopidas* 25, in 2:316; *Aristides* 7, in 2:387; *Marius* 29, in 3:200.
64. Cf. *The Wounds of Civil War,* in which both Marius and Sulla march on Rome in revenge. Marius, whose actions are more clearly approved than Sulla's, invokes "just revenge" in IV.i.62–65.
65. But see E. A. J. Honigmann, ed., *King John* by William Shakespeare. Arden Shakespeare (Cambridge, Mass.: Harvard University Press, 1954), pp. xliii–lviii for a date of 1591.

When the Dauphin decides that he will "claim this land for mine" (V.ii.94) and they learn he is plotting their death, they return to John, by whose side they are at his death, V.vii, "to rest without a spot for evermore" (V. vii.107). In *Richard II* (ca. 1595) part of the English nobility sides with forces from Brittany sent to aid the cause of Bolingbroke. Here their presence, and their course, to save England from a degenerate king, might meet with audience approval, although the question of such approval is in fact one of the major subjects of the play. In *Henry V* (1599), the Chorus to Act Two tells of Richard, Earl of Cambridge, Henry, Lord Scroop, and Sir Thomas Grey, who have conspired with the French to kill Henry. Their exposure is dramatized in II.ii; Henry's summary, "this revolt of thine, methinks, is like/ Another fall of man," (ll. 141-42) is choric, and the three are led off to execution.[66]

To turn to the tragedies, in *King Lear* (1604-5) Cordelia, arbitrarily cast off by Lear in an act creating division which would have been unanimously disapproved by a Jacobean audience,[67] returns as the Queen of France, leading a French army in conjunction with a silent "Marshal of France, Monsieur La Far" (IV.iii.10). A degree of approval is even intended for this, for positive associations attach to Cordelia throughout the play;[68] however, despite the removal of the King of France on a pretext (ll. 1-7), which allows the army to be led by the British king's good daughter, the very fact of a foreign invading army would not permit Shakespeare to present its victory in Britain. In *Macbeth* (1605-6),

66. It may be added to this account of the Histories, by way of a reminder, that *Richard III* (ca. 1593) and *1–2 Henry IV* (ca. 1597–98) are a matter of civil war. The Earl of Richmond's action, ridding England of a "usurping boar," is approved; that of the Percies, on the contrary, is condemned.

67. W. R. Elton, *King Lear and the Gods* (San Marino: The Huntington Library, 1966), p. 244.

68. *Ibid.*, pp. 75–84.

written at a time when James I expected to reunite all of Britain, Malcolm marches on Scotland with Macduff and English troops, supplied by Edward the Confessor (IV.iii.43-44), associated with Heaven and identified with Heavenly powers (*e.g.,* ll. 146-59, 237-40). As we saw in the second chapter, *Antony and Cleopatra* (1607-8) is an Empire play in which Antony's creation of independent kingships within the Empire is one of Octavius's charges against him (III.vi.1-19); more important, Antony uses foreign troops against Rome. Last, *Timon of Athens* (ca. 1605-8) presents both Timon and Alcibiades forced into exile. Timon leaves because of his hatred of humanity and Alcibiades is exiled unjustly as a result of seeking justice. The first accepts exile and dies cursing mankind; the second takes positive action, parallel to that of Coriolanus, in raising an army to march upon his native city, although finally he forgives Athens.

It is not, then, the fact of exile or of marching on one's homeland that should determine audience response; in addition to the question of the *justice* of the exile, the *kind* of invasion is important. Ingratitude apart, in only two cases is an invasion with foreign troops wholly approved. In *Titus Andronicus* the Gothic army virtually disappears after victory, as stress is laid on Rome's regeneration; and in *Macbeth,* the tyrant is "ripe for shaking" (IV.iii.238) by forces associated with Heaven and righteous government. In Shakespeare, then, approval is accorded foreign invasion only if it has positive, even religious, associations and does not thereafter harm the country. In one other play approval becomes problematic: in *King Lear,* as we have seen, the invasion fails despite Cordelia's support, but in this case continuing forces for good are represented from within by Albany, and by Edgar, who has gone through the heath experience with Lear and then brought his own father to

Dover. In contrast, the concrete political world of *Coriolanus* will not permit the disappearance of the Volscians, the Volscian army is not the army of righteousness, and no subplot has been set in motion to provide an internal cure for Rome; *Coriolanus* will end on a note of irony.

Kings had, of course, written on the subject of war and its justifications; in a passage of *Basilikon Doron* summarized by the marginal note as "Protection from forraine injuries," and referring to "Ar. 5 po., Polib 6, Dion. Hal de Rom.," James I observed:

> Ye have also to consider, that ye must not onely be carefull to keepe your subjectes from receiving anie wrong of others within; but also ye must be carefull to keepe them from the wrong of anie forraine Prince without: sen the sword is given you by God not onely to revenge upon your owne subjectes, the wrongs committed amongst themselves; but further, to revenge and free them of forraine injuries done unto them. And therefore warres upon just quarrels are lawfull: but above all, let not the wrong cause be on your side.[69]

Here revenge on one's own subjects, associated with protecting them from receiving ill from within the state, is made just, for justice exists in the eye of the rightful ruler.

In the tribunes' view a just banishment has been achieved; in Coriolanus's, the state has failed. Coriolanus, the consul-elect who still has the support of the Senate, is in Shakespeare's treatment the victim of monstrous ingratitude; and the audience would be forced to endorse, although not without horror, just and heroic revenge on a state now misled by tribunes.

This war is no sooner projected than the scene turns to Aufidius's servingmen, who, like the common people of Rome, gossip. They turn to a discussion of peace that serves to underline the previous seriousness about war. First Servingman elaborates his preference for war:

---

69. *Ibid.,* p. 97.

> Let me have war, say I; it exceeds peace as far as day does night; it's sprightly, waking, audible, and full of vent. Peace is a very apoplexy, lethargy; mulled, deaf, sleepy, insensible; a getter of more bastard children than war's a destroyer of men.
>
> (IV.v.227–31)

Although it might at first appear that this interchange is as uncomprehending as the play's opening lines, the opposing claims of war and peace here are in fact being presented ironically. The submerged metaphor is clearer in the Folio text: it is of a hunting dog, "sprightly walking" and "audible," since hounds bay on detecting the scent.[70] A peacetime sport is used to convey the way in which war is preferable to peace, which is associated with the promotion of lethargy and idleness.[71] Peace is "mulled, deaf, sleepy, insensible" (l. 230), in fact promoting disharmony because in peacetime men need each other less than at other times.[72] In this inversion, war brings about the much-desired organic unification of the state: in war, the body public is paradoxically at peace.[73] Lest the audience reject too quickly the objections to "peace" because of the comic presentation, Rome is immediately presented at peace—a false peace that is the lull before the storm.

For the first 37 lines of scene six the bliss of Rome is suggested by "tradesmen singing in their shops, and going/ About their functions friendly" (ll. 8-9). A num-

---

70. See Wilson, p. 220; James's love of the "martiall" sport of hunting with hounds is well known, as is his commendation of it to Prince Henry in *Basilikon Doron,* pp. 189–91.

71. *Basilikon Doron,* p. 187.

72. For a discussion of a major contemporary view of war as harmony, see Jorgensen, chapter 1. However, this view coexisted with an opposing one, of war as cacophany. See S. F. Johnson, "Four Books on Shakespeare: a Review," *Renaissance News* 10 (1957):42–43.

73. James's support of an unpopular peace policy is in the background of these lines quite as much as one of the contemporary references to the Coriolanus story, *Four Paradoxes,* by Thomas and Dudley Digges (1604), which cites the evils of peace; see Kenneth Muir, "The Background of *Coriolanus,*" *SQ* 10 (1959):140.

ber of them enter for a few lines in which they indicate that their families are happy and "pray" for the tribunes in gratefulness. This peace, which takes on the overtones of the association it had a few lines before in the mouth of First Servingman, is no sooner presented than it is shattered by the announcement that the Volscians are attacking again. An aedile and two messengers announce the news with increasing gravity and immediacy. The second suggests that Coriolanus, in the tribunes' state referred to as Marcius once again, is with the troops, and the third announces definitely that he and Aufidius are marching together: they have "o'erborne their way, consumed with fire, and took/ What lay before them" (ll. 79-80). The reference of fire is both to "their way," which has been burned, and to the two leaders, themselves "on fire."[74]

As if by way of reply to their initial disbelief in the reports, the tribunes are thereafter consistently blamed for bringing this calamity upon Rome. The tribunes have misled the common people, and the entire state; but the nobles must accept some blame for accepting the direction of the tribune-led people in the first place, for,

> We loved him, but, like beasts
> And cowardly nobles, gave way unto your clusters.
> (ll. 122–23)

The people now once again change their minds; one person remarks, "When I said banish him, I said 'twas pity" (l. 141). Reflecting the seriousness of the situation, Brutus remarks, "Would half my wealth/ Would buy this for a lie" (ll. 160-61), an expression of earnestness

---

74. Bradley, pp. 12 ff. The emphasis at this point is on Coriolanus's heroic behavior rather than his lack of humanity (see, *e.g.*, Traversi, p. 52). More pertinently, see Cedric Whitman's analysis of fire imagery in the *Iliad* in *Homer and the Heroic Tradition* (Cambridge, Mass.: Harvard University Press, 1958), chapter 7.

that is also ironic on the lips of a poor popular magistrate.[75]

Act Four ends with the assessment of Coriolanus, this time by his new allies. Aufidius notices his pride (IV.vii. 8) but also ominously suggests that "he hath left undone/ That which shall break his neck or hazard mine" (ll. 24-25). Although the lines suggest a return to the heroic rivalry that had existed between the two in the first act, Aufidius had during that act decided to "potch" at Coriolanus in some undisclosed way: his soliloquy now reinforces that plan. He attempts to account for Coriolanus's defection by "pride" (l. 37), "defect of judgment" (l. 39), and "nature" (l. 41), which operates in him to command peace with the same inflexibility as war; one of these (which one he leaves unmentioned) made him feared, then hated, then banished despite his merit.[76] Interest in Coriolanus shifts immediately outward: Aufidius now actively takes on the villain's role, saying practically and cynically, "our virtues/ Lie in th' interpretation of the time" (ll. 49-50).[77] Aufidius proposes a relativistic scale measuring virtues that Coriolanus would ignore; and pithily summarizes,

> One fire drives out one fire; one nail, one nail;
> Rights by rights falter, strengths by strengths do fail.
>
> (ll. 54–55)[78]

75. Plutarch, *The Philosophie, commonlie called, the Morals,* trans. Philemon Holland (London, 1603) sig. Eeee1ʳ (p. 877). STC 20063.

76. The effect is to suggest possibilities without insisting on any one; cf. *Hamlet* IV.iv.39–43.

77. Wilson, p. 225, compares this to Falstaff's "honor" speech (*1 Henry IV,* V.i.128–44). But in both cases the argument is known to be fallacious by the audience; see Robert Langbaum, *The Poetry of Experience* (London: Chatto and Windus, 1957); it was important for traditional drama that an action have a "relative position on the moral scale, a scale recognized by hero and villain alike" (p. 163).

78. Cf. *Two Gentlemen of Verona,* II.iv.192. The expression is largely commonplace: see M. P. Tilley, ed., *A Dictionary of Proverbs* (Ann Arbor: University of Michigan Press, 1950), N17 and F277; and the two compilations of B. J. Whiting, *Proverbs in the Earlier English Drama* (Cambridge, Mass.: Harvard University Press, 1938), p. 139, and *Proverbs, Sentences and Proverbial Phrases . . . before 1500* (Cambridge, Mass.: Belknap Press, 1968), N6.

Act Five

Act Five continues the attention devoted to Coriolanus and to Rome. Scene one begins with the report of the failure of Cominius's embassy of appeal before a Coriolanus who is "a kind of nothing, titleless" (l. 13), whose injury is "gaoler to his pity" (l. 65). Menenius's embassy, presented in the second scene, fares no better. These two attempts stress Coriolanus's remoteness from human feeling, and together with their summarizing repetition in V.iv.16-24, frame the seeming impossibility of the success of the women in V.iii.

For some critics V.iii is the single most important scene in the play, showing Coriolanus responding to the claims of "nature" made by his immediate family.[79] In this scene Shakespeare follows details and values from Plutarch's account; only sentimentalization, however, can read this scene apart from its political importance. When Coriolanus kneels before his mother, bending as he had when returning from Corioli (II.i.167 SD), he admits the claims of "nature," precisely, in reality, the claims that Menenius had put forth in his fable. The son returns to his mother and his fatherland; but this act comes too late. For this reason it spells his tragedy and that of the state.

As in the discussion of "policy," Coriolanus is unable to choose what is so clearly the efficacious path of denying Volumnia's appeal to nature. The qualities necessary to implement his decision to "stand/ As if a man were author of himself/ And knew no other kin" (ll. 35-37) would have been individualism and reliance on free will, qualities associated with villains in Shakespeare. On the contrary, Coriolanus's decision reflects his alliance with traditional values that deny total freedom to man's will.[80]

79. H. Heuer, "From Plutarch to Shakespeare," *SS* 10 (1957):54-59, and Wilson, p. xix. For a corrective, see Jorgensen, pp. 312-13.
80. See S. F. Johnson, "The Regeneration of Hamlet," *SQ* 3 (1952): 196-97 and n. 42.

His "injury" dictates a course of action that is justice in his own eyes, and a just revenge in all others'. The audience would have approved of the victory of "nature," expressed as "pity," over "injury," and no doubt would have colored this pagan act with Christian overtones. Approval would, however, involve not only concern for Coriolanus, but awareness that Coriolanus does not act in a vacuum, that his decisions, as always, have social consequences, and that these consequences will in turn affect Coriolanus. Although the audience might provisionally approve revenge, it would wholly approve saving Rome; in any case, it would be attentive to the immediate consequences, foreshadowed at this point in Coriolanus's remarks to Volumnia:

> You have won a happy victory to Rome;
> But, for your son—believe it, O, believe it—
> Most dangerously you have with him prevailed,
> If not most mortal to him. But let it come.
>   (ll. 186–89)

The last note, traditional for Shakespearean heroes,[81] becomes a threat for the audience in Aufidius's aside: he sees that in tentatively reconciling justice with mercy, Coriolanus has sundered mercy and honor. In taking advantage of Coriolanus's division (ll. 200-201), Aufidius, true to his villainous role, will seek to regain his "former fortune" of preeminence in the state.

There follow two scenes set in Rome. In the first, following statements of Coriolanus's inhuman greatness, comes the news of the ladies' success; in the next, the ladies return in a triumphal procession during which First Senator cries "Unshout the noise that banished Marcius,/ Repeal him with the welcome of his mother" (V.v.4-5). These words hold up the possibility of a

---

81. Cf. *Hamlet* V.ii.349, "let it be"; *King Lear* V.iii.8–26; "come . . . come"; and *Othello* V.ii.246, "let it go all."

happy resolution. In his enthusiasm, he suggests that Coriolanus need only be allowed to return; his late threat would presumably be swallowed up in Rome's gratitude for his mercy in changing sides at the last minute. Even before the final sixth scene, the area of audience concern is directed away from Coriolanus's decision itself, and to its consequences; but what the consequences will be is held in question.

Like the earlier scenes that dealt with Coriolanus with relation to the surrounding political structure, the final one begins and ends with hostile but practical political assessment. Earlier the two tribunes talked and made plans; now, like them, Aufidius plans future action. A "paper" (l. 2) has been prepared and is to be delivered to the "lords o' th' city" (l. 1), asking them to go to the market-place of Corioli to join with the common people (l. 3); Aufidius, before the united city, will "accuse" Coriolanus, who is now on his way to "appear before the people, hoping/ To purge himself with words" (ll. 7-8). Aufidius is joined by "conspirators" (8 S D), who parallel the Aediles enforcing the tribunes' will.

Aufidius charges Coriolanus with selling "the blood and labour/ Of our great action" (ll. 47-48). This accusation reflects the public, or "commonwealth," view of heroic behavior; as always, the hero is socially responsible. Aufidius and his conspirators discuss how the people will find the matter, and one conspirator remarks that they will sway to whichever of them wins. The plan is made for Coriolanus to die, an event that will cause Aufidius to rise (l. 49); Coriolanus, earlier an obstacle to Rome's unity, is now an obstacle to the rising future tyrant. The lords enter, disposed to be harsh in this "yielding" to Rome. Then Coriolanus enters, "the commoners being with him" (70 S D).

Addressed to the Lords of Corioli, Coriolanus's speech presents his actions and their results in the most favorable light possible, and includes Rome's agreement to the "terms" decided upon (ll. 83-84; cf. V.iii.197-99). This shows a new concern for Coriolanus, although his defense is made in terms of peace made with honor to the victors and (ll. 79-81) shame to Rome, but he disclaims victory. Aufidius interrupts, and, also addressing the Lords, accuses Coriolanus of being a "traitor in the highest degree" (l. 85).

The Roman tribunes had used these same terms earlier. Aufidius, who has taken over the tribunes' accusing function in the drama,[82] bases his charge on the fact that Coriolanus is really an enemy conqueror who has defeated Corioli and now, momentarily fighting with the Voscians, has betrayed his trust (l. 92). Coriolanus, in answering, reaches the same extreme heights he did when confronting the accusations of the tribunes in III.i. The difference between this and the earlier scene is that Aufidius is also Coriolanus's individual antagonist and can insult him by adding to the charge of treason the term "boy"; the effect on the audience is not like that felt at the tribunes' presumptuousness in using "shall" (III.i. 87ff). His reaction to Aufidius leads Coriolanus to cite his earlier victories, which have affected his immediate listeners on the stage: "Like an eagle in a dove-cote, I/ Fluttered your Volscians in Corioli./ Alone I did it" (ll. 115-17).[83] These, nearly Coriolanus's final words,

---

82. Cf. *Julius Caesar,* in which Antony takes on Cassius's role of misleader in the Forum speech; significantly, Cassius becomes an approved ally of Brutus and dies a hero's death (V.iii.99–103) after changing from his Epicurean philosophy (V.i.76–78).

83. For a discussion of the relations in *Coriolanus* between honor and words or deeds, see D. J. Gordon, "Name and Fame: Shakespeare's *Coriolanus,*" *Papers Mainly Shakespearean,* ed. G. I. Duthie (Edinburgh: Oliver and Boyd, 1964), pp. 40–57, and C. B. Watson, chapters 10 and 11. Concern with deeds reflects a concern with fame, or reputation, and is characteristic of tragic heroes in Shakespeare; in *Hamlet* it complements heroic virtue in V.ii.363–69. Cf. Othello's final speech (V.ii.338–56); in the plays closest in time of composition to *Coriolanus, Macbeth* and *King Lear,* the public concerns of the endings are expressed by the continuing characters, Malcolm (*Macbeth* V.viii.60–75) and Albany (*King Lear* V.iii.319–26).

bring the conspirators, and following them, the people, to make angry accusations: "He killed my son. My daughter. He killed my cousin Marcus. He killed my father" (ll. 122-23).

This confrontation of extremities is a parallel to that with the tribunes and people in III.iii;[84] the nobility of Corioli, like that of Rome, strives for Temperance. From the biased but considered views of First Lord (ll. 63-69), his later "Peace, both, and hear me speak," (l. 111) and "Peace, ho! no outrage: peace!/ The man is noble," (ll. 124-25), to the further plea for a judicious hearing (l. 127), the nobility of Corioli also attempts to take the temperate role of peacemaker. These attempts fail, like those of Cominius, Menenius, and other Roman nobles, to moderate the extremities and are cut off by violence. The conspirators' "Kill, kill, kill, kill, kill him" overshadows the Lords' words "Hold, hold, hold, hold," which complete the verse line (l. 131). With this formulation of the unreconciled conflict, Coriolanus dies.

Aufidius, in ironic fulfillment of an earlier remark (I.iii.47-48), now stands on his body (132 S D).[85] He defends his actions by referring to a heroic "rage/ Provoked by him" (ll. 136-37). He goes on to promise a full explanation of the danger posed by Coriolanus alive; Coriolanus dead, however, is, as First Lord says when he gives orders for bearing off the body, "the most noble corse that ever herald/ Did follow to his urn" (ll. 144-

---

84. Colman, p. 13, has likened the construction of *Coriolanus* to that of other "Herculean plays" in which "the obstacles to be overcome by the hero grow more formidable as the action proceeds, and the emotional oscillations grow proportionately wider. But the basic principle of construction in *Coriolanus* remains one of repetition."

85. The stage directions of *Coriolanus* are unusually full; possibly Shakespeare was no longer living in London at the time of composition of the play. Such is the suggestion of the abundant stage directions in the Folio text, which seem to be designed for the producer (or even reader) not otherwise familiar with the play. See W. W. Greg, *The Shakespeare First Folio* (Oxford: at the Clarendon Press, 1955), pp. 404, 406.

45). The penultimate speech of the play is ambiguous, however: "His own impatience/ Takes from Aufidius a great part of blame," Second Lord remarks. Whether "his" refers to Aufidius or to Coriolanus is not apparent; and although aurally the reference would probably be taken to be Aufidius, the possible meaning lingers that Coriolanus's impatience justifies Aufidius's action. The latter has purged his anger, and the final lines, ironically reinvoking Coriolanus's citation of his own bravery some thirty-five lines before, accord him now grudging praise from a Volscian:

> Though in this city he
> Hath widowed and unchilded many a one,
> Which to this hour bewail the injury,
> Yet he shall have a noble memory.
> Assist.

(ll. 151–55)

For the last time, Coriolanus is framed by political considerations. The last speakers remind the audience of the unsettled state which still exists. Aufidius, the play's ultimate demagogue, is at the end of the play still alive and unhurt, an enemy to Rome. The Volscians have the military advantage and have not accepted Coriolanus's terms of peace with Rome. In Rome, and presumably alive, are the tribunes; the Roman state remains divided between the nobility and the tribune-led commons. Whereas the nobles of both states have tried to show a wise temperance, they have differing loyalties. In Rome too is Coriolanus's own family, his wife, mother, and, ominously, his son, whom the speeches of I.iii and Coriolanus's wishes (V.iii.70-75) suggest is to be identical with his father. Whatever chastisement may have been implicit in forcing Rome to come to "terms" with the Volscians, nothing is held up at the end of the play to suggest that there will be future peace or stability. With regard to Coriolanus himself, the shift in Aufidius's attitude suggests that Coriolanus's political faults are expiated by death, much as Othello's are by his suicide. In the case of Coriolanus, death proceeds so directly from his reaction to manipulation that one might almost call it a symbolic suicide.

However this may be, Coriolanus remains a hero of equivocal social and political value. He is adversely criticized by the standard of Temperance, both private and public, brought forward in the play. When responding to the claims of "nature," he does not transcend the rivalry between them and the opposing claims of loyalty; by following the one he merely intensifies the tensions they involve. By insisting on Roman virtues that would admit no modifications, he helps to disrupt Rome. In his death, he leaves Rome on her knees, for the tragedy of the hero has not led to the regeneration of his country. Rome is threatened by a foreign army in which no one will respond to an appeal to pity, divided within by her unresolved political situation, in danger because led by evil tribunes, and without a young and righteous future leader.

The standard of Temperance and the warning of the dangers of intransigence are a response to the stiffening, in the face of a new situation, of opposing factions in early-Jacobean political circles, a specific manifestation of the larger centralizing tendencies of Counter-Reformation Europe. A tribune-led state which onstage expelled its ruler, in effect forcing him to lead foreign armies against it, was no longer concerned with the "securitie of the Prince";[86] it was moving away from its traditional government, identified not as the full republic that lasted nearly five hundred years, but as the

---

86. Forset, sig. N4^v.

relatively short-lived, tempered, Roman aristocracy.

A Classical and Renaissance formulation of a perennial human problem was to oppose tyranny and freedom, identifying the one with monarchic power, the latter with democratic. Shakespeare's response to a changed situation in Post-Renaissance, early-seventeenth century England was to show the potential tyranny of both positions. Although his moral ideal is presented, the ironic mode of *Coriolanus* prevents its implementation. But then, a play put on at the Globe and Blackfriars theaters by the King's Men would necessarily oppose political innovation; it would be conservative in tendency, to the despair of generations of later audiences.

Epilogue

Ben Jonson's *Catiline* (1611)

Following *Coriolanus* closely in date of composition, Ben Jonson's *Catiline his Conspiracie,* printed for Walter Burre in 1611, presents such a different dramatization of the concerns we have been studying as to suggest that it might be a counterstatement.[1] Like *Sejanus, Catiline* deals with the threat to republican values posed by tyranny. Catiline's conspiracy, which occurred in 63 B.C., is linked by the Prologue, the ghost of Sulla, to earlier history involving the Gracchi, Cinna, Marius, and Hannibal (I.21-25). Cethegus and Catiline evoke the public horrors of Sulla's wars (I.229-53),[2] and the former clearly identifies their intention:

> I would have seen *Rome* burn't,
> By this time; and her ashes in an urne:
> The kingdome of the *Senate,* rent a-sunder;
> And the degenerate, talking gowne runne frighted,
> Out of the aire of *Italie.*
>
> (ll. 223–27)[3]

---

1. Jonson had parodied Cominius's praise that Coriolanus "lurched all swords of the garland" (II.ii.99) in *The Silent Woman* (1610), V.iv.224–25; it seems unlikely that Jonson used the phrase independently, perhaps first.

2. The source for these lines is Lucan's pro-republican *Pharsalia.*

3. With these lines Jonson clearly establishes Sulla's ghost to be bent on the destruction of his own state, Rome. De Luna, *Jonson's Romish Plot* (Oxford: at the Clarendon Press, 1967), *passim,* argues for a political reading of *Catiline.* With reference to these two points, and to

When Catiline addresses the people, with whom he identifies himself, he puts the causes of dissatisfaction in pragmatic terms reminiscent of the plebeian complaints in *Coriolanus:* "we," he says,

>   honest, and valiant,
> Are hearded with the vulgar; and so kept,
> As we were onely bred, to consume corne;
> Or weare out wooll; to drinke the cities water;
> Ungrac'd, without authoritie, or marke;
> Trembling beneath their rods: to whom, (if all
> Were well in *Rome*) we should come forth bright axes.
> All places, honors, offices are theirs!
> .   .   .   .
>   At home, our wants,
> Abroad, our debts doe urge us; our states daily
> Bending to bad, our hopes to worse: and, what
> Is left, but to be crush'd?

> (I.354–61, 406–9)

The initial appearance of Sulla's ghost and the identification of Catiline with the spirit of evil have robbed this appeal of any chance of audience approval. As in *Coriolanus,* the real plight of the common people is admitted, but the inevitable misuse of authority attendant upon popular attempts to redress wrongs is immediately stressed. Like *Coriolanus* and unlike *Sejanus,* the leader of malcontents is disapproved by the play, for threatening Rome with destruction.

Jonson distinguishes between the current generation and its elders: the chorus in Act One stresses the degeneration of the times resulting from Rome's luxury, or "expence" (I.573), which "hath enforc'd *Romes* vertue, thence,/ Which simple poverty first made" (ll. 574-75); luxury has led to "ambition, . . . avarice,/ Riot, and

---

my study of *Coriolanus,* it is worth noting that in G. E. Bentley's listings of seventeenth-century popularity of individual characters, Sulla's ghost ranks surprisingly high. See his *Shakespeare and Jonson* (Chicago: University of Chicago Press, 1945), 1:120, 124, 125.

every other vice" (ll. 576-78). These reflections are tied
to the main action, the career of Catiline, by Act Two,
in which Sempronia, who supports his bid for election
to the consulate, speaks to Fulvia, who will reveal the
conspiracy to Cicero. To Fulvia's statement that virtue
determines nobility, Sempronia replies ironically,

> it might, at first, in *Romes* poore age;
> When both her Kings, and *Consuls* held the plough,
> Or garden'd well: But, now, we ha' no need,
> To digge, or loose our sweat for't.
>
> (II.128–31)

The election to the consulship is to be fought out between the main candidates, Catiline and the "new man"
Cicero. The Chorus of Act Two, speaking for Roman
republicanism, prays:

> O, put it in the publique voice
> To make a free, and worthy choice:
> Excluding such as would invade
> The common wealth.
>
> . . . .
>
> Such the old BRUTI, DECII were,
> The CIPI, CURTII, who did give
> Themselves for *Rome:* and would not live,
> As men, good, only for a yeere.
> Such were the great CAMILLI, too;
> The FABII, SCIPIO's; that still thought
> No worke, at price inough, was bought,
> That for their countrey they could doe.
>
> (II.372–75, 391–98)

Despite their degenerate state, the Romans rally sufficiently to elect Cicero overwhelmingly. Understated
rather like the establishment of the tribunate in *Coriolanus,* it is as if the tribunes were defeated in an election
by Cominius; Jonson's faith in the Roman people is similar to Machiavelli's, and conflicts with Shakespeare's
more orthodox reflection of political commonplaces. In

Catiline this political election is of the utmost importance, for it enables Cicero, a "new man" whom Jonson
admits to political virtue with an almost Italian appreciation of fact over theory, to play an active role as savior
of the republic. As soon as he is elected, he appears with
the old-Roman Cato, an association that assures author-
ial, and hopefully also audience, approval. When the
chorus cries "the voice of CATO is the voice of *Rome,*"
Cato adds, "the voice of *Rome* is the consent of heaven"
(III.60-61), thus securing the identification of Cicero
with positive forces.

Cicero exposes Catiline in the famous speech of Act
Four for which the play has almost always been condemned.[4] But he is lenient to a fault, and considers banishment sufficient punishment; instead of the demagogic
tribunes banishing the military and aristocratic Coriolanus, here the demagogue Catiline later directs his accom-
plices to

> Let it be given out, here in the citie,
> That I am gone, an innocent man, to exile,
> Into *Massilia,* willing to give way
> To fortune, and the times.
>
> (IV.556–59)

Dissembling innocence, he goes and seeks to win over as
allies the Allobroges, who were recently Roman enemies,
and "whose state . . . / Is discontent with the great
usuries,/ They are oppress'd with" (IV.577-79); however, they remain faithful to Rome. Like Sulla, Marius,
Julius Caesar, Lucius Andronicus, and Coriolanus, Catiline is an outcast of a Rome he considers "ingrateful"

4. Like Cato the Elder and unlike Coriolanus (chapter 6 above, n.
60), Cicero is an able speaker. In *Sejanus,* the silenced nobility awaits
destruction; but Cicero's exposure of Catiline presents a "new man"
willing to use "policy" not for self-advancement but for the general
good. Culturally as well as dramatically, this is a reversal of more
than only the *Sejanus* pattern.

and seeks to march on his homeland; and like the latter two, he raises the threat of invasion by foreign troops. But the evil in Catiline's nature and the chaos he threatens preclude any audience approval.

Indeed, he is able to face the Roman troops with only a mixture of "SYLLA's old troops, left here in Fesulae" (V.22) and with miscellaneous Roman degenerates who "never . . . did exercise their youth" and who exemplify the ills of all times. He himself is killed in battle, and the republic is saved:

> And now had fierce ENYO, like a flame,
> Consum'd all it could reach, and then it selfe;
> Had not the fortune of the common-wealth
> Come PALLAS-like, to every *Roman* thought.
> (V.663–66)

Although the republic emerges safely, the distribution of punishment to the conspirators is sufficiently ambiguous to make the end of this "comoedy"[5] more ironic than the corresponding moments in Jonson's comedies.

This is particularly true of Caesar, who becomes prominent at the same time as Cicero, and whose presence qualifies the happy ending. Caesar regards Cicero as a "popular *Consul*" (III.85); and, though presented as an ally of Catiline, Caesar is not accorded punishment.[6] The audience sees him urge Catiline on, saying "Let 'hem call it mischiefe;/ When it is past, and prosper'd, 'twill be vertue" (III.504-5);[7] and "there was never

---

5. De Luna, pp. 291–92. Since Cicero is so clearly the hero of an important action, and the play celebrates republican government, it might well be called "the tragi-comedy of Cicero."

6. The play is anti-Caesar, as A. Schlösser has pointed out ("Ben Jonson's Roman Plays," *Kwartalnik Neofilologiczny* 8 (1961):156); Boughner, *The Devil's Disciple* (New York: Philosophical Library, 1968), pp. 89–112, attributes this to reading Machiavelli (*e.g., Discorsi* I.10), but it was a Renaissance commonplace.

7. Cf. Sir John Harington's fine epigram: "Treason doth never prosper, what's the reason?/ For if it prosper, none dare call it Treason," in *The Letters and Epigrams of Sir John Harington*, ed. N. E. McClure (Philadelphia: University of Pennsylvania Press, 1930), p. 255.

any great thing, yet,/ Aspired, but by violence, or fraud"
(ll. 515-16). Later, it hears that Caesar is in Apulia
raising troops for Catiline (ll. 558-59). Cicero himself
knows about the meeting of Caesar and Catiline (ll. 773-
74), yet does not prosecute him with the others. Cicero
remarks, instead, "If there were proofe 'gainst CAE-
SAR, or who ever,/ To speake him guiltie, I would so
declare him" (V.89-90); but when a denunciation is
produced, it is called a "libell" (l. 351) and dismissed.

Caesar is reassured and allowed to go free. In return
he urges, not, like Cato, death for the conspirators, but
rather simple rustication. This divergence between the
views of the two men causes Cato to remark that Caesar

> hath very well,
> And subtilly discours'd of life, and death,
> As if he thought those things, a prettie fable,
> (V.526–28)

a view which is, he adds,

> a vaine counsaile, if he thinke them dangerous.
> Which, if he doe not, but that he alone,
> In so great feare of all men, stand un-frighted,
> He gives me cause, and you, more to feare him.
> (ll. 538–41)

After Caesar threatens Cicero, audience attention is
drawn to the report of the heroic battle against Catiline
and the victory of the Roman army.

After Catiline is dead, an allied and equally subversive force is still at work within the Roman republic.
Rome looks forward not to the tyranny of popular misleaders or of intransigent aristocrats, but of "Caesarism." Both Jonson and his audience surely knew that
some twenty years after the dramatic date of *Catiline*

the hero Cicero fell victim to the proscriptions of the triumvirate associated with this force.[8]

Certainly in the cases adduced from drama, tyranny—represented by Sulla, Tiberius, Julius Caesar, and Catiline—is clearly disapproved, in contrast to the ideals of the republic. For Shakespeare, the immoral misleaders of the people and the intransigent Coriolanus, one of those on whom consular authority would justly fall, are both dangerous, tyrannic extremes for a commonwealth that should be led by an ethically temperate aristocracy; it is Rome's tragedy that this element is so easily ignored. Jonson also shows twin prongs of tyranny threatening the state, in this case the people and aristocracy; and he also posits an ethical solution, but one that ignores known history, one based on the individual virtues of the "new man" Cicero and the "old Roman" Cato. Here, within a few years in 1608-11, we have for the last time the range of formulations traditionally permitted the mixed constitution. As in classical times, in medieval and early-Tudor England, and in Renaissance Italy, so in Jacobean England equally viable aristocratic and democratic solutions to the perennial problem of tyranny are advanced by men who shared a common knowledge of politics and a common set of assumptions that understood it to be a subdivision of moral philosophy, a means of achieving the goals of human existence.

8. It was an act of will for Jonson to make Cicero and Cato the play's last speakers; this perhaps indicates that in this play Jonson was the artist as normative social critic. Viewed in this way, it is a depressing cultural fact that the play was excessively unsuccessful on the stage. See the dedication to the Earl of Pembroke and the address "to the Reader in Ordinarie," in *Ben Jonson* 5:431-32.

Bibliography

Akrigg, G. Philip V. *Jacobean Pageant*. Cambridge, Mass.: Harvard University Press, 1962.

Alexander, Peter. *Shakespeare's Life and Art*. London: Nisbet, 1939.

Allen, Don Cameron. "Some Observations on the *Rape of Lucrece*." *Shakespeare Survey* 15 (1962):89-98.

Allen, John William. *English Political Thought: 1603-60*. Volume I: 1603-1644. London: Methuen [1938].

Anderson, Ruth L. "Kingship in Renaissance Drama." *Studies in Philology* 41 (1944):136-55.

Anonymous. *A Declaration of the Variance betweene the Pope and the Segniory of Venice*. [London: R. Barker], 1606. STC 19482.

————. "Machiavelli's Discourses." *Notes and Queries*, N.S. 5 (1958):144-45.

Appian. *Shakespeare's Appian*. Edited by E. Schanzer. English Reprint Series, no. 13. Liverpool: Liverpool University Press, 1956.

Archambault, P. "The Analogy of the 'Body' in Renaissance Political Literature." *Bibliothèque d'Humanisme et Renaissance* 29 (1967):21-53.

Aristotle. *Politics*. Translated by B. Jowett. Oxford: at the Clarendon Press, 1905.

Bacon, Sir Francis. *The Works of Francis Bacon*. Edited by J. Spedding, R. L. Ellis, and D. D. Heath. 12 vols. London: Longman, 1864-69.

Baldwin, Thomas Whitfield. *On the Literary Genetics of Shakespeare's Poems and Sonnets*. Urbana: University of Illinois Press, 1950.

————. *The Organization and Personnel of the Shakespearian Company*. Princeton: Princeton University Press, 1927.

————. *William Shakspere's Small Latine and Lesse Greeke*. 2 vols. Urbana: University of Illinois Press, 1944.

Barlow, William. *A Sermon preached at Paules Crosse*. London: 1601. (STC 1454.)

Baron, Hans. *The Crisis of the Early Italian Renaissance*. 2 vols. Princeton: Princeton University Press, 1955.

————. *Humanistic and Political Literature in Florence and Venice at the Beginning of the Quattrocento*. Cambridge, Mass.: Harvard University Press, 1955.

————. "The *Principe* and the Puzzle of Date." *Bibliothèque d'Humanisme et Renaissance* 18 (1956): 405-28.

Barroll, J. Leeds. "Shakespeare and Roman History." *Modern Language Review* 53 (1958):327-43.

Baumer, F. leV. "Christopher St. German." *American Historical Review* 42 (1937):631-51.

Bennett, H. S. *English Books and Readers: 1457-1603*. 2 vols. Cambridge, England: Cambridge University Press, 1952-65.

Bennett, Josephine W. *"Measure for Measure" as Royal Entertainment*. New York: Columbia University Press, 1966.

Bentley, Gerald Eades. *Shakespeare and Jonson: their Reputations in the 17th Century Compared*. 2 vols. Chicago: University of Chicago Press, 1945.

Bevington, David Martin. *Tudor Drama and Politics.* Cambridge, Mass.: Harvard University Press, 1968.

Bodin, Jean. *Six Bookes of the Commonweale.* Translated by Richard Knolles (1606). Edited by K. D. McRae. Cambridge, Mass.: Harvard University Press, 1962.

Boughner, Daniel. *The Devil's Disciple.* New York: Philosophical Library [1968].

Bouwsma, William J. *Venice and the Defense of Republican Liberty.* Berkeley: University of California Press, 1968.

Bowra, Cecil Maurice. *Tradition and Design in the "Iliad."* Oxford: Oxford University Press, 1930.

Bowyer, Robert. *The Parliamentary Diary of Robert Bowyer: 1606-1607.* Edited by D. S. Willson. Minneapolis: University of Minnesota Press, 1931.

Bradbrook, Muriel C. *The School of Night.* Cambridge, England: Cambridge University Press, 1936.

Bradley, Andrew Cecil. *Coriolanus.* Proceedings of the British Academy. London and New York: Oxford University Press, 1912.

Brittin, N. A. "Coriolanus, Alceste and Dramatic Genres." *Publications of the Modern Language Association* 71 (1956):799-807.

Brower, Reuben A. "Introduction," *Coriolanus,* by William Shakespeare. Signet Classic Shakespeare. New York: New American Library, 1966, pp. xxiii-1.

Brutus, Junius [pseud.]. *Vindiciae contra Tyrannos.* Translated in *A Defense of Liberty against Tyrants.* Edited by H. J. Laski. London: Bell, 1924.

Bullough, Geoffrey, ed. *Narrative and Dramatic Sources of Shakespeare.* 7 vols. London: Routledge, 1957- .

Burton, K. M. "The Political Tragedies of Chapman and Ben Jonson." *Essays in Criticism* 2 (1952):397-412.

Bush, Douglas. *Mythology and the Renaissance Tradition in English Poetry*. Minneapolis: University of Minnesota Press, 1932.

Cadoni, Giorgio. "Libertà, Repubblica e Governo Misto in Machiavelli." *Rivista Internazionale di Filosofia del Diritto* 39 (1962):462-84.

Calvin, John. *The Institution of the Christian Religion*. Translated by Thomas Norton. London, 1562. (STC 4416.)

Campbell, Oscar James. *Shakespeare's Satire*. Oxford: Oxford University Press, 1943.

Cantimori, Delio. "Il Mestiere dello Storico." *Itinerarie* 8. (Genova, 1961.)

Cartwright, Thomas. *Cartwrightiana*. Edited by A. Peel and L. H. Carlson. London: Allen and Unwin, 1951.

Caspari, Fritz. *Humanism and the Social Order in Tudor England*. Chicago: University of Chicago Press, 1954.

Castiglione, Baldassare. *The Book of the Courtier*. Translated by Sir Thomas Hoby (1561). The Tudor Translations. London: Nutt, 1900.

Catalogue of the Library of Sir Edward Coke. Edited by W. O. Hassall. Yale Law Library Publications no. 12. New Haven: Yale University Press, 1950.

Chabod, Federico. *Machiavelli and the Renaissance*. Translated by D. Moore. Cambridge, England: Bowes and Bowes, 1958.

Chambers, R. W. "The Expression of Ideas—particularly political Ideas—in the three Pages and in Shakespeare," in *Shakespeare's Hand in the Play of Sir Thomas More*. Edited by A. W. Pollard et al. Shakespeare Problems, Series 2. Cambridge, England: Cambridge University Press, 1923, pp. 142-88.

Chapman, George. *The Plays and Poems of George Chapman: The Tragedies*. Edited by T. M. Parrott. London: Routledge, 1910.

Chappell, F. "Shakespeare's *Coriolanus* and Plutarch's *Life of Cato*." Southeastern Renaissance Conference. *Renaissance Papers,* 1962, pp. 9-16.

Charney, Maurice. *Shakespeare's Roman Plays*. Cambridge, Mass.: Harvard University Press, 1961.

————, ed. *Discussions of Shakespeare's Roman Plays*. New York: Heath, 1964.

Charron, Pierre. *Of Wisdome*. Translated by S. Lennard. London: [1608]. (STC 5051.)

Church, Frederick C. *The Italian Reformers: 1534-64*. New York: Columbia University Press, 1932.

Clough, C. H. "The Relations between the English and Urbino Courts, 1474-1508." *Studies in the Renaissance* 14 (1967):202-18.

Collingwood, Robin George. *The Idea of History*. Edited by T. M. Knox. Oxford: at the Clarendon Press, 1946.

Colman, E. A. M. "The End of Coriolanus." *Journal of English Literary History* 34 (1967):1-20.

Contarini, Gasparo Cardinal. *The Commonwealth and Government of Venice*. Translated by Sir Lewes Lewkenor. London: Windet, 1599. (STC 5642.)

Cornet, Enrico, ed. *Paolo V. e La Republica Veneta*. Vienna: Tendler, 1859.

Craig, Hardin. *The Enchanted Glass*. New York: Oxford University Press, 1936.

————, ed. *Machiavelli's "The Prince": an Elizabethan Translation*. Chapel Hill: University of North Carolina Press, 1944.

Cunningham, James Vincent. *Woe or Wonder; the Emotional Effects of Shakespearean Tragedy*. [Denver:] University of Denver Press, [1951].

Curtis, M. H. "The Hampton Court Conference and its Aftermath." *History,* N.S. 46 (1961):1-16.

Curtius, Ernst Robert. *European Literature in the Latin*

Middle Ages. Translated by W. Trask. New York: Pantheon, 1953.

Daniel, Samuel. *The Civil Wars.* Edited by Laurence Michel. New Haven: Yale University Press, 1958.

Davis, Walter R. and Lanham, Richard A. *Sidney's Arcadia.* New Haven: Yale University Press, 1965.

Dean, L. F. "Shakespeare's Treatment of Conventional Ideas." *Sewanee Review* 52 (1944):414-23.

Dewar, Mary. *Sir Thomas Smith.* London: Athlone Press, 1964.

D'Ewes, Sir Simonds. *A Compleat Journal of . . . the House of Lords and House of Commons Throughout the whole Reign of Queen Elizabeth.* London: J. S[tarkey]., 1708.

Dictionary of Proverbs in England in the sixteenth and seventeenth centuries. Edited by M. P. Tilley. Ann Arbor: University of Michigan Press, 1950.

Dionysius of Halicarnassus. *Roman Antiquities.* Translated by E. Carey. 7 vols. Loeb Classical Library. Cambridge, Mass.: Harvard University Press, 1937-50.

Dipple, Elizabeth. "Harmony and Pastoral in the *Old Arcadia.*" *Journal of English Literary History* 35 (1968):309-28.

Draper, J. W. "Political Themes in Shakespeare's Later Plays." *Journal of English and Germanic Philology* 35 (1936):61-93.

Driver, Tom F. *The Sense of History in Greek and Shakespearean Drama.* New York: Columbia University Press, 1960.

Ebel, Julia G. "A Numerical Survey of Elizabethan Translations." *The Library,* 5th Series, 22 (1967): 104-27.

Eccles, C. M. "Shakespeare and Jacques Amyot: Sonnet 55 and *Coriolanus.*" *Notes and Queries,* N.S. 12 (1965):100-102.

Elizabeth I. *The Letters of Queen Elizabeth.* Edited by G. B. Harrison. London: Cassell, 1935.

Elton, Geoffrey Rudolf, ed. *The Tudor Constitution.* Cambridge, England: Cambridge University Press, 1960.

Elton, William R. *"King Lear" and the Gods.* San Marino, Calif.: Huntington Library, 1966.

Epstein, J. L. "Francis Bacon: Mediator in the Parliament of 1604." *The Historian* 30 (1968):219-37.

Erasmus, Desiderius. *De duplici Copia.* Cologne: 1551.

Farnham, Willard. *Shakespeare's Tragic Frontier.* Berkeley: University of California Press, 1950.

Ferguson, Arthur B. *The Articulate Citizen and the English Renaissance.* Durham, N.C.: Duke University Press, 1965.

Fink, Zera S. *The Classical Republicans.* Northwestern University Studies in the Humanities No. 9. Evanston: Northwestern University Press, 1945.

Forset, Edward. *A Comparative Discourse of the Bodies Natural and Politique.* London, 1606. (STC 11188.)

Fortescue, Sir John. *A learned commendation of the politique lawes of England.* Translated by Robert Mulcaster. London: Totell, 1573. (STC 11195.)

————. *The Governance of England.* Edited by C. Plummer. Oxford: at the Clarendon Press, 1885.

Frye, D. C. "Commentary in Shakespeare: the Case of *Coriolanus." Shakespeare Studies* 1 (1965):105-17.

Frye, Northrop. *Anatomy of Criticism.* Princeton: Princeton University Press, 1957.

Fulbecke, William. *A Historicall Collection of the Factions, Tumults, and Massacres. . . .* London: Ponsonby, 1601. (STC 11412.)

Fussner, F. Smith. *The Historical Revolution.* New York: Columbia University Press, 1962.

Gaetano, Armand L. De. "The Florentine Academy and

the Advancement of Learning through the Vernacular: the Orti Oricellari and the Sacra Accademia." *Bibliothèque d'Humanisme et Renaissance* 30 (1968): 19-52.

————. "G. B. Gelli and the Rebellion against Latin." *Studies in the Renaissance* 14 (1967):131-58.

Garrett, Christina H. *The Marian Exiles*. Cambridge, England: at the University Press, 1938.

Gerber, Adolph. "All of the five fictitious Italian Editions of Writings of Machiavelli and three of those of Pietro Aretino printed by John Wolfe of London (1584-88)." *Modern Language Notes* 22 (1907): 2-6, 129-35, 201-6.

————. *Nicholas Machiavelli: die Handschriften, Ausgaben und übersetzungen seiner Werke im 16. und 17. jahrhundert*. Gotha: Druck von Friedrich Andreus Perthes Aktiengesellschaft, 1912-13.

Giannotti, Donato, *Opere politiche e letterarie*. Edited by F.-L. Polidori. 2 vols. Firenze: Felice le Monnier, 1850.

Gierke, Otto von. *Natural Law and the Theory of Society: 1500-1800*. Translated by E. Barker. Cambridge: Cambridge University Press, 1950.

————. *The Political Theories of the Middle Age*. Translated by F. W. Maitland. Cambridge, England: at the University Press, 1927.

Gilbert, Allan H. *Machiavelli's "Prince" and its Forerunners*. Durham: Duke University Press, 1938.

Gilbert, Felix. *Machiavelli and Guicciardini: Politics and History in Sixteenth-Century Florence*. Princeton: Princeton University Press, 1965.

————. "Bernardo Rucellai and the Orti Oricellari: A Study on the Origin of Modern Political Thought," *Journal of the Warburg and Courtauld Institutes* 12 (1949):101-31.

————. "The Date of the Composition of Contarini's

and Giannotti's Books on Venice." *Studies in the Renaissance* 14 (1967) :172-84.

————. "Sir John Fortescue's *Dominium regale et politicum.*" *Mediaevalia et Humanistica* 2 (1943) :88-97.

————. "The Venetian Constitution in Florentine Political Thought." *Florentine Studies: Politics and Society in Renaissance Florence.* Edited by N. Rubinstein. London: Faber and Faber, 1968, pp. 463-500.

Gordon, D. J. "Name and Fame: Shakespeare's *Coriolanus,*" in *Papers Mainly Shakespearean.* Collected by G. I. Duthie. Edinburgh: Oliver and Boyd, 1964, pp. 40-57.

Gottfried, R. B. *Geoffrey Fenton's "Historie of Guicciardin".* Indiana University Publications, Humanities Series No. 3. Bloomington: Indiana University Press, 1940.

Granville-Barker, Harley. *Prefaces to Shakespeare.* 2 vols. Princeton: Princeton University Press, 1951.

Great Britain. Public Record Office. *Calendar of State Papers, Venetian, 1555-56.*

Greg, Walter Wilson. *The Shakespeare First Folio.* Oxford: at the Clarendon Press, 1955.

Grendler, Paul F. "Francesco Sansovino and Italian Popular History: 1560-1600," *Studies in the Renaissance* 16 (1969) :139-80.

Greville, Fulke, First Lord Brooke. *The Life of Sir Philip Sidney.* Edited by N. Smith. Oxford: at the Clarendon Press, 1907.

————. *Poems and Dramas.* Edited by Geoffrey Bullough. 2 vols. Edinburgh: Oliver and Boyd, [1939].

————. *The Remains: being poems of Monarchy and Religion.* Edited by G. A. Wilkes. Oxford: Oxford University Press, 1965.

Gross, Manfred. *Shakespeares "Measure for Measure"*

und die Politik Jakobs I. Neumunster: Wachholtz Verlag, 1965.

Guicciardini, Francesco. *Dialogo e Discorsi del Reggimento di Firenze.* Edited by R. Palmarocchi. *Scrittori d'Italia* 140. Bari: Laterza, 1932.

————. *Opere Inedite.* Edited by G. Canestrini. 10 vols. Firenze: 1857-67.

Hale, John Rigby. *Machiavelli and Renaissance Italy.* New York: Collier, 1963.

Harington, Sir John. *Letters and Epigrams of Sir John Harington.* Edited by N. E. McClure. Philadelphia: University of Pennsylvania Press, 1930.

————. *Nugae Antiquae.* Rev. Ed. 3 vols. London: Dodsley, 1779.

Hart, Alfred. *Shakespeare and the Homilies.* Melbourne: Melbourne University Press, 1934.

Harvey, Gabriel. *Gabriel Harvey's Marginalia.* Edited by G. C. Moore Smith. Stratford: Shakespeare Head Press, 1913.

————. *Letterbook of Gabriel Harvey.* Edited by E. J. L. Scott. Westminster: Camden Society, N.S. 33, 1884.

Haydn, Hiram. *The Counter-Renaissance.* New York: Scribner, 1950.

Heuer, H. "From Plutarch to Shakespeare: a Study of *Coriolanus.*" *Shakespeare Survey* 10 (1957):50-59.

Hexter, J. "Seyssel, Machiavelli and Polybius vi: the Mystery of the Missing Translation." *Studies in the Renaissance* 3 (1956):75-96.

Heywood, Thomas. *An Apology for Actors* (1612). Edited by R. H. Perkinson. New York: Scholar's Facsimiles and Reprints, 1941.

————. *The Rape Of Lucrece.* University of Illinois Studies in Language and Literature, vol. 34, No. 3.

Edited by Alan Holaday. Urbana: University of Illinois Press, 1950.

Hinsley, Francis Harvy. *Sovereignty.* London: Watts, 1966.

Honig, E. "*Sejanus* and *Coriolanus:* a Study in Alienation." *Modern Language Quarterly* 12 (1951):407-21.

Honigmann, E. A. J. "Shakespeare's Plutarch." *Shakespeare Quarterly* 10 (1959):25-33.

————. "*Timon of Athens.*" *Shakespeare Quarterly* 12 (1961):1-20.

Hoppe, H. R. "John Wolfe, Printer and Publisher, 1579-1601." *The Library,* 4th Series, 14 (1933-34): 241-88.

Howell, Roger. *Sir Philip Sidney.* Boston: Little, Brown, 1968.

Hudson, Winthrop Still. *John Ponet (1516?-1556): Advocate of Limited Monarchy.* Chicago: University of Chicago Press, 1942.

Jacquot, Jean. *George Chapman.* Paris: Société d'Editions "les belles lettres," 1951.

Jaeger, Werner. *Paideia I.* Translated by G. Highet. New York: Oxford University Press, 1939.

James I. *Basilikon Doron of James VI.* Edited by James Craigie. 2 vols. Edinburgh: Scottish Text Society, 3rd Series, 1944-50.

————. *The Political Works of James I.* Edited by C. H. McIlwain. Cambridge, Mass.: Harvard University Press, 1918.

Johnson, A. F. "English Books printed Abroad." *The Library,* 5th Series, 4 (1949-50):273-76.

Johnson, Samuel Frederick. "Early Elizabethan Tragedies of the Inns of Court." 2 vols. Ph.D. Dissertation, Harvard University, 1947.

————. "Four Books on Shakespeare: a Review." *Renaissance News* 10 (1957):42-43.

————. Review of T. S. Dorsch, ed. *Julius Caesar* by William Shakespeare. Arden Edition. Cambridge, Mass.: Harvard University Press, 1955. In *Shakespeare Quarterly* 8 (1957):391-94.

————. "The Regeneration of Hamlet." *Shakespeare Quarterly* 3 (1952):187-207.

Jonson, Ben. *Ben Jonson.* Edited by C. H. Herford and P. Simpson. 11 vols. Oxford: at the Clarendon Press, 1925-52.

————. *Sejanus.* Edited by Jonas A. Barish. Yale Ben Jonson. New Haven: Yale University Press, 1965.

Jorgensen, Paul Alfred. *Shakespeare's Military World.* Berkeley: University of California Press, 1956.

Kantorowicz, Ernst H. *The King's Two Bodies.* Princeton: Princeton University Press, 1957.

Kempner, Nadja. *Raleghs Staatstheoretische Schriften.* Leipsig: Tauchnitz, 1928.

Killorin, Joseph. "Hobbes and Honor." Ph.D. Dissertation, Columbia University, 1968.

Kitto, Humphrey D. F. *Poiesis: Structure and Thought.* Berkeley: University of California Press, 1966.

Knappen, Marshall Mason. *Tudor Puritanism.* Chicago: University of Chicago Press, 1939.

Knight, G. Wilson. *The Imperial Theme.* London: Oxford University Press, 1931.

Knights, Lionel Charles. *Shakespeare's Politics: with some Reflections on the Nature of Tradition.* Proceedings of the British Academy. London: Oxford University Press, 1957.

Kuhl, E. P. "Shakespeare's *Rape of Lucrece." Renaissance Studies in Honor of Hardin Craig.* Edited by Baldwin Maxwell et al. Stanford: Stanford University Press [1941], pp. 160-68.

Langbaum, Robert. *The Poetry of Experience.* London: Chatto and Windus, 1957.

Lathrop, H. B. *Translations from the Classics from*

Caxton to Chapman. Madison: University of Wisconsin Press, 1933.

Law, R. H. "The Roman Background of *Titus Andronicus.*" *Studies in Philology* 40 (1943):145-53.

————. "The Text of Shakespeare's Plutarch." *Huntington Library Quarterly* 6 (1943):197-203.

Layman, Beverly Joseph. "The Political Thought of Fulke Greville." Ph.D. Dissertation, Harvard University, 1953.

Lefranc, Pierre. *Sir Walter Ralegh: Ecrivain.* Paris: Armand Colin, 1968.

Levin, Harry T. "The Shakespearian Overplot." *Renaissance Drama* 8. Edited by S. Schoenbaum. Evanston: Northwestern University Press, 1965, pp. 63-72.

————. "Introduction," *Coriolanus,* by William Shakespeare. The Pelican Shakespeare. Baltimore: Penguin, 1956.

Lewkenor, Samuel. *A Discourse . . . for such as are desirous to know the situation and customes of forraine cities. . . .* London: J. W., 1600. (STC 15566.)

Lievsay, John L. *The Englishman's Italian Books: 1550-1700.* Philadelphia: University of Pennsylvania Press, 1969.

————. "Paolo Sarpi's Appraisal of James I," in *Essays in History and Literature Presented to Stanley Pargellis.* Chicago: The Newberry Library, 1965, pp. 109-17.

Livius, Titus. *Ab Urbe Condita* I. Translated by B. O. Foster. Loeb Classical Library. London: Heinemann, 1922.

Lodge, Thomas. *The Wounds of Civil War.* Edited by J. W. Houppert. Regents Renaissance Drama Series. Lincoln: University of Nebraska Press, 1969.

Luciani, Vincenzo. *Francesco Guicciardini e la Fortuna dell'Opera Sua.* Translated by V. de Southoff. Firenze: L. S. Olschki, 1949.

————. "Ralegh's *Cabinet-Council* and Guicciardini's Aphorisms." *Studies in Philology* 46 (1949):20-30.

Lumley Library: the Catalogue of 1609. Edited by Sears Jayne and F. R. Johnson. London: British Museum, 1956.

Luna, Barbara de. *Jonson's Romish Plot: a Study of "Catiline" and its Historical Context.* Oxford: at the Clarendon Press, 1967.

MacCallum, Mungo William. *Shakespeare's Roman Plays and their Background.* London: Macmillan, 1910.

Machiavelli, Niccolo. *I Discorsi.* Palermo: Antonielli, 1584. [London: Wolfe, 1584.] (STC 17159.)

————. *The Discourses.* Edited by L. J. Walker, 2 vols. New Haven: Yale University Press, 1950.

————. *The Florentine Historie.* Translated by T. B., Esq. London: T.C., 1595. (STC 17162.)

————. *Lettere.* Edited by F. Gaeta. Milan: Feltrinelli, 1961.

————. *The Prince and the Discourses.* Edited by Max Lerner. New York: Modern Library, 1950.

————. *Opere.* 8 vols. Milan: Feltrinelli, 1960-   .

Maclean, H. N. "Fulke Greville: Kingship and Sovereignty." *Huntington Library Quarterly* 16 (1952-53):237-71.

MacLure, Millar. *George Chapman: a Critical Study.* Toronto: University of Toronto Press, 1966.

Mahood, Molly M. *Shakespeare's Wordplay.* London: Methuen, 1957.

Maxwell, J. C. "Shakespeare's Roman Plays: 1900-1956." *Shakespeare Survey* 10 (1957):1-11.

McConika, James K. *English Humanists and Reformation Politics.* Oxford: at the Clarendon Press, 1965.

McGrath, Patrick. *Papists and Puritans under Elizabeth I.* London: Blandford, 1967.

McIlwain, Charles Howard. *The Growth of Political Thought in the West from the Greeks to the end of the Middle Ages*. New York: Macmillan, 1932.

McNair, Philip. *Peter Martyr in Italy*. Oxford: at the Clarendon Press, 1967.

Mohl, Ruth. *Studies in Spenser, Milton, and the Theory of Monarchy*. New York: King's Crown Press, 1949.

―――. *The Three Estates in Medieval and Renaissance Literature*. New York: Columbia University Press, 1933.

Montaigne, Michel de. *The Complete Works of Montaigne*. Translated by D. M. Frame. Stanford: Stanford University Press, 1958.

―――. *Essais*. Edited by P. Villey. 3 vols. Paris: Alcan, 1930.

Mosse, George Lachmann. "The Influence of Jean Bodin's *République* on English Political Thought." *Mediaevalia et Humanistica* 5 (1948):73-83.

―――. *The Struggle for Sovereignty in England*. East Lansing: Michigan State College Press, 1950.

Muir, K. "The Background of *Coriolanus*." *Shakespeare Quarterly* 10 (1959):137-45.

―――. "Menenius's Fable." *Notes and Queries* 198 (1953):240-42.

―――. "Samuel Harsnett and *King Lear*." *Review of English Studies,* N.S. 2 (1951):11-21.

―――. "Shakespeare and Lewkenor." *Review of English Studies* 7 (1956):182-83.

Nardi, Jacopo. *Istorie della Citta di Firenze* (1582). 2 vols. Firenze, 1842.

Neale, John E. *Elizabeth I and her Parliaments: 1559-1581*. London: Cape, 1953.

―――. *Elizabeth I and her Parliaments: 1584-1601*. London: Cape, 1957.

―――. *The Elizabethan House of Commons*. London: Cape, 1949.

————. "Peter Wentworth." *English Historical Review* 39 (1924):36-54, 175-205.

Neumeyer, Peter F. "Ingratitude is Monstrous: An Approach to *Coriolanus,*" *College English* 26 (1964): 192-98.

Notestein, Wallace. *The Winning of the Initiative by the House of Commons.* (Proceedings of the British Academy.) London: Oxford University Press, 1924.

Oliver, H. "Coriolanus as Tragic Hero." *Shakespeare Quarterly* 10 (1959):53-60.

Orsini, Napoleone. *Studii sul Rinascimento italiano in Inghilterra.* Firenze: Sansoni, 1937.

Panofsky, Erwin. "Et in Arcadia Ego," *Philosophy and History: Essays presented to Ernst Cassirer.* Oxford: at the Clarendon Press, 1936, pp. 223-54.

Parks, George B. *The English Traveller to Italy.* Stanford: Stanford University Press, 1954.

Parliamentary Debates in 1610. Edited by S. R. Gardiner. Westminster: Camden Society, 1862.

Parliamentary History of England . . . to . . . 1803. Volume 1: 1066-1625. Edited by William Cobbett. London, 1806.

Paul, Henry N. *The Royal Play of "Macbeth."* New York: Macmillan, 1950.

Pearson, Andrew F. Scott-. *Thomas Cartwright and Elizabethan Puritanism: 1535-1603.* Cambridge, England: Cambridge University Press, 1925.

Pédech, Paul. *La Méthode Historique de Polybe.* Paris: Société d'Edition "les belles lettres," 1964.

Pellegrini, Giuliano. *Un Fiorentino alla Corte d'Inghilterra nel Cinquecento: Pettruccio Ubaldini.* Studi di Filologia Moderna, N.S. 7. Torino: Bottega d'Erasmo, 1967.

Perkinson, R. H. *"Volpone* and the Reputation of Venetian Justice," *Modern Language Review* 35 (1940): 11-18.

Phillips, James Emerson, Jr. "George Buchanan and the Sidney Circle," *Huntington Library Quarterly* 12 (1948):23-55.

————. *The State in Shakespeare's Greek and Roman Plays*. New York: Columbia University Press, 1940.

Pineas, Rainer. *Thomas More and Tudor Polemics.* Bloomington: Indiana University Press, 1968.

Plutarch. *The Philosophie, commonlie called, the Morals. . . .* Translated by Philemon Holland. London: Hatfield, 1603. (STC 20063.)

————. *Plutarch's Lives of the Noble Grecians and Romans Englished by Sir Thomas North*. Introduction by George Wyndham. 6 vols. The Tudor Translations. London: Nutt, 1895.

Poems on the Affairs of State. vol. 4. London, 1707.

Pole, Cardinal Reginald, "Pro Ecclesiaticae Unitatis Defensione," *Pole's Defense of the Unity of the Church*. Translated with an Introduction by J. G. Dwyer. Westminster, Md.: Newman Press, 1965.

Polybius. *The hystories of Polybius . . . Englished by C. W[atson]. Annexed an abstract of the worthy acts perpetrate by King Henry the fift*. London: Bynneman, 1568. (STC 20097.)

————. *The Histories*. Translated by W. R. Paton. 6 vols. Loeb Classical Library. Cambridge, Mass.: Harvard University Press, 1954-55.

Ponet, John. *A Short Treatise of politike power*. [Strasburg], 1556. (STC 3965.)

Praz, Mario. "The Politic Brain: Machiavelli and the Elizabethans," in *The Flaming Heart*. New York: Doubleday Anchor, 1958, pp. 90-145.

Proser, Matthew. *The Heroic Image in Five Shakespearian Tragedies*. Princeton: Princeton University Press, 1965.

Proverbs in the Earlier English Drama. Edited by B. J.

Whiting. Cambridge, Mass.: Harvard University Press, 1938.

Proverbs, Sentences and Proverbial Phrases from English Writings mainly before 1500. Edited by B. J. and H. W. Whiting. Cambridge, Mass.: Belknap, 1968.

Rabkin, Norman. *Shakespeare and the Common Understanding.* New York: Free Press, 1967.

Racin, John Jr. "The Early Editions of Sir Walter Ralegh's *The History of the World." Studies in Bibliography* 17 (1964):199-209.

Ralegh, Sir Walter. *The Works of Sir Walter Raleigh.* 8 vols. Oxford: at the Clarendon Press, 1829.

Rees, Ennis S. *The Tragedies of George Chapman.* Cambridge, Mass.: Harvard University Press, 1954.

Reynolds, Beatrice. *Proponents of Limited Monarchy in Sixteenth Century France: Francis Hotman and Jean Bodin.* New York: Columbia University Press, 1931.

Ribner, Irving. *The English History Play in the Age of Shakespeare.* rev. ed. London: Methuen, 1965.

———. *Jacobean Tragedy.* London: Methuen, 1962.

———. "Machiavelli and Sidney: the *Arcadia* of 1590." *Studies in Philology* 67 (1950):225-35.

———. "The Tragedy of Coriolanus." *English Studies* 39 (1953):1-9.

Richmond, H. M. *Shakespeare's Political Plays.* New York: Random House, 1967.

Ridolfi, Roberto. *Opuscoli: di Storia Letteraria e di Erudizione.* Firenze: Bibliopolis, 1942.

Ringler, William A., Jr., ed. "Introduction," *The Poems of Sir Philip Sidney.* Oxford: at the Clarendon Press, 1962.

Rose, Paul Lawrence. "The Politics of *Antony and Cleopatra," Shakespeare Quarterly* 20 (1969):379-89.

Rosen, William. *Shakespeare and the Craft of Tragedy.* Cambridge, Mass.: Harvard University Press, 1960.

Roth, Cecil. *The Last Florentine Republic.* London: Methuen, 1925.

Sargent, R. "The Source of *Titus Andronicus.*" *Studies in Philology* 46 (1949):167-83.

Sarpi, Paolo. *An apology or apologiticall answere made unto Cardinall Bellarmine.* 1607. (STC 21757.)

————. *A full and Satisfactorie answer to the late unadvised Bull, against Venice.* 1606. (STC 21759.)

————. *History of the Quarrels of Pope Paul V. with the state of Venice.* Translated by C. P[otter]. London: 1626. (STC 21766.)

Schanzer, Ernest. *The Problem Plays of Shakespeare.* London: Routledge, 1963.

Schlösser, A. "Ben Jonson's Roman Plays." *Kwartalnik Neofilologiczny* 8 (1961):123-60.

Scott, Mary A. *Elizabethan Translations from the Italian.* Baltimore: Modern Language Association, 1895-99.

Sellers, H. "Italian Books printed in England before 1640." *The Library,* 4th Series, 5 (1924):105-28.

Sen Gupta, Subodh C. *Shakespeare's Historical Plays.* Oxford: Oxford University Press, 1964.

Shakespeare, William. *The Complete Works.* Edited by G. L. Kittredge. Boston: Ginn, 1936.

————. *Coriolanus.* Edited by J. Dover Wilson. The New Shakespeare. Cambridge, England: Cambridge University Press, 1960.

————. *Henry VI, Part II.* Edited by A. C. Cairncross. Arden Shakespeare. London: Methuen, 1957.

————. *Julius Caesar.* Edited by T. S. Dorsch. Arden Shakespeare. Cambridge, Mass.: Harvard University Press, 1955.

————. *King John.* Edited by E. A. J. Honigmann.

Arden Shakespeare. Cambridge, Mass.: Harvard University Press, 1954.

——. *Measure for Measure*. Edited by J. W. Lever. Arden Shakespeare. Cambridge, Mass.: Harvard University Press, 1965.

——. *The Merchant of Venice*. Edited by J. R. Brown. Arden Shakespeare. Cambridge, Mass.: Harvard University Press, 1955.

——. *The Poems*. Edited by F. T. Prince. Arden Shakespeare. Cambridge, Mass.: Harvard University Press, 1960.

——. *Titus Andronicus*. Edited by J. C. Maxwell. Arden Shakespeare. Cambridge, Mass.: Harvard University Press, 1953.

Sidney, Sir Philip. *The Complete Works of Sir Philip Sidney*. Edited by A. Feuillerat. 4 vols. Cambridge, England: at the University Press, 1912-26.

Smith, Logan Pearsall. *Life and Letters of Sir Henry Wotton*. 2 vols. Oxford: at the Clarendon Press, 1907.

Smith, Sir Thomas. *De Republica anglorum*. Edited by L. Alston. Cambridge, England: at the University Press, 1906.

Sommers, Alan. "*'Wilderness of Tigers'*: Structure and Symbolism in *Titus Andronicus*." *Essays in Criticism* 10 (1960):275-89.

Spencer, T. J. B. "Shakespeare and the Elizabethan Romans." *Shakespeare Survey* 10 (1957):27-38.

Spenser, Edmund. *The Poetical Works of Edmund Spenser*. Edited by J. C. Smith. 3 vols. Oxford: at the Clarendon Press, 1909.

Spivack, Charlotte. *George Chapman*. New York: Twayne, 1967.

Starkey, Thomas. *A Dialogue between Reginald Pole and Thomas Lupset*. Edited by K. M. Burton. London: Chatto and Windus, 1949.

——. *England in the Reign of King Henry the*

Eighth. 2 vols. Edited by J. M. Cowper. London: Early English Text Society, 1871-78.

State Trials. *A Complete Collection of State Trials 2.* Edited by T. B. Howell. London: Bagshaw et al., 1816.

Stevenson, David Lloyd. *The Achievement of "Measure for Measure."* Ithaca: Cornell University Press, 1966.

Stirling, Brents. *The Populace in Shakespeare.* New York: Columbia University Press, 1949.

Stone, Lawrence. *The Crisis of the Aristocracy.* Oxford: at the Clarendon Press, 1965.

Strathmann, E. A. "A Note on the Ralegh Canon." *Times Literary Supplement,* 13 April 1956: 228.

Strype, John. *Life of Sir Thomas Smith.* Oxford: at the Clarendon Press, 1820.

————. *Life and Acts of John Whitgift.* 2 vols. Oxford: at the Clarendon Press, 1822.

Talbert, Ernest William. *The Problem of Order.* Chapel Hill: University of North Carolina Press, 1962.

Thomson, S. H. "Walter Burley's Commentary on the *Politics* of Aristotle," in *Mélanges Auguste Pelzer.* Louvain: Bibliothèque de l'Université, 1947 pp. 557-78.

Thucydides. *The Peloponnesian War, The Greek Historians.* Edited by F. R. B. Godolphin. 2 vols. New York: Random House, 1942.

Tillyard, Eustace M. W. *The Elizabethan World Picture.* New York: Modern Library, n.d.

————. *Shakespeare's History Plays.* London: Chatto and Windus, 1944.

Traversi, D. A. "Coriolanus," *Scrutiny* 6 (1937):43-58.

Tudor Plays. Edited by E. Creeth. New York: Anchor Doubleday, 1966.

Venezky, Alice S. *Pageantry on the Shakespearean Stage.* New York: Twayne, 1951.

Villari, Pasquale. *Niccolo Machiavelli and his Times.* 4 vols. Translated by L. Villari. London: Kegan Paul, 1883.

Villiers, J. I. de. "Ben Jonson's Tragedies," *English Studies* 45 (1964) :433-42.

Von Fritz, Kurt. *The Theory of the Mixed Constitution in Antiquity.* New York: Columbia University Press, 1954.

Waith, Eugene. *The Herculean Hero in Marlowe, Chapman, Shakespeare and Dryden.* London: Chatto and Windus, 1962.

Walbank, Frank William. *A Historical Commentary on Polybius.* 2 vols. Oxford: at the Clarendon Press, 1957.

Wallace, Willard Mosher. *Sir Edwin Sandys and the First Parliament of James I.* Philadelphia: University of Pennsylvania Press, 1940.

Walton, Izaac. *The Lives.* New York: Scott-Thaw, 1903.

Watson, Curtis B. *Shakespeare and the Renaissance Concept of Honor.* Princeton: Princeton University Press, 1960.

Weinstein, Donald. "The Myth of Florence," *Florentine Studies: Politics and Society in Renaissance Florence.* Edited by N. Rubinstein. London: Faber and Faber, 1968, pp. 15-44.

White, Helen Constance. *Social Criticism in Popular Religious Literature of the Sixteenth Century.* New York: Macmillan, 1944.

Whitman, Cedric. *Homer and the Heroic Tradition.* Cambridge, Mass.: Harvard University Press, 1958.

Wilkinson, B. "The 'Political Revolution' of the Thirteenth and Fourteenth Centuries in England," *Speculum* 34 (1949) :502-9.

Williams, P. Review of *Proceeding in Parliament, 1610.* Edited by E. R. Foster. 2 vols. New Haven: Yale

University Press, 1966. In *Renaissance Quarterly* 21 (1968):481-83.

Willson, David Harris. "The Earl of Salisbury and the 'Court' Party in Parliament, 1604-10," *American Historical Review* 36 (1931):274-94.

——. *King James VI and I*. London: Cape, 1956.

Wilson, F. P. "Shakespeare's Reading." *Shakespeare Survey* 3 (1950):14-21.

Zeeveld, W. Gordon. *Foundations of Tudor Policy*. Cambridge, Mass.: Harvard University Press, 1948.

——. "*Coriolanus* and Jacobean Politics." *Modern Language Review* 57 (1962):321-34.

Zocca, Louis R. *Elizabethan Narrative Poetry*. New Brunswick: Rutgers University Press, 1950.

Zurich Letters: A.D. 1558-1579. Edited by H. Robinson. Parker Society. Cambridge, England: at the University Press, 1846.

Index

253